Beginning Android Web Apps Development

Develop for Android using HTML5, CSS3, and JavaScript

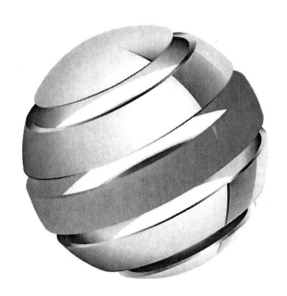

Jon Westfall
Rocco Augusto
Grant Allen

Apress®

Beginning Android Web Apps Development: Develop for Android using HTML5, CSS#, and Javascript

Copyright © 2012 by Jon Westfall, Rocco Augusto, Grant Allen

ISBN-13 (pbk): 978-1-4302-3957-4

ISBN-13 (electronic): 978-1-4302-3958-1

Trademarked names, logos, and images may appear in this book. Rather than use a trademark symbol with every occurrence of a trademarked name, logo, or image we use the names, logos, and images only in an editorial fashion and to the benefit of the trademark owner, with no intention of infringement of the trademark.

The use in this publication of trade names, trademarks, service marks, and similar terms, even if they are not identified as such, is not to be taken as an expression of opinion as to whether or not they are subject to proprietary rights.

While the advice and information in this book are believed to be true and accurate at the date of publication, neither the authors nor the editors nor the publisher can accept any legal responsibility for any errors or omissions that may be made. The publisher makes no warranty, express or implied, with respect to the material contained herein.

President and Publisher: Paul Manning
Lead Editor: Mark Beckner
Technical Reviewer: Stephen Hughes
Editorial Board: Steve Anglin, Ewan Buckingham, Gary Cornell, Louise Corrigan,
    Morgan Ertel, Jonathan Gennick, Jonathan Hassell, Robert Hutchinson,
    Michelle Lowman, James Markham, Matthew Moodie, Jeff Olson, Jeffrey Pepper,
    Douglas Pundick, Ben Renow-Clarke, Dominic Shakeshaft, Gwenan Spearing,
    Matt Wade, Tom Welsh
Coordinating Editor: Adam Heath
Copy Editor: Chandra Clarke
Compositor: MacPS, LLC
Indexer: SPi Global
Artist: SPi Global
Cover Designer: Anna Ishchenko

Distributed to the book trade worldwide by Springer Science+Business Media New York, 233 Spring Street, 6th Floor, New York, NY 10013. Phone 1-800-SPRINGER, fax (201) 348-4505, e-mail orders-ny@springer-sbm.com, or visit www.springeronline.com.

For information on translations, please e-mail rights@apress.com, or visit www.apress.com.

Apress and friends of ED books may be purchased in bulk for academic, corporate, or promotional use. eBook versions and licenses are also available for most titles. For more information, reference our Special Bulk Sales–eBook Licensing web page at www.apress.com/bulk-sales.

Any source code or other supplementary materials referenced by the author in this text is available to readers at www.apress.com. For detailed information about how to locate your book's source code, go to www.apress.com/source-code.

Dedicated to my wife, Karey, and to my parents, Alan & Dianne

—Jon Westfall

I dedicate this book to my daughter Rose... and Perry White, who is too good of a reporter to not know Clark Kent is Superman. You Perry are a true gem.

—Rocco Augusto

Contents at a Glance

Contents

Chapter 9: HTML5 Location-Based Applications 145

Chapter 10: Using Cloud Services: A Transport Application 167

Chapter 11: Pushing the Limits with Audio and Video 187

About the Authors

Jon Westfall is a researcher and technologist working in New York City at Columbia Business School. His current appointment is as the Associate Director for Research and Technology at the Center for Decision Sciences, a center within Columbia Business School at Columbia University in New York City. Additionally, he holds an appointment as a Lecturer in the Columbia University Psychology department, periodically teaching a course in Judgment and Decision Making. In addition to his research, he also has career ties in information technology, where he has worked as a consultant since 1997, founding his own firm, Bug Jr. Systems. As a consultant, he has developed custom software solutions (including native Windows 32 applications, Windows .NET applications, Windows Phone 7 and Android mobile applications, as well as ASP, ASP.NET, and PHP web applications). He has also served as a senior network and systems architect and administrator (on both Windows and Unix networks, and hybrids) and has also been recognized as a Microsoft Most Valuable Professional (MVP) 2008 – 2012. In his spare time, he enjoys writing both technical books as well as fiction. His novel, Mandate, as well as other writings are available via his website at http://jonwestfall.com. He can be contacted through his website, and followed on Twitter (@jonwestfall).

Rocco Augusto is a Web Developer based out of the City of Roses – Portland, Oregon. Rocco first started dabbling in the art of Web Design and Development in middle school when the code bug bit him and refused to let go. When not tinkering away at some new markup or design idea you can usually find Rocco enjoying some time with his beautiful wife, daughters, and their unruly puppies.

Grant Allen has worked in the IT field for over 20 years, as a CTO, enterprise architect, and database administrator. Grant's roles have covered private enterprise, academia, and the government sector around the world, specialising in global-scale systems design, development, and performance. He is a frequent speaker at industry and academic conferences, on topics ranging from data mining to compliance, and technologies such as databases (DB2, Oracle, SQL Server, MySQL), content management, collaboration, disruptive innovation, and mobile ecosystems like Android. His first Android application was a task list to remind him to finish all his other unfinished Android projects. Grant works for Google, and in his spare time is completing a Ph.D on building innovative high-technology environments. Grant is the author of Beginning DB2, and lead author of Beginning Android 4, Oracle SQL Recipes, and The Definitive Guide to SQLite.

About the Technical Reviewer

 **Steven Hughes** has been a Microsoft Windows Phone MVP for the past decade for his passion and dedication in the mobile community. Steven became involved with handheld computers since the early '90s including the beta testing and the prototype design of several hardware and software designs. His passion and knowledge of mobile technology and the mobile industry has advised and consulted many on its use and has earned the nickname 'fyiguy' as result. Steven loves to share information and help people; you may see his contributions and articles on several websites, publications, podcasts, and other productions pertaining to mobile technology. Steven is also the Chief News and Review Editor for BostonPocketPC.com and has written several detailed reviews and articles on various facets of mobile technology as well. Steven is a Moderator in the Microsoft Answers forums and also co-manages the New England Windows Phone User Group. Steven is employed as a Biomedical Engineer for the VA New England Healthcare System. When he has some free time he generally spends it with his family or outdoors playing soccer, hitting the slopes, strumming his guitar, catching a movie in his self-constructed custom home theater, or riding the trails on his mountain bike.

Acknowledgments

I'd like to acknowledge my editors here at Apress (Mark Beckner, Adam Heath, Chris Nelson, & Jonathan Gennick), as well as my co-authors Rocco & Grant and technical editor, Steven, for their hard work in this project. On a personal note, the support given to me by my wife, Karey, my parents, Alan & Dianne, and my extended family (especially Dan, Sue, Greg, Scott, & Mark) cannot be overstated. I'm also greatful for the support of my mentors, Eric Johnson and Elke Weber, my colleagues, Cindy Kim, Margaret Lee, Ye Li, ChristophUngemach, SooBaik, Galen Treuer, and Min Bang, and my current and former interns, Katherine Chang, Meaghan Gartner, Mary Reiser, Yechao Liu, Soo Jung Lee, & Nina Rouhani. Finally, I'd like to thank my friends who encouraged me to become as geeky as I am, directly and indirectly. This includes Steve Jocke, Tony Rylow, Ashley Newman, Maria Gaglio, Marie Batteiger, JD Jasper, Jason Dunn, Don Sorcinelli, Eric Hicks, Darius Wey, Jack Cook, Johan van Mierlo, Annie Ma, Holly Feiler, Dot Bertram, & Cathy Bischoff.

—Jon Westfall

Introduction

Both of the first author's (Jon's) parents were artists. They each could draw fantastical pictures that resembled real life, and were shocked to see that their son could barely muster up a stick figure. If you've always felt that your inner artist was best expressed through what you could build with the help of a computer and the Internet, then this book can guide your virtual paintbrush. The finished product? A mobile web application for Android devices, which can in turn inspire creativity and productivity in millions of prospective users. It is our hope that this book will give you all that you need to get up and running and creating your masterpieces in no time.

Who This Book Is For

This book is written at a beginner's level. For the most part, we assume nothing as we write about everything from what HTML is to how to apply CSS to querying databases and displaying content using JavaScript. For some, this may mean that they would like to skim certain introductory materials (and assuredly miss many bad jokes). However, even advanced users will likely gain something from the tricks we unroll our sleeves to reveal.

How This Book Is Structured

We've split the content in this book into several chapters, with three "unofficial" parts.

In **the first part,** we introduce you (Chapter 1) to the basic languages of the web: HTML, CSS, JavaScript, and more. We then jump into two applications (Chapters 2–3) quickly to get your feet wet, and then back out to discuss planning concerns you might need to address when designing your own apps (Chapters 4–6)

In **the second part,** we start to jazz things up a bit. We go into building impressive user interfaces (Chapter 7) and working with visual content (Chapter 8). We then show you two more applications (Chapters 9–10) that speak to the unique nature of mobile applications: Using location information to guide your apps (and users), as well as tapping into the cloud for information and data.

Finally, **in the last part,** we talk about the next level of interactivity to add to your applications. We touch on adding audio and video (Chapter 11), doing things behind the user's back to provide impressive functionality (Chapter 12) and wrapping it all up and uploading to the web or building a full app for your formerly browser-bound creation (Chapter 13).

While we've grouped chapters into a logical order, after Chapter 1 you should feel free to explore the rest of the content. While many topics build upon one another, reading what interests you first may help you get a good grasp of what concepts from earlier chapters you'll definitely want to check out. At the same time, there are nuggets of information in each chapter that will stand upon their own, especially discussions on design, psychology, and user experience! We hope you enjoy the journey!

Downloading the code

The code for the examples shown in this book is available on GitHub at
`https://github.com/jonwestfall/Beginning-Android-Web-Apps-Development`.

Contacting the Author

We're always happy to hear from our readers, and if you have questions, comments, or thoughts
about the book (or life in general), you can contact any of us through our personal websites or
social media.

Jon Westfall: `http://jonwestfall.com`   Twitter: `@jonwestfall`
Rocco Augusto: `http://nerdofsteel.com/`   Twitter: `@therocco`
Grant Allen: `http://www.artifexdigital.com`   Twitter: `@fuzzytwtr`

Chapter 1

Harnessing the Power of the Mobile Web

Welcome to the first chapter of this book. In this chapter, we'll endeavor to not only tell you about what you'll find in this book, but to also compare it to what has come before. You see, quite simply, it is only now that the true power of mobile web applications and mobile-optimized websites is being realized, despite the existence of the "web" on mobile phones in some form for 10 years.

Before we show off the neat stuff we have planned for this book, it's probably best to make sure everyone is on the same page, lingo-wise. So we'll start talking about the basic terms in web design. In the second section, we'll talk about the precursors to today's mobile web. And finally, in the last section, we'll talk about the concepts that will guide this book and give you a sneak peek at some of the applications we'll be developing!

Basics of Web Design

There are a few concepts that it's best to discuss up front. Forgive us if you've heard this all before. However, if you're completely new to web design (i.e., you've never written a single web page or blog), then this should be a good place to start. And, if we're starting at the beginning, then we should start with the lingua franca of the web: HTML.

Getting Started: HyperText Markup Language (HTML)

In the late 1980s, the computer language we know today as HTML was born. HTML isn't a true programming language, per se, in that it isn't compiled. Rather, HTML is interpreted by special software called a **web browser**. Browsers, such as Microsoft Internet Explorer, Mozilla Firefox, and Google Chrome on your Desktop computer, and Dolphin HD, Opera Mini, and Skyfire on your Android device, download HTML files from a **web server**, interpret them, and display them. This entire process is fairly simple. A web server can be any sort of computer that makes a list of files available to other computers on the network over something called HyperText Transport Protocol (HTTP, as in http:// at the beginning of web addresses, which are also called **URLs**). Browsers download these HTML files over HTTP and read them, looking for special features known as **tags**. These tags function in the same way as tags in older word processor programs did—specifying how text and other elements of the page should look when displayed in the viewer. Consider the web page in Figure 1–1.

This is normal text. However let's get fancy and make **this bold** (this is *italicized*). The tag to the left just made this a new line.

The tag to the left here just made this a new paragraph.

Figure 1–1. *An example web page named hello.html*

Let's look at the HTML code that made up the page shown in Listing 1–1:

Listing 1–1. *hello.html*

```
<html>
<head>
<title>This is the text that appears in the browser's Title bar!</title>
</head>
<body>
This is normal text. However let's get fancy and make <strong>this bold</strong> (this
is <em>italicized</em>).
<br /> The tag to the left just made this a new line.
<p> The tag to the left here just made this a new paragraph.</p>
</body>
</html>
```

The code might look a bit strange, but let's walk through it line by line. The first line, which simply reads <html>, lets the browser know that it's reading an HTML document. You'll notice that the last line of the document, </html>, is similar. This line "finishes" the HTML object—closing the tag and telling the browser that the page is over. By having sets of tags like this, the browser knows what formatting to apply and where to stop applying it.

The second through fourth lines of the code are known as the page header. This is where programmers store important information that the browser needs to know in order to format the page properly. In this case, the only tag I've placed within the header is a title tag, which specifies what should be shown in the title bar of the user's web browser. The header would be the location where one would most commonly finds certain documents, such as Cascading Style Sheets, JavaScript, and META information for search engine optimization, special instructions for different browsers, favicons (those little icons that appear next to a bookmark entry in your browser), and other important information about the page that is not related to the documents'content, which brings us to line 5 - the bodytag.

The bodytag tells the browser that the content to display to the user is about to be given. From here, we see straight text—the same that's in the rendered page shown in Figure 1–1. However, you'll notice a few special tags we've added in. The first, , tells the browser that the text between it and its end tag should be in bold to give it a stronger visual oomph. A second tag, <em>, does the same by emphasizing the content orby making the content italic.[1] A third tag, <br />, starts a new line (br stands for line break!). The <br /> tag is a little different than most HTML tags. Since the tag does not require itself to enclose content on the page in the same thatthe <strong> and <em> tags do, this tag closes on itself. Finally, the <p> tag starts a new paragraph.

At their cores, all web pages are some form of HTML, although most we'll discuss in this book are much more complicated. Thankfully, we'll walk you through them, so you won't be overwhelmed!

If this is your first outing into the world of HTML and web applications, then it would probably be a good idea to familiarize yourself with the basics of HTML before jumping full on into the book. One of the best resources on the Internet for learning HTML and browsing through basic code examples can be found at the W3Schools (http://www.w3schools.com/). Once you've gotten your feet a little wet with HTML, or in case you're already soaked from the neck down, it would be time to move on to some of the more intermediate portions of web application design and technologies that we will be using in this book.

Getting Stylish: Cascading Style Sheets (CSS)

Imagine that you're writing up a simple web page to aid in your parenting—a family chore list. It might look something like the list in Figure 1–2.

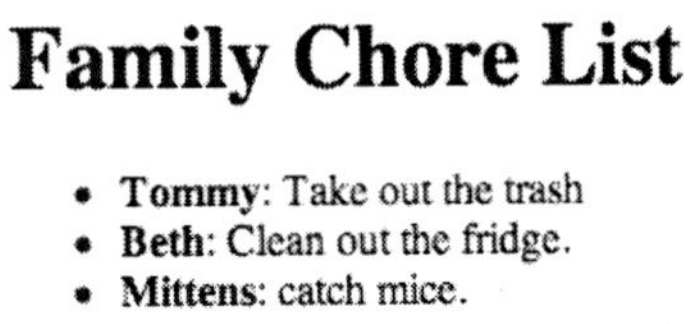

Family Chore List

- **Tommy**: Take out the trash
- **Beth**: Clean out the fridge.
- **Mittens**: catch mice.

Figure 1–2.*Family Chore List*

By just glancing at the finished product, there does not appear to be a lot going on here.We have a standard boring black and white document that completely lacks any style or individuality. Let us take a look at the code behind the scenes shown in Listing 1–2.

Listing 1–2. *chores.html*

```
<html>
<head>
<title> Family Chore List </title>
</head>
<body>
<h1>Family Chore List</h1>
```

---

[1] It's worth noting that the <b> and <i> tags you may be used to were used in HTML 4 for the same purpose as <strong> and <em> respectively. Their use has been deprecated in HTML5 in favor of the tags above.

```
<ul>
<li><strong>Tommy</strong>: Take out the trash</li>
<li><strong>Beth</strong>: Clean out the fridge. </li>
<li><strong>Mittens</strong>: catch mice. </li>
</ul>
</body>
</html>
```

Let us break down the teensy morsel of code within the bodyelement. Here, the unordered list on the page is created using the ul tag. An unordered list is great to use anytime you want to create a bulleted list of items. If your list requires a little more order,you might opt to use the ol, or ordered list,HTML tag.

While the page is fairly nice and simple, you might want to spice it up. Perhaps around Christmas time, you'd like splash some color on your family chores page that would make even the most bah humbug elf smile with glee (see Figure 1–3).

Figure 1–3. Christmas Chore List with green and red adding a holiday feel

Perhaps on the Fourth of July, you might want to fill your family with patriotic gusto (see Figure 1–4).

Figure 1–4. Patriotic Chore List with the red, white, and blue

Each time we change the colors, we modify the HTML source code by adding in appropriate tags. Take a look at the patriotic version of chores.html in Listing 1–3.

Listing 1–3. patriotic chores.html

```
<html>
<head>
<title> Family Chore List </title>
</head>
<body bgcolor=blue>
<font color=red><h1>Family Chore List</h1></font>
<font color=white>
<ul>
<li><strong>Tommy</strong>: Take out the trash</li>
<li><strong>Beth</strong>: Clean out the fridge. </li>
<li><strong>Mittens</strong>: catch mice. </li>
</ul>
```

```
</font>
</body>
</html>
```

Making modifications straight to the HTML is fine for small pages. However, imagine how much time adding those font tags might take if there were 12 children and countless pets to coordinate. Or perhaps you have multiple pages, one for each child and you don't want them to feel left out if their sibling has nice color combinations and they don't. Never fear–we can use something called a Cascading Style Sheet, or CSS, to keep it all in check. Basically, a CSS file is a small document consisting of a set of styles to be applied to an HTML document that can be changed at anytime, affecting every page it is connected to, without ever having to edit the original HTML document(s). Listing 1–4 provides an example CSS file.

Listing 1–4. *patriotic.css*

```
body {background-color: blue}
h1 {color: white}
li {color: red}
```

Notice how the format of the file is simply the HTML tag you wish to edit (H1 for example and the attributes you'd like to give it). In this case, we want the color of text within h1 to be white.We can simplify chores.html to include a link to this CSS file, as shown in the code of Listing 1–5.

Listing 1–5. *chores.html with CSS reference*

```
<html>
<head>
<title> Family Chore List </title>
<link rel="stylesheet" type="text/css" href="patriotic.css" />
</head>
<body>
<h1>Family Chore List</h1>
<ul>
<li><strong>Tommy</strong>: Take out the trash</li>
<li><strong>Beth</strong>: Clean out the fridge. </li>
<li><strong>Mittens</strong>: catch mice. </li>
</ul>
</body>
</html>
```

We'll get exactly the same output as is shown in Figure 1–4. Now, imagine how this works if we scale upward. First of all, the parents no longer need to edit the HTML tags directly to change styles. Depending on the holiday, they simply could have multiple CSS files they could link to (simply changing the fourth line of the code in Listing 1–5). Second, they could extend the CSS even further to specify spacing, fonts (Mittens hates serifs), and more. Finally, if they have more than one page, they could simply link the CSS sheet at the top of each page to their current "theme" and all the pages would look alike. While the examples above are extremely simple, they illustrate the power of CSS. We'll examine CSS inmore detail as we continue through the book!

Getting Interactive: JavaScript

Sometimes great design isn't enough to make your point. Sometimes you want to do something a bit flashy, or something unique, or something downright useful. One of the simplest ways to do that is by using JavaScript. JavaScript is a scripting language that runs inside the viewer's web browser. For example, perhaps you've gone to a site before and gotten a pop-up message like the one in Figure 1–5.

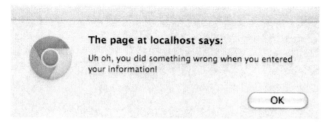

Figure 1–5. *A JavaScript warning*

Typically, you see these messages while filling out a forms page or perhaps in an online shopping cart telling you that your item is out of stock or some such annoying message. While you might be used to seeing these messages on web pages on your computer, they can also be shown in a mobile web browser (see Figure 1–6).

Figure 1–6. *A JavaScript warning on an Android phone*

The code that creates these messages is remarkably simple. Listing 1–6 integrated the code into the chores.html page we saw in the CSS example above.

Listing 1–6. *chores.html with JavaScript reference*

```
<html>
<head>
<title> Family Chore List </title>
<link rel="stylesheet" type="text/css" href="patriotic.css" />
<script type="text/javascript">
function ShowWarning() {
alert("Mittens - your mousing numbers are down this week - NO CATNIP FOR YOU");
}
</script>
</head>
<body onload=ShowWarning();>
<h1>Family Chore List</h1>
<ul>
<li><strong>Tommy</strong>: Take out the trash</li>
<li><strong>Beth</strong>: Clean out the fridge. </li>
<li><strong>Mittens</strong>: catch mice. </li>
</ul>
</body>
</html>
```

Let's start by talking about the new section of code right below the CSS link, inside the headsection, with the tag script. The scripttag tells the browser that a section of scripting code (in this case, of the type text/javascript) is about to be given. The browser then interprets the code. Since it's in the headsection, the browser simply stores this code for later use. This piece of code is called a function, which you can think of as a list of commands wrapped up in a "shortcut". Here the command is another function named alert. As you can imagine, JavaScript functions can get quite complex, with functions including other functions and interacting with user input.

Once the function is loaded into the browser's menu, we need to tell the browser when we want to execute it. In this case, I've changed the bodytag to include the line onload=ShowWarning();. This tells the browser that, when the page is loaded, I want it to run the function ShowWarning. The two parentheses indicate a spot where I could include information to pass to the function. This becomes useful for creating things like calculators or for checking input in a form. For example, I could write up something like Listing 1–7.

Listing 1–7. *chores.html with JavaScript reference passing a variable*

```
<html>
<head>
<title> Family Chore List </title>
<link rel="stylesheet" type="text/css" href="patriotic.css" />
<script type="text/javascript">
function ShowWarning(catname) {
alert(catname + " - your mousing numbers are down this week - NO CATNIP FOR YOU");
}
</script>
</head>
<body onload=ShowWarning("Mittens");>
<h1>Family Chore List</h1>
```

```
<ul>
<li><strong>Tommy</strong>: Take out the trash</li>
<li><strong>Beth</strong>: Clean out the fridge. </li>
<li><strong>Mittens</strong>: catch mice. </li>
</ul>
</body>
</html>
```

The code in Listing 1–7 will produce the exact same message as the code in Listing 1–6. However, in Listing 1–7, I've passed the feline's name as a variable. The function ShowWarning now expects that I'll pass a variable to be named "catname", and it can use that information in its code. When I call ShowWarning() in the bodytag, I simply add the cat's name to be passed to the function. I can pass more than one thing, if I want to. As mentioned, this could get quite complex, depending on how much I want to chastise poor Mittens.

As you can see, coupling JavaScript along with HTML and CSS can produce pages that look good, are easy to update, and can interact with the user. But sometimes you might need to produce a document that doesn't give style information–it just gives general information. A prime example of this is given in the next section, as we start to get into the wonderful world of XML!

Getting Informative: Extensible Markup Language (XML)

If you spend any time on the Web, you may have noticed an odd little icon on some pages that looks something like this.

Figure 1–7. An RSS icon

This little orange icon tells the reader about an RSS feed that the current website has available. RSS feeds look pretty uninteresting and unintelligible to a user (take a look at Figure 1–8 for the start of an RSS feed). However, other web pages and scripts can use them to grab a lot of information from one source and display it in different ways to the user.

```
<?xml version="1.0" encoding="UTF-8"?>
<?xml-stylesheet type="text/xsl" media="screen" href="/~d/styles/rss2full.xsl"?><?xml-stylesheet typ
<channel>
    <title>JonWestfall.Com</title>
    <link>http://jonwestfall.com</link>
    <description>More Than You Want To Know!</description>
    <lastBuildDate>Thu, 16 Jun 2011 13:21:06 +0000</lastBuildDate>
    <docs>http://backend.userland.com/rss092</docs>
    <language>en</language>
    <!-- generator="WordPress/3.1.3" -->

    <atom10:link xmlns:atom10="http://www.w3.org/2005/Atom" rel="self" type="application/xml" href="
        <title>Keep your Android Tablet Up To Date Daily With Increased Battery Life!</title>
        <description>Recently I found that I had a problem with my Samsung Galaxy Tab (Although you
&lt;p&gt;&lt;a href="http://feedads.g.doubleclick.net/~a/EFCCCh7JV-yrNNUlTsPwYhvAs_A/0/da"&gt;&lt;im
&lt;a href="http://feedads.g.doubleclick.net/~a/EFCCCh7JV-yrNNUlTsPwYhvAs_A/1/da"&gt;&lt;img src="ht
&lt;a href="http://feeds.feedburner.com/~ff/jonwestfall?a=FFCZ10Xe7kc:Yhg4XtccZAQ:yIl2AUoC8zA"&gt;&l
&lt;/div&gt;&lt;img src="http://feeds.feedburner.com/~r/jonwestfall/~4/FFCZ10Xe7kc" height="1" width
        <link>http://feedproxy.google.com/~r/jonwestfall/~3/FFCZ10Xe7kc/</link>
            <feedburner:origLink>http://jonwestfall.com/2011/05/keep-your-android-tablet-up-to-date-
    <item>
```

Figure 1–8. The start of a blog's RSS feed, showing new entries

For example, Figure 1–9 is the beginning of the RSS feed for my personal blog. Each element contains a variety of data that isn't very pretty to look at but provides all the information one might want to view my blog in a special piece of software called an RSS reader. While certain applications, like Microsoft Outlook, have built-in RSS readers, many prefer to use a dedicated reader client. One popular RSS reader is Google Reader, which can take the link to my RSS feed and produce a nice view of my blog so that the Google Reader user can quickly see` what articles I've posted recently.

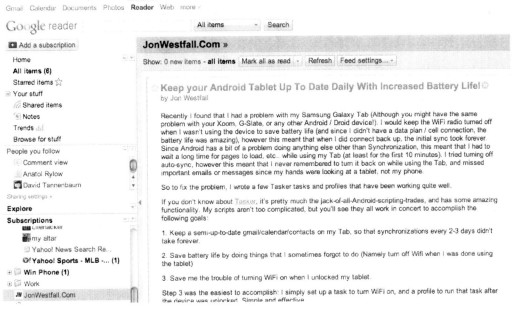

Figure 1–9. My personal blog, displayed within Google Reader

Now, you might be asking why I'd want people to view my website somewhere other than at its usual web address. The simple answer is that it might be more convenient for my users to view all the blogs they read (mine and others) within one piece of software. Software, such as Google Reader, can keep track of hundreds of RSS feeds, from news sources, blogs, and even just simple status updates like my Twitter feed. All of these pieces of information are retrieved by Google Reader in a format known as Extensible Markup Language (XML). XML isn't a format you'd want to have your human viewers see, but it is one that you'd want to use if you were sharing information between web pages or between web services.

While the example above shows XML as an output, the web application that powers my blog (WordPress) produces the XML so other sites like Google Reader can use it. XML can also be used as an input. For example, I might want to take data (such as sports scores) and display them on my webpage. Most likely, those sports scores will be available in XML, which my web page can then open and **parse**. Parsing is simply a fancy term that means "read, interpret, and display". My webpage will read the scores, interpret them if necessary (i.e., calculate something, aggregate something), and then display them to the user in some meaningful way.

So to recap, we've now seen how to build a basic webpage, how to make it look pretty (easily), and how to make it interact with a user. Finally, we talked about how webpages and programs get data between each other by using XML. As we move through the book, we'll talk in depth about each of these areas and give you plenty of examples of how to use them. In fact, coming up in Chapter 2, we'll discuss how to get data from a very popular web service and display it in the first full application we'll create!

JSON: Human-Readable Data Interchange

If you have a brilliant idea for a mobile web application that relies on the application programming interface, or API, of other services, such as Twitter or Foursquare, then chances are you will be quickly introduced to JSON (JavaScript Object Notation), which is one of my favorite technologies.

JSON is a human-readable, super-lightweight data interchange technology that is based on JavaScript. Basically, it is a JavaScript object that can be used to transmit simple data structures and arrays of information. When it comes to working with external data in your web application, I have fallen in love with JSON for its ease of use when compared to other technologies such as XML. As with all technologies though, your mileage may vary.Figure 1–10 shows an example of what a JSON document would look like.

view-source:nerdofsteel.com/json


```
{
  "title": "nerd.of.steel: json",
  "link": "http://www.nerdofsteel.com/",
  "items": [
        {
      "title": "Chalkboard Project - CLASS Project",
      "description": "  <p>The Chalkboard Project is a non-partisan nonprofit working to unite Oregonians
to make K-12 public schools among the nation's best. For this project I was hired on as the Lead Developer
in charge of all front end and back end development of the Chalkboard&#8217;s <span
class='caps'>CLASS</span> project, which is targeted toward educational leaders conversing about how to
better support teacher and learning in the state of Oregon.</p>",
      "image": "<img src='http://www.nerdofsteel.com/images/160t.png' alt='' />",
      "link": "http://educators4reform.org/",
      "width": "418"
  },    {
      "title": "Ready... Set... Teach!",
      "description": "  <p>The Chalkboard Project is a non-partisan nonprofit working to unite Oregonians
to make K-12 public schools among the nation's best. For this project I was hired on as the Lead Developer
in charge of all front end and back end development of the Chalkboard Project's teacher focused blogging
site.</p>",
      "image": "<img src='http://www.nerdofsteel.com/images/165t.png' alt='' />",
      "link": "http://oregonteacherblog.chalkboardproject.org/",
      "width": "349"
  },    {
      "title": "Chalkboard Project Blog",
      "description": "  <p>The Chalkboard Project is a non-partisan nonprofit working to unite Oregonians
to make K-12 public schools among the nation's best. For this project I  was hired on as the Lead Developer
in charge of all front end and back end development of the Chalkboard Project&#8217;s blog.</p>",
      "image": "<img src='http://www.nerdofsteel.com/images/157t.png' alt='' />",
      "link": "http://blog.chalkboardproject.org/",
      "width": "481"
  },    {
      "title": "Vestas Extreme Safety",
      "description": "  <p>Vestas Americas is responsible for the sales and service of wind turbines in the
United States and Canada. The internal Extreme Safety site is a content management system devoted to
allowing the engineers to share stories, injury reports, photos and videos related to their job at Vestas.
I was hired on as the Lead Developer in charge of all front end and back end development for the
site.</p>",
      "image": "<img src='http://www.nerdofsteel.com/images/170t.png' alt='' />",
      "link": "http://vestasextremesafety.com",
      "width": "427"
  },    {
      "title": "Earthbound Soundboard",
      "description": "  <p>I got the hankering for some good ol&#8217; EarthBound fun so I made this
```


Figure 1–10. *Rocco Augusto's portfolio in JSON format from nerdofsteel.com*

The Mobile Web, Yesterday and Today

Many of us first started using the Internet in the late 1990s or, if you weren't alive in the late 1990s, perhaps you've used it your whole life! While we might be very familiar with the Internet on our desktop, getting it onto a small screen that can fit in our pocket might seem a bit strange, especially with different jargon and marketing-speak that is often heard when it comes to the Web. We'll start by discussing how fast the data arrives on your phone and then what sorts of data can be sent.

Knowing the Speeds (Or "What is 3G anyway?")

Often in commercials for the latest smartphone, you'll hear a number such as "4G" or "faster than 3G". The "G" stands for the generation of the technology. You rarely hear about 2G, second generation, and there is a good reason for it. The onslaught of data onto a smartphone coincided with the emergence of the third generation of cellular network data standards. However, 1G and 2G did exist and, if you owned the first iPhone (Released in 2007), you only had 2G speed, using protocols including GPRS, EDGE, and 1X. Data coming to you over 2G was just about twice as fast as a dial-up modem, around 115KbpsSo while email and text-based web pages would load reasonably fast, anything with too many images or multimedia would take approximately eternity[2].

Around 2001, the initial designs for what we consider 3G (or third generation) data networks were drafted andcould reach theoretical speeds of over 7Mbps These networks, which include protocols like UMTS, WCDMA, and EV-DO, can move data much faster than their 2G counterparts. For the first time, thisallowed forinnovations such as streaming movies and music directly to a phone. The limiting factor in showing complex web pages was no longer the speed of the data connection but the speed of the phone. By 2007, most telecom providers had adopted and "rolled-out" a 3G network and devices, such as mobile broadband cards, became common.

In the past few years (2008-2010), new and approved versions of current 3G technologies have become available. While there is considerable argument about what exactly the differences between the 3G technologies we were privy to before and this newer 3G-based technology that is being dubbed "4G" are, it is obvious that newer protocols, such asHSPA, HSPA+, WiMAX, and LTE, are faster than their 3G predecessors. Unfortunately, while all of the major carriers are gradually moving forward with their plans to increase data speeds and network capacity, those updates and changes will not become immediately apparent to the end user until they purchase a phone with the right internal hardware to take advantage of these numerous changes.

One common trap that many web developers who target mobiles may fall into, at least early on, is the notion that speed is all one needs to consider when developing a mobile app. If I know my users will need a 3G network to use the feature I'm developing, it might be tempting to skip streamlining other areas of the app, given the fact I know I'll have a faster data connection. However, as mentioned above, speed isn't the only factor one needs to consider.The actual processing and software power of the device (i.e., the capabilities of its web browser) can also slow down an app. If you want evidence of this, use your own Smartphone or Tablet on Wi-Fi instead of cellular data and observe how certain sites and apps still lag when connecting to the Internet, despite a connection much faster (generally) than 3G or 4G. We'll discuss how to avoid programming bloated unresponsive apps as we continue through the book.

Languages and Protocols, Yesterday and Today

Now that we know how fast we can go, we should probably talk a bit about how web pages were shown to handheld users over the past 10 years and the current state of the mobile world.

In the beginning, handheld devices, such as the earliest modern personal digital assistants (PDAs), had no direct connection to the Internet. This meant that any content

---

[2] At least it felt that way.

the user wanted to read from the web needed to be downloaded first and then stored on the device or cached. A very popular service for this, AvantGo, operated for a little over a decade before closing up shop in 2009. While these services were somewhat annoying (in that you needed to manually synchronize your PDA physically to your computer regularly to get the content you wanted), they generally presented content in a very basic and easy to read manner. Ironically enough, this type of presentation has experienced a bit of a revival as users today find content while online and otherwise busy (i.e. at work) and wish to save it to read later. One popular service, Read It Later (`http://readitlaterlist.com/`), even has a mobile client that shows these saved web pages in a similar format to the old "offline cache" system popular in the late 1990s! Figure 1–11 shows a cached article on Read It later.

Hafner's 2-run HR lifts Indians over Rockies 4-3

by TOM WITHERS, us.rd.yahoo.com
June 22nd 2010

CLEVELAND (AP)—Josh Tomlin(notes) came through with another quality outing and designated hitter Travis Hafner(notes) hit a two-run homer in his last start for a while, leading Cleveland to a 4-3 win over the Colorado Rockies on Wednesday night before the Indians leave for three NL cities.

Figure 1–11. *Read It Later, on Android, shows the cached version of a Yahoo! Sports article*

As PDAs with built-in Wi-Fi radios and smartphones became available, users could connect directly to a web page and view its content. Before direct access to the Internet, however, many telecoms delivered phones with WAP browsers. WAP, or Wireless Application Protocol, was an extremely simple data servicethat allowed users to navigate simple menus to get to the information they wanted. These menus were typically all text, with perhaps 1–2 images here and there, and were designed to be quick portals to things like web–based email, perhaps movie times, or weather information. Phones with WAP browsers weren't connecting to the Internet, per se, as they could only view what their provider had put on the menu, but at least they could view it wherever they had cell coverage, as opposed to downloading it and reading it offline.

A similar concept to WAP was the Java Platform, Micro Edition, and often abbreviated j2me. j2me allowed users to load small java applets on their phone that could connect to specific services in the same way WAP did, providing a similar experience. While j2me (Java Platform, Micro Edition) was available on phones 2-3 years ago, along with the ever–popular feature phone–friendly Brew MP operating system from Qualcomm, it was limited by odd security settings and precautions that providers might put on a phone. Oddly enough, it was available on phones that already had working web browsers that could go anywhere. This madeone wonder why you might load up a special Gmail j2me applet when you could simply visit the mobile version of Gmail.

Finally, by about 2005, most smartphones on the market contained a fairly decent web browser that one could open, type in a URL, and view an actual web page. These web pages were typically one of the following two varieties: normal web pages crammed onto a smaller screen (see Figure 1–12) or specially created mobile versions of a website (see Figure 1–13). Both had their advantages and disadvantages. The normal page usually looked horrible on a small screen, with information flowing off the page, unreadable, or in technical terms, unrenderable (rendering is the process by which a web page is shown in a browser). While the information was usually horribly displayed, if one had enough patience and skill, one could usually find what they needed.

Figure 1–12. *My personal blog, desktop-view, displayed in a mobile browser*

Mobile versions, on the other hand, are generally easier to navigate, as they are specially designed for smaller screens using variants of the HTML language like XHTML or CHTML. These pages look nice and are very usable, but usually lack specific content.

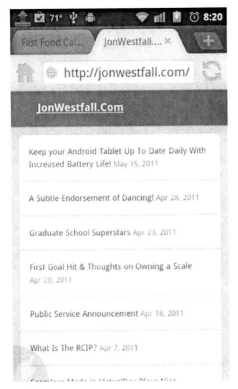

Figure 1–13. *My personal blog, displayed in a mobile view, in a mobile browser*

The goal of this book is to help you create mobile optimized versions of a website that contain much the same content as the desktop version might, while still being useable. As you might expect, users who find your page easy to use will be more likely to overlook some missing pieces. However, users who need 20 minutes (or as one of our editors pointed out, 20 seconds!) to find the latest game score or weather report will likely flock elsewhere.

Concepts We Like—And What's Ahead!

As we wrap up this chapter, we'd like to take a moment and discuss a few guiding principles that we like to keep in mind and hope you will to, not only as you read this book, but as you start programming your own web applications.

Concept 1: Think Like A User

Think about a website you own, one you've contributed to, or just one that you visit frequently, and ask yourself this: What do most people do when they visit this site? The answer might come quickly. However, it might be worth thinking deeper about just how "average" that answer is.

For example, a friend of mine recently published a few blog posts on The Huffington Post, a site known for the rapidity and outspoken way in which comments are quickly posted on an article. When he sent me the link to his article, I pulled it up and read through it. When I was done, I closed my browser and went about my day. Later in the week, my friend asked me if I saw the article and after I said I had, he asked "What did you think of all those comments?" The answer was simple. I didn't think anything about those comments, certainly not even enough to read them. However, in his mind, since they were feedback on his own work, the comments were much more interesting than the article itself (after all, to an author, their own work seems pretty familiar and uninteresting). Now imagine if my friend had designed the website on which his work was published. You might not be surprised if you saw user comments highlighted, perhaps even displayed prominently to the side of the article or somewhere else other than at the bottom, in smaller print. For my friend, the "average" user would be more interested in the comments than the article, when in fact, the opposite is likely true.

Thankfully, my friend isn't a programmer. But as programmers, we must keep track of what our users are doing with our website or application. If we focus all of our attention on a feature a user finds trivial, while ignoring needed updates or enhancements to core features users find essential, we may lose those users en masse.

Concept 2: Don't Annoy the User

The best example of concept 2 that I can give comes from the evil word "monetization", or simply the idea that "Hey, I did a lot of work, I'd like some sort of repayment in the form of legal tender!" Monetization typically comes from selling advertising; something that users understand is a fact of life. If you want something for free, you expect that in some way you might be subjected to an ad every now and then to keep it free. Most find this preferable to paying for content and, indeed, many publishers report earning more money through advertising than through sales of their paid products!

However, just because you're advertising to people doesn't mean you need to jam advertisements in their face! You need to use tasteful ads, ads thatpique the user's interest, and ads that don't annoy the user. Ads in every paragraph or on the top, sides, and bottom of every page are rarely effective.

Similarly, unnecessary content or special effects may also annoy a user. For example, recently I came across a page that used a special login button that had a nice raised edge and looked good on my desktop browser. However, on my Android smartphone, the browser was confused: Was this a button or an image? When I tapped on it, nothing happened. Finally, through a really odd motion of tapping and slightly holding and moving my finger, I got it to log in. The problem would have been solved, if the author of such a page had simply done one of the following:

1. Tested the page with a mobile browser

2. Used a standard web form button

In this instance, form took precedence over function. Don't get me wrong, fancy designs are fine, as long as they don't detract from usability.

Concept 3: Test-Retest Reliability

In my (Jon's) day job, I research how individuals make decisions and the effects of those decisions. In my research life, the concept of test-retest reliability means that results from one run through of a given task should be the same as the second time through (and subsequent). I'll borrow that concept from research methodology to discuss a view on testing your content.

Similar to Concept 1, users are all different. Most of them will have a slightly different setup than you have when designing a web page or an app. For example, right now I'm using a 27" monitor, something that as a designer I find very useful, but wouldn't expect most people to have. Thus, if I design a web page, I probably shouldn't assume that people's browser window is 1565 pixels wide and 912 pixels high, like mine is right now. This becomes especially important when working with smaller screens. Some Android phones and tablets have relatively large screens, while others have smaller screens. Testing your app or web page on a variety of devices (perhaps with the help of friends) ensures that your users get the best and most optimal experience every time they visit the site. One must also be careful about repeat visits, since browsers may cache content it should update. On the other hand, some of the techniques we'll highlight in future chapters make use of templates or frameworks that will make the browser cache your friend. These techniques reuse content the user has already downloaded!

Concept 4: Keep it Simple Stupid!

Nowadays, you cannot walk down the street without seeing some parent shove their smartphone in front of their toddler's face to keep them busy on long car rides or while at the store. Before this time of magical touch–based, Internet–enabled phones and tablets and before the time of broadband Internet, which I (Rocco) also like to refer to as "the time before time," it was considered a great privilege to get into a basic computer class. It was one of those things that was expected of someone in primary school to do if they ever wanted to have any sort of successful spreadsheet loving job when they graduated from high school.

Growing up religiously watching Star Trek with my father every week, you can imagine how ecstatic I was when I went into the sixth grade and was finally able take my first official computer class. I mean, come on! How could you not want to be like Scotty and whip up the formula for Transparent Aluminum in a matter of seconds on a computer that you were, just a second ago, talking into the mouse and trying to give it voice commands?! This is why that entire summer before school started was spent going to the library checking out every computer book I could find to prepare for what I thoughtmight be in store for my upcoming beginner's class to computers. That excitement quickly turned to disappointmentwhen I learned that the world of computers was not as glamorous and exciting as Star Trek and every movie with a computer hacker in it made it appear to be. Instead, the most I learned out of that class was how to make a copy of the Beverly Hills Cop theme song and put it on a floppy disk, as well as how to open a HyperCard application (though strangely enough we never learned to write a HyperCard application.)

That first year, as much of a disappointmentas it was, became the catalyst to my determination/obsession with computersthat lead me to sign up for a computer class again during my seventh grade year. Unbeknownst to me,this computer class, this minuscule hour a day out of my lifewould eventually lead to what has been a lifelong obsession. See, this was the year that AOL was starting to get really popular in the United States.Most importantly, this yearsaw the birth of HTML 2.0. My teacher at the time saw where this technology was going and embraced a vision of a future where information was exchanged freely. Every day in class, he would hammer home that one day the "people that create the Internet pages" (this was before the term Web Developer was coined) would one day be paid as much as doctors and lawyers and would be just as valuable and important. Of course, we all thought he was a crazy old man but his excitement for this future that he envisioned was enough to get me hooked and eventually I started believing in it and preaching it as well. He believed in this vision so much that the only work we had to do all year was create the school's entire website.

Out of everything I learned from that class, the most important rule I learned was the KISS principle, an acronym for "Keep it Simple Stupid." As much as I loved this teacher for what he gave me in terms of knowledge, there was no denying that he was a grouchy old jerk. Every time we had a brilliant idea for our school's website, such as adding animated GIF flames and sprites of Beavis and Butthead, he would always just say "Keep it simple stupid!" As annoying as it was as a child to constantly be shot down and basically called an idiot daily, it did wonders in teaching me the art of patience and restraint. It made me realize that even though Feature X, Y, and Z would be awesome on any given project I was working on, it was more important to put them on the backburner so I can get Feature A, B, and C coded and delivered. Now when I am working on a project, I sit down and map out exactly what I need to do to launch my project. I set aside any cool ideas I have for extra features that are not mandatory to a launch so I can work on them later whenthe task at hand will not sidetrack me.

No matter who you are and no matter how long you have been designing or developing, one thing always rings true. The hardest part of any project is starting that project. The more awesome features that aren't needed in your project that you end up adding in because they're awesome (e.g., adding flames to a hot rod to make it go faster), the harder it is for you to decide where to start with your project to get the ball rolling. So remember, no matter how incredible that idea you just had is, if it is not absolutely necessary to get your project off the ground and garner interest in it, then try to think twice before adding it to the project at this time. Make a mental note or physical note of this idea and come back to it later. A perfect example of this would be a program such as Twitter. When Twitter was released a few years back, it was a very sparse program built around the very simple idea of "What are you doing now?" As time went on, more new and exciting features were added as needed. Twitter has now developed from a silly little site where you could tell the world what you were eating for lunch into a heavily invested in web application that breaks such newsworthy events as the death of Michael Jackson and even played a vital role in getting information out of Internet-deprived countries in the midst of civil war.

Remember that Rome was not built overnight. It was a constantly evolving empire that was building upon itself everyday and you should look at your next web project the same way. Start small and add on as you can while not overwhelming yourself in the process. In essence—*Keep it simple, Stupid!*

Coming Up

Now that we've talked about the nuts and bolts of web design, the acronyms, the odd stories, and the concepts, let's talk a little bit about what you'll find in this book.

Starting off in the next chapter (just pages away!), we'll develop a simple application utilizing one of the most popular services on the Web today, Twitter. Twitter is a great web phenomenon so we'll stick with it for another small application in Chapter 3. Then we'll take a step back and look at the bigger picture—issues like how you develop an app in the first place (Chapter 4), and how to deal with different screen resolutions and browser platforms (Chapters 5 & 6). In Chapter 7 we're going to show off jQuery Mobile—and importantly, show you how to make your app look professional and 'pretty' with it. Chapter 8 will continue with this theme by showing off some nice resources to use in your user interface design. With that out of the way, we'll play around with location based and cloud based applications, and then finish the book with discussions on using audio and video, Ajax, and prepping your product to 'ship'. It's a lot of material to cover, but we know you're up for the trip! Also, if you haven't noticed, our trend is to give you a lot of information by example, then move back into a more textbook-like narrative. This way, hopefully, you'll stay engaged through this nail-biter of a computer book! (OK, that was a bit sarcastic, although we truly hope this approach will make for "fun" reading.)

So, without further procrastination, let's begin with our first application!

Chapter 2

Twitter Applications: Who's That Tweet?

Now that we have covered what we will be learning throughout the course of this book, it's time to get our hands dirty by jumping in and creating our first mobile web applications. Both of these applications will be very simple applications that interact with the Twitter API. An API, or an application programming interface, is an interface used to interact with a specific application based off a set of rules or parameters given to the application by the user. More often than not, one would use an API to gather and parse data from the application's infrastructure without ever needing to directly connect to the application's database to fetch that information.

The first application we will build is the application "Who's That Tweet?", which will parse through a small predefined list of verified Twitter users and display a random tweet on the page, as well as a list of four possible individuals that might have created that tweet.

The second small web application we will build is called "I Love Ham", which will also be borrowing Twitter's fire hose of data to create a quick and fun form of entertaining for mobile users on the go. "I Love Ham" will focus on very basic game mechanics. The user is presented with two predefined rhyming Twitter searches to choose from. If they choose the Twitter search that receives the most results back, then they are the winners. Both of these mobile web games will rely heavy on HTML5, JavaScript, and a fantastic piece of technology called JSONP.

In this chapter, we'll get you up and running with a development environment on your own personal computer (think of it as your own mini-Internet, which will connect to Twitter on the real Internet, but mostly live just on your computer) and discuss the Who's That Tweet? application. In the next chapter, we'll continue by discussing the I Love Ham application. Let's get started!

JSONP

You might remember us talking about JSON in chapter one. JSON is a wonderful piece of technology and chances are if you have worked in the web development field in the past few years, then you have probably run across it once or twice. If you've surfed the web in the past day, you've also probably run across a website using it! If you have ever worked with the APIs of Flickr, Twitter, or Gowalla, then chances are you are also very familiar with JSON. For those that skipped over chapter one completely, JSON is a human readable data interchange technology that is made to be lightweight and is also an open standard. As a technology, JSON is fairly young with its usage being traced back originally to a little after the turn of the century with the JSON.org (http://www.json.org) website launching in 2002.

If you are familiar using JavaScript and creating objects, then JSON should look relatively familiar to you. However, JSON is to not be confused with a JavaScript object as they are not the same. As much as I love JSON, there is one tiny little annoying thing that most developers are not aware of until they spend hours ripping out their own hair prematurely making themselves go bald and that is a really nasty, little, pesky thing called cross-domain scripting.

To understand what cross-domain scripting is and why there are hardcoded rules in place in your browser to prevent you from doing it, you have to first understand what cross-site scripting (XSS) is. XSS is a type of vulnerability in web sites and applications that allows an attacker or intruder to basically inject their own scripts and content into the site or system. An intruder might use an XSS vulnerability to upload a script to your server that would allow them to simulate a Bash shell (a common UNIX shell or command-line interface) for your server in their very own browser, or worse yet, possibly use that vulnerability to steal thousands of usernames and passwords from your database.

Due to these concerns, your browser will not load JSON data from a domain outside of your site's server in most cases. In order to grab and use that data, it would have to be grabbed on the backend server side before the page is loaded and then served to the user. This doesn't seem like that big of a deal until you start building applications that have thousands upon thousands of users. Then parsing that external data can end up impacting the performance of your server. To get around this performance issue and delegate some of those external data parsing requirements to the end user, we will use JSONP or "JSON with padding", which will allow our application to request the JSON data we need because it will be wrapped (or padded) within a JavaScript object.

Setting Up Your Development Environment

Before we can get started coding, we will need to set up a development environment. For the sake of simplicity, I will assume that we are using a Windows-based operating systems so I will only go through the steps of setting up a basic WAMP (Windows, Apache, MySQL, and PHP) server for us to test our code on. I know not everyone uses

Windows–based systems but chances are, if you are using Linux or OS X, then you are already familiar with setting up an *AMP environment for testing.

For our testing environment, we will be using the open source and freely available WAMP server called Uniform Server (http://www.uniformserver.com/). You can download the WAMP server from their website. The version I am using, and the version that will be shown in the screenshots in this chapter, will be from version "7.1.2–Orion."

Setting up the test environment is fairly simple. Just find the downloaded file that you grabbed from the website and run the self-extracting EXE file. Once you do that, open the folder. Before running the server, I wanted to go over a few helpful programs that the Uniform Server team included to make our lives easier. The first application is called Pre-Check (Run_pre_check.exe).[1] Let's run this application and look at the results in Figure 2–1.

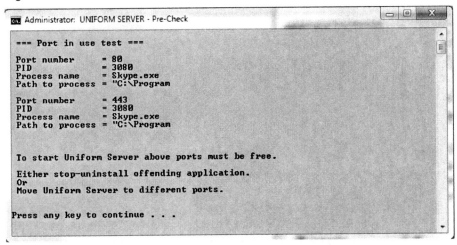

Figure 2–1. *Uniform Server's Pre-Check application showing that ports 80 and 443 are currently in use*

As you can see, if I tried to run the server at this moment in time, it would fail. I currently have Skype open and it is running on the classic HTTP ports (Ports 80 and 443) that I need to run the server. There's a one program to port rule in networking, so we need to do a bit of simple tweaking. While you do have the ability to edit some configuration files to change which ports you will use, for the sake of simplicity, I will just shut down Skype so we can run on a default set up.

Now that we have freed up our ports, we can run the "Start.exe" application that will open up and place an icon in your system tray. Right click the Uniform Server icon in your system tray. It looks like a blue box with the numeral 1 in it as seen in Figure 2–2 below. Choose the "Install and Run All Services" option at the top of the menu. Now, if you open up your web browser and point it toward http://localhost/, you should be

---

[1] You may need to run this, and other commands, as an administrator in Windows. To do so, right click on the command and choose "Run as administrator."

presented with the default Uniform Server starter page (localhost is simply another name for the computer you're currently working on, as is the IP address 127.0.0.1).

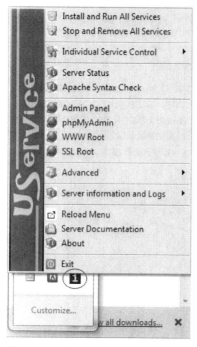

Figure 2–2. *Uniform Server menu as seen in your system tray*

Now that our server is up and running, we are *almost* ready to get started writing some code. The one last thing we have to do is familiarize ourselves with the server's default WWW root folder. If you open up the folder where you extracted your copy of Uniform Server, you will see a folder called www (see Figure 2–3). Anything that you place in this folder will be visible to any user that is viewing your site via a browser. Since we are going to be using our own project files, you can feel free to delete everything in this folder to start fresh. Later you might make use of these files when setting up your production server. However, for development purposes, they are not needed.

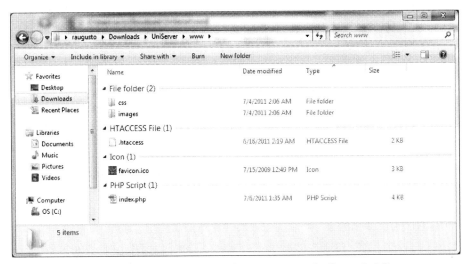

Figure 2–3. *The default WWW folder view that will house your application project files*

Now that you have managed to set up your own web server for local development and cleaned up the root folder, it is time to start some coding! If you need any help with your Uniform Server or just want to dig around a little deeper to see what you can do with this server, you can run the "help.bat" batch file in the Uniform Server directory and that will present you with some very in-depth documentation (see Figure 2–4).

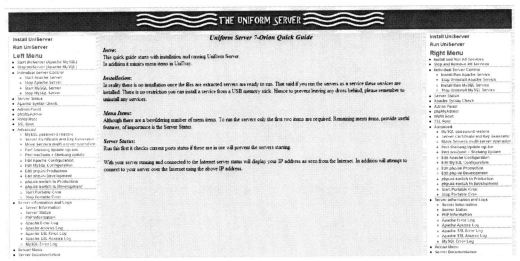

Figure 2–4. *Uniform Server quick help documentation*

Your First Mobile Web Application

Grab yourself some coffee and do a little stretching because now it is time to start some coding. The first application we are building, "Who's That Tweet?", will be a small and simple game that takes a collection of verified Twitter users and celebrities and randomly displays one of their tweets. The user will then be presented with a list of four Twitter users that could have possibly created that Twitter post. If the end user chooses the right Twitter user to go along with that post, then they will get 100 points added to their score and move on to the next random post. If not, they will be presented with a visual cue that their guessing skills were inferior and will move on to the next random Twitter post.

The first thing we are going to do is create a very basic HTML layout, or foundation, for our game. After that, we will move on to styling that bland skeleton layout with a little CSS3 and, once it looks pretty, we will finally move on to writing our JavaScript, which will tie everything together in our first mobile web application.

The HTML

Listing 2–1 contains the basic HTML for our game.

Listing 2–1. *Basic HTML for Who's That Tweet?*

```
<!DOCTYPE HTML>
<html>
<head>
<meta charset="utf-8">
<meta name="viewport" content=" initial-scale=1.0; maximum-scale=1.0; minimum-scale=1.0;
user-scalable=0;" />
<title>Who's That Tweet?</title>
<link href='http://fonts.googleapis.com/css?family=Droid+Sans&v1' rel='stylesheet'
type='text/css'>
<link rel="stylesheet" type="text/css" href="css/style.css">
<script type="text/javascript" src="js/jquery-1.6.1.min.js"></script>
<script type="text/javascript" src="js/main.js"></script>
</head>
<body>
    <header>
      <div class="score"><strong>Score:</strong> <span>0</span></div>
      <h2>Player 1</h2>
    </header>
    <section>
      <div id="tweet">
        <div class="avatar"></div>
        <div class="content"></div>
      </div>
      <ul></ul>
    </section>
  </body>
</html>
```

The HTML markup for the page is very bland and basic. Starting from the head element, the first thing you might notice that is slightly different from standard Desktop–based web development is the use of the meta element with the name "viewport". This element is extremely important when it comes to mobile design and development, and we'll talk more about it in Chapter 10. With it, you can control whether or not a user can zoom the content on your page or even how much the user can zoom into your page. Here we have the zoom of our viewport set to the default value and have turned off the option to let the user zoom in and out of the page so we do not have to worry about an end user accidentally double tapping the display causing your soon-to-be web application to zoom in or out while frustrating your user.

Once inside the body element, you might notice that we are using several of the "new" HTML5 elements such as header and section. The header element is a newer tag that is used to semantically structure your code to indicate the introduction to a page or article on the web. In our header area, we are using it to house the current score of the player, which we will update after each round with JavaScript, as well as the player's name. Keeping simplicity in mind for the sake of this demo, we will leave the player named Player 1.

Next up we have the section element, which is used to house the main content of our demo. Like header, the section element is a new HTML5 tag that is used to semantically mark the section of a document or a page. Back in the old xHTML days, we would usually designate sections of a page with a tidal wave of endless div tags, which could be extremely confusing to search engines and screen readers for the visually impaired. Now, with the proper use of the section tag, it should be fairly trivial for search engines and screen readers to better guess at what information on the page is the important information that should be read aloud or searched.

Inside the main content section of the page, we have a div container with the ID of tweet, which will be used to house the random tweet that we pull from the array of verified users, as well as an empty ul (unordered list) element that will be used to contain the four random verified Twitter users that we will display to the end user.

Inside of the #tweets container, we see two div containers—.avatar and .content. For those who are unfamiliar with CSS, anytime you see the hash tag (#) when referring to code in this book, it means that we are referring to the ID of an element. If we are referring to a tag by its class attribute, it will have a period sign in front of it as, such as .avatar above.

Now that we have the basic structure setup, it is time for one of my favorite parts of the whole process—styling the page with CSS!

The CSS

In the last chapter, we discussed CSS. Here, you'll learn more about it by seeing it in action. However, don't get discouraged if you don't follow everything that's going on. We'll talk more about it throughout this chapter and in the future.

With the CSS here, we are not going to do anything super fancy. However, we will take advantage of Android's Webkit[2] rendering engine to use some of the newer CSS3 features that have become popular over the past couple years. Let us start off with some basic styling resetting and general layout styles and then crawl through our CSS file section by section. In Listing 2–2, we will comb through the basic HTML elements on the page and reset their margin and padding, or how they are spaced apart from each other on the page, as well as reset the size of fonts and the type of font used throughout the document.

Listing 2–2. *Who's That Tweet? CSS File – Part 1*

```
/*** RESET ***/
html, body, header, section, div, p, ul, li, h2 {
    margin:0;    padding:0;
}
ul, li {
    list-style:none;
}

/*** GLOBAL CSS ***/
html, body {
    width:100%;
    overflow-x:hidden;
}
body {
    font-size:14px;
    font-family: 'Droid Sans', Arial, Helvetica, sans-serif;
    background:#06c;
}
h2 {
    font-size:14px;
}
```

If you have written any CSS in the past, this first bit of styling code should look very basic and familiar. We start off by resetting the margin and padding of several of the page elements to zero to guarantee that whatever styles we assign to the page will be positioned correctly across the vast array of Android–powered devices. This can be important especially when you keep in mind that Android is a rapidly developing platform with newer versions being released two times a year or more.

Next thing we are doing is removing any bullets that might be attached to unordered lists (ul) and list items (li) elements and then setting the pages default font and font size, as well as the applications background color.

Last but now least, we will be utilizing the "Droid Sans" web font. See, over the past couple years as the web has been evolving, designers and developers alike have been screaming and begging for a new and easier way to use those gorgeous fonts you see time and again in print advertisements on their applications and web sites they are working on. I mean seriously, who wants to stare of Arial or Times New Roman all day

---

[2] Webkit is an open source web browser engine, which means people can make web browser software using it. Android uses a custom version of it, as does Apple's iOS.

long? One of the incredible features of CSS3 is the use of including True Type fonts in your project. From now on, you don't have to rely on poorly compressed images or horribly intrusive Flash solutions to utilize beautiful typography.

Google has even gone out of their way to do us a favor by creating a free and open database of web safe fonts to be used to your heart's content. You can visit the Google Web Fonts website at `http://www.google.com/webfonts`. Once you find a font that you would like to use, Google will give you some HTML code to add to your layout to load the fonts into your browser and call it from your CSS file, as we have called "Droid Sans" as our page's default font (see Figure 2–5).

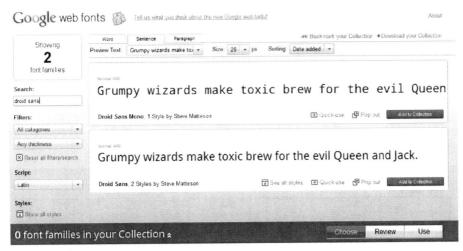

Figure 2–5. *Viewing the Droid Sans font on the Google Web Fonts website*

In Listing 2–3, we will provide the user with a stylish header that will rest on the top of their browser and will house the player's fake name as well as their score.

Listing 2–3. *Who's That Tweet? CSS File, Part 2*

```css
/*** HEADER ***/
header {
    width:100%;
    font-weight:bold;
    text-transform:uppercase;
    text-shadow: 1px 1px 1px rgba(255,255,255,0.5);
    line-height:40px;
    background-image: -webkit-gradient(
        linear,
        left bottom,
        left top,
        color-stop(0, rgb(135,135,135)),
        color-stop(0.8, rgb(201,201,201))
    );
    -webkit-box-shadow:0 0 15px rgba(0,0,0,0.5);
    box-shadow:0 0 15px rgba(0,0,0,0.5);
}
header h2 {
    margin-left:10px;
```

```
    }
.score {
    float:right;
    margin-right:10px;
}
```

The HEADER section of the CSS is where we will have a little fun and utilize some of the magic of CSS3. Before the widespread use of CSS3, if you wanted to create a section of your page that made use of a gradient background, then you would have to rely on creating images in a graphics design program and splice them to suite your needs. Now, just like magic, you can add some not-as-simple-as-it-should-be code to your CSS to create the same gradient effects you would get with Photoshop with just a few lines of code. On top of those new nifty gradients, we can also add in a drop shadow to our header with only one tiny little line of CSS code. It's like magic!

Listing 2–4 could be considered the entree of our CSS file in that it contains a majority of the properties that will be used to make our page look awesome.

Listing 2–4. *Who's That Tweet? CSS File, Part 3*

```
/*** SECTION ***/
section {
    margin:20px 10px;
    padding:10px;
    border-radius:7px;
    background:#aaa;
    -webkit- box-shadow:0 0 20px rgba(0,0,0,0.5);
    box-shadow:0 0 20px rgba(0,0,0,0.5);
}

section.fail {
    background:#990000;
    color:#fff;
}
section.win {
    background:#009900;
    color:#fff;
}
section.fail li, section.win li {
    border-bottom:1px solid #fff;
}
section.fail li:first-child, section.win li:first-child {
    border-top: 2px groove #fff;
}
section #tweet {
    width:100%;
    margin-bottom:10px;
    padding-bottom:10px;
}
section .avatar {
    float:left;
    width:48px;
    height:48px;
}
section .content {
    margin-left:58px;
    min-height:48px;
```

```
}
section .person {
    margin-left:42px;
}
section ul {
    width:100%;
    clear:both;
}
section li {
    margin:0;
    padding:5px 5px 5px;
    height:32px;
    line-height:32px;
    border-bottom:1px solid #666;
}
section li .avatar {
    width:32px;
    height:32px;
}
section li .avatar img {
    width:32px;
    height:32px;
}
section li:first-child {
    border-top: 2px groove #666;
}
```

The `section` portion of the CSS, like the HTML document before it, is where most of the magic happens. The first thing you should notice is another new nifty feature of CSS3 created by the Powers That Be to make our lives easier–border–radius. Now, instead of spending hours trying to splice together images correctly to have rounded corners in your document, or worse, relying on bloated JavaScript libraries to take care of our border radius needs, we can pass off that work to the browser's rendering engine and be done with it.

Here we utilize the border-radius CSS property to give our `section` container a nice modern smartphone look and then top it off with a nice drop shadow. Afterward, we define two sets of styles for the `.win` and `.fail` classes that we will call each round via JavaScript as a visual indicator of whether the user chose correctly.

Figures 2–6, 2–7, and 2–8 show our game view, the view after an incorrect answer and the view after a correct answer, respectively. Now, let's learn about the JavaScript we need for producing the user feedback views.

Figure 2–6. *Who's That Tweet? running in an Android 2.3 web browser*

Figure 2–7. *Who's That Tweet? display after failing to choose the correct owner of the tweet*

Figure 2–8. *Who's That Tweet? display after selecting the right poster of the tweet*

The JavaScript

Now that we have our page laid out and styled, it is time to make it dynamic with some JavaScript. All of the application demos throughout this book will make use of the jQuery JavaScript framework. If you are unfamiliar with jQuery, it is a fantastic, JavaScript library that is used the world over and makes cross-platform JavaScript development trivial when compared to the olden days of Internet Explorer 6's dominance.

There is a bit of JavaScript here, so I will break it up as I did with the CSS before it and explain what is going on one section at a time. When coding up this demo, I added a slew of helpful comments in the code along the way that should further help those new developers amongst us in understanding what is going on.

Listing 2–5 will walk us through a set of default variables that will be used in our application, as well as give us a very meaty array filled with some of Twitter's most popular verified users.

Listing 2–5. *Who's That Tweet? Javascript File, Part 1*

```
/**
 * Who's That Tweet
 * @author: Rocco Augusto
 * @file: js/main.js
**/

/* This array holds a list of verified
```

```
        Twitter accounts that we will use
        to pull in random tweets for each
        round
*/
var defaultIcon =
'https://si0.twimg.com/sticky/default_profile_images/default_profile_3_normal.png';
var currentRound = [];
var correct = '';
var tweets =  [
    'jimmyjohns',
    'sugarsammyk',
    'wilw',
    'JeriLRyan',
    'pattonoswalt',
    'trutriciahelfer',
    'AndrewWK',
    'ChristianKane01',
    'charliesheen',
    'levarburton',
    'edwardjolmos',
    'Rosie',
    'kevinrose',
    'jason',
    'leolaporte',
    'aplusk',
    'StacyKeibler',
    'LilianGarcia',
    'nicolerichie',
    'rainnwilson',
    'ericschmidt',
    'pennjillette',
    'nerdist',
    'Scobleizer'
];
```

Here we define a few global variables that will be used throughout the application. The first being the defaultIcon variable which contains a long URL for the image of the default user Twitter avatar we will be using throughout the script. We could have done without the variable and just added the code to our script when we needed it but it is always good practice when coding to cache as much of your code for reuse as possible. Now when we want to add the defaultIcon anywhere in our script, we do not have to remember some big long complicated URL that in most cases will just visually muck up our code.

Next we create an empty array called currentRound which will house all of the data we pull in from Twitter for the round we are on. We create a predefined array of verified users to randomly choose from. For this list, I just did a Google search for verified Twitter users and copied the names of all the users I found on the first page of the Google search.

If this were a real game based off of the Twitter API and not a demo, we would want to utilize an online server with a list of all Twitter verified accounts but, since we are starting small, an array will work just fine for now.

Listing 2–6 shows the second part of the main JavScript file for Who's That Tweet.

Listing 2–6. *Who's That Tweet? Javascript File, Part 2*

```
// this function will grab a random user from
// the tweets array.
function getRandom() {
    var l = tweets.length;        // grab length of tweet array
    var ran = Math.floor(Math.random()*l);       // grab random user

    // check if randomly selected user is in list
    if(currentRound.indexOf(tweets[ran]) == -1) {
        if(currentRound.length == 0)
            correct = tweets[ran];        // make first random user the correct user

        //push random user to currentRound array
        currentRound.push(tweets[ran]);

        // grab three additional random users
        if(currentRound.length < 4)
            getRandom();
    }
    else {
        // if random user is already in list then start over
        getRandom();
    }
}
```

In Listing 2–7, our next function will go through and select a random user from our
tweets array and then grab three other random users for the user to choose between as
seen in the function getRandom(). In this function, we use the JavaScript Math object to
do the heavy lifting in choosing our random user.

Listing 2–7. *Who's That Tweet? Javascript File, Part 3*

```
// grab the user avatars for users in currentRound array
function buildQuiz() {
    var l = currentRound.length;
    for(i=0;i<l;i++) {
        $.getJSON('https://twitter.com/status/user_timeline/' + currentRound[i] +
'.json?count=10&callback=?', function(data) {
            var img = data[0].user.profile_image_url;
            var name = data[0].user.screen_name
            var h = '';

            // crete the html that will be injected into the game screen
            h += '<li rel="' + name + '">';
            h += '   <div class="avatar"><img src="' + img + '" alt="" /></div>';
            h += '   <div class="person">' + name + '</div>';
            h += '</li>';

            // add users and images to page
            $('section ul').append(h);
        });
    }
}

function init() {
    //reset the correct answer and currentRound array
    correct = '';
```

```
    currentRound = [];
    $('ul, section').removeClass();
    $('ul').empty();

    getRandom();

    //display the default twitter account icon
    $('#tweet .avatar').html('<img src="' + defaultIcon + '" alt="" />');

    //grab a random tweet from the correct user
    $.getJSON('https://twitter.com/status/user_timeline/' + correct +
  '.json?count=10&callback=?', function(data) {
        var ran = Math.floor(Math.random()*data.length);

        console.log(data.length);
        console.log(ran);

        $('#tweet .content').html(data[ran].text);

        // randomize the currentRound array so the correct user isnt always first
        currentRound.sort(function() {return 0.5 - Math.random()});

        // grab avatars and display usernames
        buildQuiz();
    });
}
```

In our next two functions, we will initiate the application by calling the function init().
This function resets all the variables to start a fresh new game, parses the JSONP
Twitter API feed for the randomly selected verified Twitter account, and then passes
everything off to be built and displayed to the user through the buildQuiz() function.

Once the document loads into the browser and the DOM (Document Object Model - a
cross-platform representation of all of the objects in an HTML document) is ready to be
manipulated, the code below (Listing 2–8) runs. In jQuery, you can run your code when
the document is ready–the ondocumentready event in JavaScript land–by using the
following shorthand $(function() { ... code goes here });

Once the document is ready, we will call the init() function, which will reset everything
on the page, grab a random user, and build the quiz as we went through before. We will
also assign the click event to all list items that will be written to the page so they end up
working like buttons. Once a user clicks a list item, the application will replace the
defaultIcon with the correct avatar from the user that posted the Tweet, update the
score if the user chooses correctly, and assign the gameover class to the game, which
will then tell the application to start a new round if the screen is tapped again.

Listing 2–8. *Who's That Tweet? Javascript File, Part 4*

```
$(function(){
    // run the init() function and start the application
    init();

    // check for correct user on user selection
    $('ul li').live('click', function() {
        var name = $(this).attr('rel');
```

```
        var img = $('li[rel="' + correct + '"] img').attr('src');
        var score = $('.score span');

        // restart the game if game over
        if($('ul').hasClass('gameover')) {
            init();
        }
        else {
            // swap out default avatar for correct avatar
            $('#tweet .avatar img').attr('src', img);

            if(name == correct) {
                score.text(parseInt(score.text())+100);
                $('section').addClass('win');
            }
            else {
                $('section').addClass('fail');
            }

            // add gameover class to page
            $('ul').addClass('gameover');
        }
    });
});
```

And there you have it! For those of you coding along, congratulations, you have officially completed your first mobile web application. You can fire up your trusted Android device now (if you haven't already done so already), connect to the same network that your computer is on, and view your new application on it. To do so, just point your device's browser to the IP address of your computer. You can find your IP address by opening a command prompt (Windows) and running the ipconfig command (see Figure 2–9) or by opening a terminal (OS X/Linux) and running the ifconfig command.

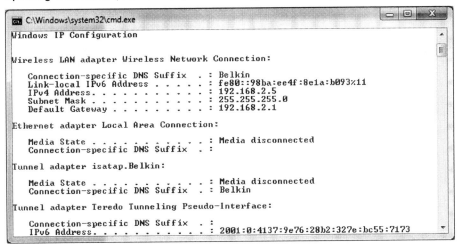

Figure 2–9. *The command prompt on Windows 7 displaying our server's IP address*

There you have it – your first application.

Summary

We've covered a lot of "applied" ground here, such as setting up your development server, writing CSS and JavaScript files, and testing out your new application. We'll continue this "applied" writing with another example in the next chapter before stopping to talk a bit more about the core concepts of web design. Now let's talk about ham in Chapter 3!

Twitter Applications: I Love Ham

Now that we have one mobile web application under our belt, I want us to explore using the Twitter API to do something a little different from the same old classic "displaying Twitter messages applications" that are cropping up left and right. As we discussed in Chapter 2, using the Twitter API gives you access to the alwaysplentiful "fire hose" of data that can be used for all types of applications and games—basically anything you can imagine.

One idea for which I have always loved using Twitter came from a series of old web shows that were around a few years ago. While the name of this game changed from show to show, the main principle behind the game was always the same. A user is presented with two different search terms that rhyme and would have to guess which term results in a higher number of tweets. While the rules are simple, this little game, which we will build and call "I Love Ham," can yield hours of fun. So without further ado, let's fire up our local development environments and start writing some code!

The HTML

The following, Listing 3–1, sets up the basic HTML document that will become the basis for our application.

Listing 3–1. *HTML for I Love Ham*

```
<!DOCTYPE HTML>
<html>
<head>
<meta charset="utf-8">
<title>I Love Ham</title>
<linkhref='http://fonts.googleapis.com/css?family=Droid+Sans&v1' rel='stylesheet'
type='text/css'>
<linkrel="stylesheet" type="text/css" href="css/style.css">
<script type="text/javascript" src="js/jquery-1.6.1.min.js"></script>
<script type="text/javascript" src="js/main.js"></script>
```

```
<meta name="viewport" content="width=320, height=device-height, user-scalable=no,
initial-scale=1.0, maximum-scale=1.0, minimum-scale=1.0" />
</head>
<body>
<section>
<h2>Which one of these fabulous tweets has more search results?!</h2>
<ul id="choices">
</ul>
</section>
</body>
</html>
```

The HTML markup that we are using in this application is going to be a bit sparser than it was in "Who's That Tweet?", the previous application we built, and it looks pretty similar too! For the sake of simplicity, I left the naming convention of the folder tree layout pretty much the same (see Figure 3–1):

- /index.html

- /css/styles.css

- /js/main.js

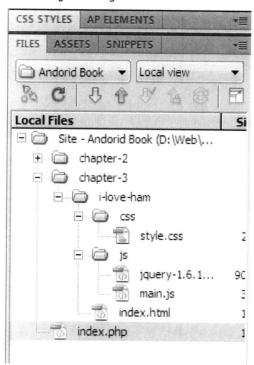

Figure 3–1. *A clean and easy to read file structure, as seen in Adobe Dreamweaver CS 5.5, will save you plenty of time and frustration down the road!*

When creating files and organizing your project's folder structure, I found that it is often useful to stick to naming schemes that are human readable, easy to understand at a glance, and consistent throughout projects. If you end up naming files "supercooldocument12-667.html," you make the documents harder for your end users to find, and it can cause issues down the road if you ever come back to your application to make future updates and edits.(Trust us: you'll completely forget what those files do.) Another tip would be to name files with the current date or to use a version control system to keep things straight. So remember, when it comes to naming files, keep it simple and/or meaningful!

The CSS

Our CSS is going to look similar to the previous application we built, as well. There are a few key differences here and there and a few neat CSS properties that we are showcasing in this application, such as the text-shadowCSS property, which allows you to apply some pretty fantastic shadow effects to your text live in the client's browser. This doesn't rely on having a designer to whip up some overly compressed image with the new fancy text as we would have done back in the old days (and by old days, I mean a few years ago!).

Listing 3–2 covers the basic resetting of spacing and font sizes of common elements that will be used throughout our application.

Listing 3–2. *CSS for I Love Ham -Part 1*

```
/*** RESET ***/
html, body, header, section, div, p, ul, li, h2 {
margin:0;
padding:0;
}

ul, li {
list-style:none;
}

/*** GLOBAL CSS ***/
html, body {
width:100%;
height:600px;
overflow-x:hidden;
}

body {
font-size:14px;
font-family: 'Droid Sans', Arial, Helvetica, sans-serif;
background:#993366;
}

h2 {
font-size:18px;
color:#fff;
text-shadow:1px 1px 5px rgba(0,0,0,0.9);
}
```

Our h2 tag is going to be the lucky recipient of our text-shadow. If you look in the HTML markup for this application, you can see that this h2 tag houses a blurb of text that will be presented to the user. Depending on the current state of the game, the text will change up to four times and will be updated by the application'sJavaScript. As previouslymentioned, if we were doing this the old way, we would have had to create four separate images containing the text we wanted and either manually inject those images into the page when needed or assign them as background images to CSS classes to be assigned to our blurb container as needed. While that would not have been hard to do, it would have required more code to be written as well as more graphical resources to be loaded on the device, which if the user is in an area with a slow data connection, can cause a noticeable moment of lag or cause the user to become emotionally disconnected fromyour app!

In Listing 3–3, we're going to set up the list items:

Listing 3–3. *CSS for I Love Ham– Part 2*

```
/*** SECTION ***/
section {
margin:20px 10px;
padding:10px;
}

sectionul {
width:100%;
margin:25px 0;
}

section li {
margin:10px 0;
padding:10px 5px 10px;
min-height:22px;
line-height:32px;
border-radius:7px;
background:-webkit-gradient(linear, 0% 0%, 0% 100%, from(#a1a1a1), to(#A1A1A1), color-
stop(.6,#8A8A8A));
-webkit- box-shadow:0 0 20px rgba(0,0,0,0.5);
box-shadow:2px 2px 10px rgba(0,0,0,0.8);
}
```

You will also notice we are doing something a little different with the List Items in our CSS as well. Here, we are adding a nice gradient background to the buttons to give them a little more oomph. Unlike the previous gradient backgrounds we created in our first application, this one is using a three color gradient system to give it more of a beveled effect. Also, just like our text-shadows, using CSS helps cut back on wasting our client's resources, for example loading images that we do not use. I know I'm really hammering that point home, but that's because it is a truly important rule to follow! Never carelessly waste your client's resources, especially when living in the current world of outlandish data caps or slow data connections. Last but not least in our CSS file (See Listing 3–4), I am going to introduce you to two very handy CSS selectors to familiarize yourself with—the :beforeand :afterselectors.

Listing 3–4. *CSS for I Love Ham– Part 3*

```
sectionli.fail {
background:#990000;
color:#fff;
}

sectionli.win {
background:#009900;
color:#fff;
}

sectionli.fail, section li.win {
border-bottom:1px solid #fff;
}

sectionblockquote {
margin:0;
padding:0;
}
sectionblockquote:before {
content: "\201c\ ";
font-size:26px;
float:left;
margin-right:5px;
padding-left:5px;
}

sectionblockquote:after {
content: "\201e\ ";
font-size:26px;
margin-left:5px;
padding-left:5px;
}
```

Now, these selectors are neat, as they allow you to add content either before or after the element they are attached to. Here, I am attaching them to the blockquote element, which is an older HTML element used to semantically mark that content as a quote that should stand out from the rest on thepage.

Now, if you look at the content property, you might be a little confused. In most cases, people usually add something meaningful to this field like a ">" in place of bullets on an unordered list, or an ellipsis after a blurb of content that links back to an article. Not a lot of people are aware, however, that you can also include Hex code in this property to display characters that are not commonly found on the keyboard, such as the quotation marks I want to add at the beginning and end of my blockquote content!

The JavaScript

Now that we have a good understanding of how everything is laid out, it is time to jump in and figure out how all the gears, pulleys, and sprockets are put together and get this application working! First, just as in our previous application, we start off declaring our global variables here that will be used throughout the application. In JavaScript, it is very important to understand the difference between using a global variable and a local variable.

In a nutshell, and I would like to take a moment to stress the fact that this is the most basic of explanations, a local variable is a variable that can be used inside a function but is not available for use inside of a different function or as a part of your script. Functions are basically "short-cuts" that can be reused. For example, I might create a function that does a bit of math on given input (called "function arguments,"that is, the information you put inside () after a function call) and re-use that same function throughout my code. Local variables are used inside function blocks but are not accessible outside. Think of the inside of your function as a small world apart from the rest of your code in terms of these variables!

A global variable, on the other hand, as you probably guessed by now, is accessible globally so you can call it in any function or object in your JavaScript file. While there are those out there that would scoff at the use of global variables because they *can*cause problems down the line. For example, a global variable could be updated from a variety of functions, causing confusion as to how the variable is changing during the debug process. However, for the sake of learning, since this is a book for beginners, we will use them in our examples.

Listing 3–5 sets up a list of global variables to be used throughout our JavaScript file, as well as an array filled with rhyming demo choices to keep our users entertained for hours... or minutes.

Listing 3–5. *Javascript for I Love Ham -Part 1*

```
/**
 * I Love Ham
 * @author: Rocco Augusto
 * @file: js/main.js
**/

var correct = '';
var choice = '';
varresultLength = 0;
var tweets = [
['I love ham','Earthquake in Japan'],
['Android is awesome', 'I just hit an opossum'],
['Ice cream sandwich','I fell out of my hammock'],
];
```

Unlike our previous game, we will have a smaller array of choices to be presented to our users. While I would have loved to add 50 to 100 different rhyming examples, unfortunately I was only witty enough to create three off the top of my head. For the time being, I think three is good, but if you are following along at home, try to put in as many as you can think of! I'm sure a good lot of you are a bit more witty than I am!

Listing 3–6 walks up through the `init()` function of our application and grabs our Twitter JSON feed from the API.

Listing 3–6. *Javascript for I Love Ham -Part 2*

```
functioninit() {
window.scrollTo(0, 1);

//reset the correct answer and currentRound array
correct = '';
choice = getRandom();
$('ul, section').removeClass();
$('ul').empty();

//find out which item has more search results
for(i=0;i<choice.length;i++){
var position = i;
$.getJSON('http://search.twitter.com/search.json?rpp=100&q=' +
choice[i].replace(/\s/g,'%20') + '&callback=?', function(data) {
//check the length of results for each search
//then set them to the "correct" variable
correct.push(data.results.length);
});
}

// generate the buttons for this round
buildQuiz();
}
```

Here we have our init() function, which will be called and run later in the application after the DOM (Document Object Model) has loaded. When using the Twitter API, there are several parameters youcould send with yoursearches. Let's run through them quickly!

   ▧   Rpp tells the API how many results we want back per page. In this
        case, we are pulling in the maximum of 100 results per search.

   ▧   Q is the parameter that will house our search query.

   ▧   Callback is triggered to make sure the API sends back data in a
        JSONP format so we are not presented with any cross domain
        security issues!

Another thing you will notice above is i in the search query, where we are calling in the term to search at that time. In that part, I am using the replace() method to search our string for all spaces and replace them with %20, which is the URL encoded version of a space. This allows the search to be sent via a normal HTTP request without messing up where the page really gets pointed to on the web. To get a better understanding of why this is necessary, imagine this—someone sends you a link to http://someawesomesite.com/some awesome page. Since the URL is broken up, if the person you sent that link to clicks it, then they would most likely be navigated to a page with the URL of http://someawesomesite.com/some, and the rest of the URL would be ignored, but clicking a URL that looked like http://someawesomesite.com/some%20awesome%20page would take the user exactly where they intended to go. Always make sure there are no breaks in the URLs that you create (see Figure 3–2)!

www.androidthoughts.com/news/show/112817/amazon-cloud-player-unlimited-music-storage-as-long-as-you-pay.html

Figure 3–2. *Notice the preceding URL from Android Thoughts uses hyphens instead of spaces to present the user with a much more friendly and human readable URL*

After we grab the JSONP data from Twitter, we are going to parse the data for the `data.resultsfield` and then grab the length of that array, the number of records in it, and then push them off to the `correctarray` that we created earlier, as can be seen in Listing 3–7.

Listing 3–7. *Javascript for I Love Ham -Part 3*

```
// this function will grab a random user from
// the tweets array.
functiongetRandom() {
var l = tweets.length;  // grab length of tweet array
var ran = Math.floor(Math.random()*l);  // grab random user

return tweets[ran];
}

functionbuildQuiz() {
var h = '';

for(i=0;i<choice.length;i++){
h += '<li>';
h += '  <blockquote>' + choice[i] + '</blockquote>';
h += '</li>';
}

// write buttons to the page
$('ul').html(h);
}

$(function(){
// run the init() function and start the application
init();

// check for correct user on user selection
$('ul li').live('click', function() {
var id = $(this).index();
```

```
var not = (id == 0) ? 1 : 0;
var result = '';

// restart the game if game over
if($('ul').hasClass('gameover')) {
init();
$('h2').text('Which one of these fabulous tweets has more search results?!');
}
else {
if(correct[id] > correct[not]) {
//congratulate the player
result = 'Congratulations! you are a total rock star!';
$('sectionli:eq('+ id + ')').addClass('win');
}
else if(correct[id] == correct[not]) {
//if it is a tie
result = 'It is a tie! You\'re a winner by default!';
}
else {
//shame the player into playing again
result = 'Boo! You failure!';
$('sectionli:eq('+ id + ')').addClass('fail');
}

// addgameover class to page
$('ul').addClass('gameover');
$('h2').text(result + 'Tap a button to play again!');
}
});
});
```

Before we continue, it's worth nothing that we've placed a backslash in the "You're a winner" line. This is because we've used an apostrophe, which JavaScript normally interprets as the closing of a string. By placing the backslash before it, we've 'escaped' it, telling JavaScript to use an 'alternate' meaning for the following apostrophe (in this case, the alternate meaning is to simply treat it as part of the string).

The rest of the functions are pretty similar to what we already created, so we will skip going over them to jump down to code that controls what happens when a button is pressed. Here in this code, we are grabbing the index, or position in the unordered list, of the button pressed. We then compare the value of that searchwiththe value of the other search. If your choice is the one with the greater number, then you win, and the blurb at the top of the page changes with a nice message congratulating you on your accomplishment or a message of failure if you choose poorly. In our logic statement, we also have instructions for what to do in case of a tie game and in casetwo searches have the same exact number of votes.

Now go ahead and save your work, fire up your browser, and run your newly designed application (see Figure 3–3)! While it is simple, I am sure you are starting to get a good idea of how, using HTML5, CSS3, and JavaScript, you can make a pretty fun and responsive web application in real-time!

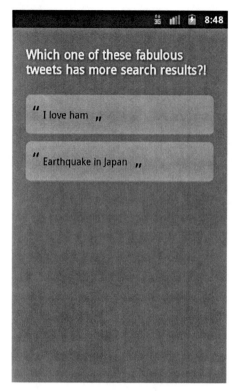

Figure 3–3. *I Love Ham running on an Android 2.3 device*

Summary

Not too shabby, if I do say so myself! We managed to take a little bit of code and a whacky idea and very quickly turn it into a nice looking proof-of-concept to play around with. We've shown another example of tapping into the Twitter API through JavaScript, and we've set up the stage for extending this to other aspects – not just searching Tweets, but also using trending topics and mentions. With a little more time and effort, we could build upon this very basic Twitter application and turn it into a full-fledged game that could suck hours away from our users' lives!

Chapter **4**

Basic Planning and Structuring of Your Application

Thus far, we've gotten you straight into coding a few apps, given you some background information on screen resolutions, JavaScript, and CSS, and we've given you a giant bag of free (and cheap) "stuff" in the form of various resources that you can use while developing. It would not be difficult for you to, given this information, go completely crazy coding all sorts of neat things and putting them out there for the world to see and use. The only problem is, without you actually considering what you're building, the world might not be too keen on actually using what you've built. And nothing can make one more depressed than spending hours and hours on a project that only you (and perhaps a few friends) will ever see.

In this chapter, we're going to talk about application development in two different ways: Planning your application, which involves understanding what you're building and how you can make sure you don't overlook vital pieces; and structuring your code, which is a much simpler idea but just as important for reasons we'll discuss. This is the "bringing order into chaos" chapter, and we hope that you'll heed our warnings and advice!

Know Thy Audience

If you have any sort of passion for creating something, than you might have had the experience before of thinking, "I wish that I had a tool that did [insert witty idea here] … I know, I'll just build it!" At this point you most likely went out and hacked something together for your own use, and then realized that others might be interested in using it as well. I know I do this all the time whenever I create a new web or mobile application, building for my own needs or for people that have needs like my own. Perhaps these people are your audience.

Or maybe you are just one of those people who see problems that others don't. You know that if you put something out there to solve a certain problem, others will latch on and praise your name. Perhaps they are your audience.

Or finally, maybe you're an innovator that thinks you have tapped into the next great game, service, or program that people will be clamoring to use. If you put a little effort into it (maybe only 50–100 hours of coding), you can see the dollar signs adding up from the addicted masses—they're certainly your audience, right?

Well, perhaps your passion, ingenuity, and innovation will be enough, and the audience will magically appear. But let's think about this for a moment; in each of the preceding examples, you're taking a rather large leap in assuming that your passions, problems, and joys will generalize to a lot of other people out there. If you were in a company and pitched these products to others, the first question would be, "How do we know we have an audience?" Simply answering, "I'd buy it," is not enough. You've got to have some idea of who you're targeting and whether they're interested.

Giving People What They Want

There are a number of ways you might start researching your next application. Sometimes a need jumps out at you, or you see an obvious opportunity. Other times you might think something would be a hit but have no idea whether it truly will or not. While you can watch Twitter and Facebook for complaints you could remedy, or perhaps use some sort of survey to understand what your audience wants, we'll present a very easy method here that speaks to one universal rule: Know what people are looking for. The followingmethod should give you some indication of how people are spending their time online, and thus let you know where you may have an opportunity.

We start with a popular advertising system on the web, Google's Adwords. It is free to sign up, and even if you never place a single ad, one tool Adwords offers that you might find very useful is the External Keyword Tool (`https://adwords.google.com/select/KeywordToolExternal`). This tool tells you how many people are searching Google for a particular keyword. It's a great way to see if people are actually interested in something you want to build.

For example, a project that I've considered building for some time (and actually have built up, in some sense) would be a web site for aspiring writers to hone their skills. I envision a web site where a person would get a topic, write some form of prose (short story, essay, poem, etc.) and have others vote on the piece. Winners of topics would have some "cred" given to them, and perhaps win real prizes.

How do I find out if there is a market for this? Well, I might use the Keyword Tool to do a few simple searches, like those in Figures 4–1, for the keywords "writing contest" and "writing help."

Search terms (2)			
Keyword	Competition	Global Monthly Searches ?	Local Monthly Searches ?
writing contest	▨	246,000	135,000
writing help	▨	90,500	60,500

Go to page: 1   Show rows: 50 ▾ |◄ ◄ 1 - 2 of 2 ► ►|

Figure 4–1. *Google Keyword Search for "writing contest" and "writing help"*

One should remember that Keyword Search is designed to be usedbyadvertisers, so a bit of deciphering the unfriendly mangled mess of language that is "Marketing SEO Speak" is important. First, I know that "writing contest" has about 2.5 times more traffic (in terms of monthly searches on Google) than "writing help." This is useful information in that it suggests that there are more people looking for contests and recognition versus constructive comments on their writing. If my web site or app is going to have both of these elements, it seems the contest angle might be better used. If, however, I'm not completely sure what my app or web site will be, I might find the Keyword Ideas list (Figure 4–2) to be particularly helpful:

Keyword ideas (100)			
Keyword	Competition	Global Monthly Searches ?	Local Monthly Searches ?
contest writing	▨	246,000	135,000
help with writing	▨	90,500	60,500
help in writing	▨	90,500	60,500
help for writing	▨	90,500	60,500
help on writing	▨	90,500	60,500
help writing	▨	90,500	60,500
essay writing contest	▨	49,500	33,100

Figure 4–2. *Partial Keyword Ideas list for the search terms above*

Here the "competition" column might be useful in telling me where to go. You see "competition" according to Google Adwords is how many other advertisers out there are trying to get their ads to appear when people search for the keyword listed. I'd have stiff competition for "contest writing" (or another item farther down the list, "free help writing a business plan"), but very little competition for "essay writing contest" (or another item not shown: "persuasive writing contest").

Using the External Keywords tool in Adwords, I can get an idea of not only for what people are searching, but also for what other companies are advertising. This can help you better understand if an audience exists for your product (by using keywords you suspect they'd use in Google) and if there are already a lot of alternatives you'd be up against. While word-of-mouth advertising can work well for some products, you shouldn't underestimate the power of search traffic!

Who Is My User?

Provided that you know an audience exists for your product, you now must figure out who your user is. Recently, in attending a course filled with bright, young future

MBA–holding executives, I was amazed to find them annoyed at the idea of "targeting" or finding their niche users and marketing specifically to them. They balked at the idea of not marketing to "everyone," without realizing that:a) "everyone" might not be interested and b) the target user is more motivated to actually use your product than a generic "everyman" (or "everywoman") out there.

Learning about your users is best accomplished by studying either your own product (in its early stages) or other products or web sites already in existence. If you're building an app that's going to track commuter transit arrival and departure times and delays, perhaps look around at whom competing apps or services are targeting. There is a good chance you'll be targeting the same group, and so putting some time and effort into considering that group's needs and desires in a product is time well spent.

Let's talk through an example of this, with the fictional transit application I mentioned earlier. Identifying an audience can be difficult, and you may need to consider more than one group of people. One group that seems logical to consider is busy commuters or business travelers. If I want to target this group, I might ask and answer a few questions, such as:

- What features in my app or web site will be attractive to busy people?

- What features, nuances, or procedures in my app will slow down a fast–moving person?

- What features can my app have that would actually be useful to someone who uses public transportation?

- How can I easily signal to my busy user that something important is going on (i.e., a late arriving bus or train)?

- How will my application be used? Will it be used to plan a trip, or at the last minute to reroute? Or both?

The list can go on from there, but you get the picture. By developing a hypothetical "user" and putting yourself in his or her shoes, you can better understand what you need to do to make his or her life easier. Make it easier, and you'll gain a user or customer! Then simply rerun the same research on your next demographic, perhaps this time "leisure travelers" or "tourists."

Not all of this research has to take place in your head; resources exist to tap into what your potential users are saying. Perhaps take a look at the reviews of your potential competitors, and see what people are loving and hating about those apps. You can also check out user groups and forums, and even conduct simple Twitter searches to get a handle on the "issues" in a given area.

As I mentioned a few paragraphs back, you might also already be in a position to have this information at hand. If you've developed a web site or application in the past, you might have used a product such as Google Analytics (http://google.com/analytics) or Flurry Analytics (http://www.flurry.com). These products can track who uses your application and give you invaluable information that you can later use to define your "user."

For example, in one application that I wrote, I had a simple form that people could use to tell me a bit more about themselves. From there, I found out that the average user of my app was between 25 and 34 years old, as seen in Figure 4–3.

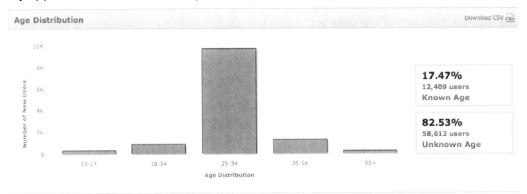

Figure 4–3. *The age distribution for an application*

This information can be useful in a number of ways. First, I might think about features this group would find important and focus on those in future releases. Or perhaps I'll shift my small advertising budget away from the teen to early 20's market and focus more on 25– to 34–year–olds to attract new users. The more I know about my users, the better I can understand their needs, and the better my web site or application can serve them.

One word of caution though: you might notice that my application only has known information for 17% of users. It happens to be that the portion of my application that records this information may be more useful to certain demographics, which could skew my data. Without getting deeply into discussion about this particular program, it is good to note that you should never rely on one source, especially if you have only a small bit of data, or feel you may have a skewed sample.

Once I have information from a variety of sourcesabout my audience and my users, I can create a plan.

Having a Plan

Planning is quite possibly the easiest thing to overlook as a new developer eager to play, build, and profit. In this section, we'll discuss issues regarding what type of application to build, how that application should look, and how the user should move through it. By understanding all of these from the start, we can keep our priorities in order, and when coding, simply implement what we've already worked out. Let's start by looking at the different types of mobile applications or interfaces we could build.

All Mobile Is Not the Same

The title of this book includes the words "web apps," which inherently acknowledges that there are other sorts of apps out there. Let's talk about the three types of mobile interfaces or applications.

Native Applications

If you've owned or used an Android phone (which I hope you have, if you're reading this book), you've probably used a few of the applications on it. The web browser is one of these applications, the contacts application is another, and the calculator application is still another. These applications, for Android, are generally written using Java and compiled using special tools known as the Android Software Development Kit, or SDK. These tools are free to download and use, to create applications that you can publish in the Android Marketplace.

These applications are called "native" applications in that they execute straight from the phone. The user has a dedicated icon for them, and tapping it opens the application (See Figure 4–4). These applications can store data easily on the phone, and can interface with one another if the user allows. Typically they must be downloaded and installed via the Marketplace or a publisher's web site but can also be "side–loaded" or installed on a device by downloading and running the application's APK package on your handset.

Figure 4–4. *FAILboard Pro:a native Android application*

Native applications tend to be faster because all pieces of the application live in the phone's memory and they also have deeper access to the hardware of the phone, which the web browser does not have. By the same token, native applications come with risksto the end–user; the application just installed might really be a trojan trying to steal information, or the developers, in a haste to push out an update, did not pay attention to what they were doing and left a security vulnerability in place. This is similar to what happened to Skype in 2011, when someone discovered that usernames and passwordswere being saved on users' handsets in unencrypted human–readable text, which anyone could easily retrieve. Luckily, a fix for the problem was quickly made available. For developers, developing a native application may take more time and may also come with a steeper learning curve, especially if the developer is already versed in HTML, CSS, JavaScript, and other web technologies.

Mobile Web Sites

A mobile web site, or website optimized for mobile devices, is generally viewed by users after they navigate either directly to it or to the regular web sitewhich redirects them to the mobile version. These are still websites, and do not normally store data on the user's device or interact with it very closely. Essentially, they are just there to be a presentation and not really to interact intensely with your users. This is generally the most basic way for a company or web site to improve the mobile user experience. Mobile web sites allow you to conduct some basic operations, but do not interact with you other than to provide a few simple pages of text and perhaps a form or two.

Because of this, these web sites lack the "full featured-ness" of their bigger brothers on the desktop (i.e., the full web site) and also may not be particularly optimized for smartphone or tablet screens (e.g., tablets may see a too–big version, smartphones may see a too–small version, depending on which device the web site is targeting). While developers may like this approach, as it's fairly simple to create, update, and test, end–users do not think of these mobile web sites as applications. If your goal is to build something for interactivity or to be seen as a tool, then you will probably want to avoid the simplicity of this approach in favor of a Web Application.

Web Applications

Finally we get to the union of the first two types of applications we've discussed, and the type of application we've been developing in this book. Web applications attempt to bring the seamlessness of a native app with the relative ease of coding and updating that comes from a mobile web site. For example, our earlier apps in this book (see Chapters 2 and 3) had buttons users could easily push, just like the native app shown in Figure 4–4, but lived inside of a web browser. If the user were to create a shortcut to the application (or the application itself could ask the user if they'd like to create one), then the app could have its own icon just like a native app does. There are also techniques that web apps can use to integrate themselves into the operating system just like native apps do.

It is best to think of it this way: web applications, just like regular applications, are meant to be interacted with instead of just viewed.

So Which Do I Build?

By now, you might be wondering what direction you really want to go. And honestly, while this book focuses on the benefits of web applications (as they are generally easier to program than native applications, are more full featured than mobile sites, and are accessible to beginner programmers), you might not be able to use just one solution. Again we refer to the idea of knowing your user. If your user is in an area where they'll always have cellular service, then perhaps a web app will be just as useful as a native application. If the user uses a variety of different devices (e.g., Android, Windows Phone, or iOS powered), then a web app might be the easiest way to be on all three of those platforms at once.

In the end, you must develop your mobile strategy to accommodate your user. Later in this book (Chapter 13), we'll tell you how you can "cheat" a bit by turning a web app into a native app with little to no work (thus allowing you to have at least a web app and a native application for Android).

Once you've chosen how you want to build your mobile strategy, you should consider avoiding the urge to jump right in and code something. A good developer plans out his or her applications, whether they are native, web-based, or mobile web sites. This step can be grouped under the idea of structuring your application, which we'll discuss next.

Structuring Your Application

In this section, we're going to talk about the process of designing your application from the ground up. This takes the form of three steps, a wireframing or mockup stage, a graphical designing phase, and a code structuring stage. Let's start by talking about design.

Wireframing / Mockup

It can be very tempting to have an idea, and then immediately begin coding it up without thinking about how the end product is going to look. This can be a bad idea for a number of reasons:

- It might lock you into a design that doesn't really look that good in the end (i.e., it's too cluttered). Or you might realize that your design isn't as efficient as it could have been if you hadn't jumped right into creating buttons and boxes!

- It might prevent you from innovating because you don't "feel like" changing things to add new features.

- It might stop you from soliciting feedback until the end of the project, when it may be too time consuming to change things. It's easier to show your design to users to see if they find it intuitive, and then tweak a drawing, rather than show them an app and then recode to make the design better.

To prevent these things, many designers create wireframe diagrams or "mockups" of their applications. For example, a very crude mockup for a transit app like the one we discussed earlier might look like this (Figure 4–5).

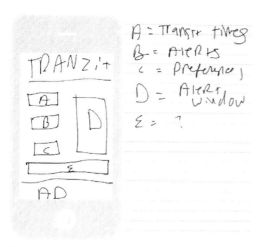

Figure 4–5. *A crude mockup of the Tranzit application*

As I mentioned, this is a rather crude mockup; in fact, it's probably not even version .0001 of the design I'd eventually have. In mocking it up though, I do realize something. I built buttons for transit times, alerts, and preferences; I set aside space for alerts; and I even set aside some space at the bottom for an advertisement. However, I have another bit of screen, labeled "E," that I have no idea what I might do with. With a mockup, I can simply erase and redraw to get it right. If I were developing this in real life, though, I might end up with an empty space there without really realizing it until it was already near version 1.0.

Obviously, you can create mockups however you like. Figure 4–5 was created using an application on my tablet which lets me draw freehand (as you can probably tell). One could also lay out a mockup in a web editor with actual images, buttons, and more (even though the buttons would not actually work). Another option is to use a program such as PowerPoint or Keynote, where it is easy to draw boxes, make animations, and create many similar drawings.

HotGlooand Other Mockup Tools

If you are looking for a web-based tool for creating your mockups, then you might want to check out HotGloo. The product home page is shown in Figure 4–6 (http://www.hotgloo.com/). This tool, which comes complete with a monthly subscription, is probably one of the best and easiest-to-use wireframing tools that I have used. Some wireframing tools I have used provide you with only the basic wireframes, but HotGloo allows you to do a lot of your visual designing and wireframing simultaneously, saving you time.

Other products that you may want to consider include LucidChart (http://www.lucidchart.com) and Pencil Project (http://pencil.evolus.vn), which may integrate into existing tools you already use, such as Microsoft Visio.

Figure 4–6. *The HotGloo web site, which we can safely assume was wireframed in HotGloo*

User Movement: Navigation or Storyboard

Once you have your wireframe completed, it is then time to sit down and connect the dots to figure out how you are going to structure the content on your site, mapping out all of the pages and the sections to which they will belong. This part of the process is called site mapping and can be pretty easy and fun if you take your time with it. If your application isn't particularly linear (e.g., perhaps it's a game), you can also think of this as storyboarding. In the simplest terms, it's laying out content in an organized and logical manner.

While creating your map it is best to try and keep content that is similar in similar sections or groups. This will make it easier when building your app as you can easily see at a glance what pages in your application need to be associated with each other.In the case of a game, think of this as presenting your information in a logical manner:keeping all of the "gold" and things you can buy with it together, orall of the "life points" and enhancements affecting them together, and so on.

Take a look atFigure 4–7 following to get a better idea of how a traditional sitemap looks. Notice how it is very similar to those family tree projects that we were all forced to do in grammar school? Well, it is pretty much the same principle. The parent pages (or sections) of the site each have child pages that are associated with that section or category.

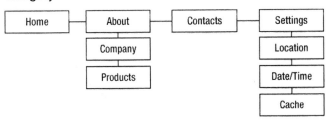

Figure 4–7. *A simple sitemap for demo application*

For this sitemap, I used a graphic design tool to create the mockup for this book; butwhenever I am working on a project for personal use, or when I am sitting down with a client that wants to see something quickly, I will sketch the sitemap and wireframes out on a napkin or piece of notebook paper.

Use whatever you have available to create your sitemap. No matter how it is created, the important thing is that yousit down and thinkthrough how your pages are organized to make building and developing easier on your end.

The last thing any developer wants to do is get 80% through working on a project, only to have to go back and do something over again because a mistake was made due to a lack of proper planning!

Now that we know how the app looks and how the content is organized, we can begin coding. Let's spend the last few pages of this chapter discussing how best to structure our development environment for maximum productivity.

Structuring Your Development

With the high-level information set, you'll also want to consider good practical rules for development that can keep you organized and efficient while writing your app. Following, we'll discuss some ideas for structuring your code and the directories in which it will be kept.

Code Structure

Now that you have your wireframes completed and you have a rough idea of where you want all the elements on your page to go, it's time to start figuring out how you are going to structure your code so you are not doing more work than is needed when building your applications.

You're probably scratching your head right now thinking,"How difficult can it be? I'm just writing text to a page."You would be right. However, let's say you have ten different pages in your application. You push out an update to your web application and realize that you have a problem with something in your footer.

If not properly prepared, our hapless developer may have copy and pasted the same footer throughout ten different HTML pages that make up the application. Now that it is time to update that code, our fictional developer has to update ten different HTML files with the new footer information.

An easier way to properly structure this code would have been to take the footer information, which is the same throughout the entire site, and create a separate file for it. Then in your code you can include that file into your page templates and display it on every page as before. If you ever have to change that code in the future, with this method all you have to do is change the code in one file, making your life a lot easier.

Let's take a look at the sample following. In Listing 4–1 we have a very sparse page that is using PHP to pull in that extra page code that we would like to have on each page.

Listing 4–1. *Using a PHP Include Statement We Will Pull In Extra Code to be Included On Our Page*

```
<!DOCTYPE HTML>
<html>
<head>
<meta charset="utf-8">
<title>Super Cool Web Application</title>
</head>
<body>
<header>Super Awesome Header</header>
<article>
<header>Article Header</header>
<p>Fusce luctus accumsan odio. Cras vel sodales mi. Suspendisse et arcu quis magna
feugiat ultrices sit amet non erat. Etiam malesuada dui venenatis eros gravida aliquet.
Aliquam erat volutpat. Nullam dapibus cursus ultricies. Suspendisse congue accumsan
purus non scelerisque. Phasellus ut sapien libero, vel luctus velit.</p>
</article>

<!-- This is where we use PHP to include another file into our document -->
<?php include('footer.php'); ?>

</body>
</html>
```

If you look toward the bottom of that listing you will notice that I am pulling in the page
footer.php (see Listing 4–2). I am doing this by wrapping my include function in the
<?php ?> tags. This tells your page to execute PHP code if your server supports it, and
in this code is looking for the footer document that is in the same relative path as the
document listed previously. If you are using the Uniform Server local development server
that we discussed earlier in the book, then this should work like a charm. Otherwise we
may need to specify a relative path; for example, if I put all of my "included" files into a
directory named "includes," my code may read: include('includes/footer.php'). We'll
talk about directory structure in a moment, so once you're done here you'll know how
the relative path will look to your files.

Now that we know what it looks like to include a file in your document using PHP, we
are going to take a look at what the innards of that PHP file look like, so you can see
how simple it is to structure your code in an easy, reusable fashion.

Listing 4–2. *A Look Inside the footer.php File*

```
<footer>
<ul>
<li><a href="#">Home</a></li>
<li><a href="#">About</a></li>
<li><a href="#">Contact</a></li>
<li><a href="#">Privacy Policy</a></li>
<li><a href="#">Terms and Conditions</a></li>
</ul>
<p>&copy; 2011 Super Awesome Site, Inc. All rights reserved.</p>
</footer>
```

As you can see here, the code in this document is pretty basic. We have an unordered
list that is floated to the right of the document and some copyright text that will float to
the left of it. We will just imagine that somewhere off in the distance there is a stylesheet
created for this document that makes everything pretty.

Now the cool thing about PHP is that it runs on the server, not on the client side. That means that none of the PHP code you include in your HTML document (whether this means including other documents into your template, or custom created classes, functions, etc.) will ever be visible to the client. What the client will see when he or she loads the page and views the source is just one seamless HTML document (see Listing 4–3).

Listing 4–3. *Viewing Our Faux Article In a Browser Would Show One Complete HTML Document, With No Server Side PHP Code*

```
<!DOCTYPE HTML>
<html>
<head>
<meta charset="utf-8">
<title>Super Cool Web Application</title>
</head>
<body>
<header>Super Awesome Header</header>
<article>
<header>Article Header</header>
<p>Fusce luctus accumsan odio. Cras vel sodales mi. Suspendisse et arcu quis magna
feugiat ultrices sit amet non erat. Etiam malesuada dui venenatis eros gravida aliquet.
Aliquam erat volutpat. Nullam dapibus cursus ultricies. Suspendisse congue accumsan
purus non scelerisque. Phasellus ut sapien libero, vel luctus velit.</p>
</article>

<!-- This is where we use PHP to include another file into our document -->
<footer>
<ul>
<li><a href="#">Home</a></li>
<li><a href="#">About</a></li>
<li><a href="#">Contact</a></li>
<li><a href="#">Privacy Policy</a></li>
<li><a href="#">Terms and Conditions</a></li>
</ul>
<p>&copy; 2011 Super Awesome Site, Inc. All rights reserved.</p>
</footer>

</body>
</html>
```

Folder Structure

In the previous example we discussed segmenting your files into small structures to make them more manageable. With more files, you'll probably also want to create directories to store specific files grouped by function.

In Figure 4–8, I created a mock folder structure for a make–believe application. Just like separating your code in your documents, it is also good practice to neatly arrange your folder structure in such a way that you can easily find the files you need throughout the development life of your app.

Figure 4–8. *A neatly organized mock folder structure as seen in the file browser of Adobe Dreamweaver CS5.5*

Here we are sticking with a very basic structure in which all of the resource directories (such as our css, img, and js folders) are in the Document Root folder of the site, and there is a template folder which will hold the template code for the different pages of our web application.

Inside of the template folder there is an includes folder which we will use to house documents that are used throughout the application, such as markup code for the header or footer, and maybe even some random blocks of content. Referring to our example in the previous section on relative paths, the include line in our index.php file in Figure 4–8 would reference the footer file as include ('template/includes/footer.php'). This not only keeps things separated, it makes logical sense as well. The footer is part of the template, and it's included in pretty much everything, hence it lives in the includes directory, within the template directory.

Now when it comes time to develop our application or make an update in the future we won't have to try and remember where all of our code is located because we can easily and logically find it at a glance.

If we want to edit the information on the contact page we will just edit the template file located at /template/contact.php. If we see a problem with the header file we can easily jump into /template/includes/header.php and make any changes we need to our hearts' content, and then have those changes reflected throughout the entire application.

Summary

Hopefully now that you reached the end of yet another chapter you have a better idea of what kind of thought process and work goes into the creation of a web application, or even a web site, before the actual coding begins. If you were working for an agency or studio, or other developer–centric business, then you would probably be on a team of people and each person would be responsible for their own tasks and taking care of different parts of planning before it was handed off to you as a developer. (You'd probably also have a lot more in terms of testing teams, development milestones, builds, etc.) If you are working for yourself, however, you now know what to do to make your life a little more bearable and your workload just a bit more tidy.

Chapter 5

Handling Multiple Screen Resolutions with CSS 3

One of the hardest things to deal with when designing websites is the myriad of different user configurations you might encounter. Modern web browsers and operating systems are highly configurable, and different options can affect how your web application is viewed. In this chapter, we'll talk specifically about screen resolution—or the number of pixels on the screen—and how one can accommodate varying resolution settings using CSS 3.

A History of Tired Eyes and Resolution Evolution

If you've ever used a computer late into the night, perhaps after a long day of work, you might have discovered a helpful trick: You can change the size of the objects on the screen to make reading them easier on your eyes. This generally involves changing your computer's display resolution. The resolution is simply the number of pixels that are displayed by your screen and is given in two numbers—the first for the number of pixels wide, the second for the number of pixels tall (i.e., height). By changing resolution, most often by scaling it down from something high, such as 2560 x 1600 (incidentally, what I'm using as I type this page at 7 PM at night), to something lower (perhaps 1600 x 1200—a good 11 PM resolution) you're taking away individual pixels, which means that items on your screen will appear larger.

In the late 1990s, as people began to surf the web in larger numbers, the standard resolution was known as VGA (for Video Graphics Array) and it was commonly set as 640 x 480. As time went by and monitors became larger, cheaper, and more efficient, most users adopted SVGA (the S being for Super—honestly!), at 800 x 600. This gave way to XGA (Extended Graphics Array—thankfully not Xtreme) at 1024 x 768, and larger. Today, my monitor is displaying WQHD (Wide Quad High Definition) at the aforementioned 2560 x 1600.

As you can imagine, web designers have struggled with screen resolutions for years, ever since 640 x 480 went out of style. They eventually diverged into two camps—those who supported designing for one resolution (a "fixed-width"), and those who designed for multiple resolutions ("flexible-width"). The fixed-width folks believe that the best web design is one in which you are absolutely sure that all users are seeing your website as close to the way you designed it as possible. This means picking a resolution, such as 1024 x 768, and designing your page to make use of that space (see Figure 5–1). If the user has a larger resolution set, your page will simply have extra space at the sides, but the tables and placement will remain where you want them, within your 1024-pixel width (see Figure 5–2). If the user has—horrifyingly—a smaller resolution, then your content will take up more of the screen than they have to give, and they'll be forced to use the absolutely dreaded horizontal scroll bar for your page.

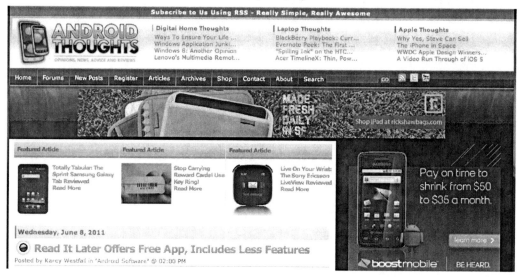

Figure 5–1. *An example of a Fixed-Width Webpage at 1024 x 600 resolution*

Figure 5–2. *The same page at 2048 x 1536 resolution. Note the wide black bars on the sides*

In comparison, a flexible-width layout will try to accommodate resolutions of all sizes (see Figures 5–3 and 5–4).

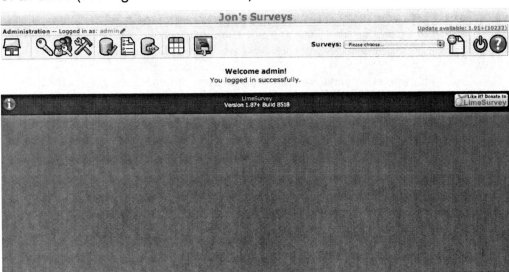

Figure 5–3. *An example of a Flexible-Width Webpage at 1024 x 600 resolution*

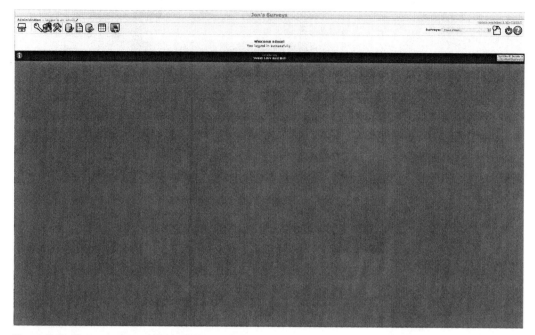

Figure 5–4. *The same page at 2048 x 1536 resolution*

By now, you might have started looking at your smartphone or tablet and thought, "Hmm… wonder what the resolution is on this thing?" You know what? That's what most of the designers of mobile web pages are wondering too. Currently, with Android activations hovering around 350,000 new devices a day, designers and developers alike are realizing they need to make drastic changes in their approach to web application development in order to stay relevant with the vast array of devices we use daily to view the web. It's a hard game to play if you favor a fixed-width approach: What resolution do I build my mobile app for? There are some easy answers ("Well, most people have iPhones, I'll just build for that"), but they have their downfalls ("What?!? They made a BIGGER iPhone called an iPad… uh oh…"). By targeting specific devices, you also tend to annoy users of any device other than your target.

In this chapter, we'll offer you a bit of "screen resolution." That is to say, we'll attempt to solve the problem by discussing how your mobile web application can actually be intelligent enough to understand the resolution, and even the orientation, of the device that your user is using and adapt automatically for it. It's almost as if you'll be coding up a small brain that says "Hmm, this device has a lot of width; let's show everything we can" or "Oh, no; this is a small screen. We can't show this information side by side!" As a designer, we can harness the small brain and make it even more intelligent, by letting it display the same content in a variety of different ways to different devices and—by extension—different users. Let's begin with an example.

The Daily Droid

Imagine you've decided to start publishing a daily newspaper for Android users and you've come up with a great title: The Daily Droid. The only problem is that some of your users are using a Motorola Xoom, which has a resolution of 2048 x 1536; some are using a Samsung Galaxy Tab (a 1024 x 600 resolution); and still others are using the Roccwest XTreme, which for some odd reason has a resolution of 1280 x 800. If you were to target one of these devices, the other two wouldn't look quite right using a fixed width. Thankfully, we can write one page that will look fine in all three—see Figures 5–5 through 5–7:

Figure 5–5. *The Daily Droid at 1024 x 600 resolution*

Figure 5–6. *The Daily Droid at 1280 x 800 resolution*

Figure 5–7. *The Daily Droid at 2048 x 1536 resolution*

Comparing these figures side by side can be very surprising—the content is exactly the same, but the layout has shifted quite markedly. The even more amazing part is that this is the same page—our developer was able to create it once and make it smart enough to react appropriately at these three different resolutions[1].

But what about our friends without tablets? Well, with a tiny bit of work, we can also accommodate them with the Daily Droid Smartphone Edition, as shown in Figure 5–8 (portrait orientation) and Figure 5–9 (landscape).

Figure 5–8. *The Daily Droid at 480 x 859 resolution*

---

[1] In this case, the developer (Rocco) had no idea what resolutions the guy writing the narrative (Jon) was going to pick, and yet the page still looks great.

Figure 5–9. *The Daily Droid at 859 x 480 resolution*

Let's take a look at the code behind the Daily Droid to discover both how the page is built, and how we determine if it should say "Smartphone" or "Tablet" edition. We'll go over the HTML in the next section and then the CSS in the following section. Reading through the following code, you should, based on the comments, get a sense of what each section is doing.

The Daily Droid's Base HTML Code

We've broken the HTML it into several parts, so you can go through it in manageable pieces. In the first part, shown in Listing 5–1, we create the initial HTML layout and specify the two different headers.

Listing 5–1. *HTML Code for The Daily Droid part 1*

```
<!DOCTYPE HTML>
<html>
<head>
<meta http-equiv="Content-Type" content="text/html; charset=utf-8">
<meta charset="utf-8">
<title>The Daily Droid</title>
<meta name="description" content="An Android Responsive Web Design Demonstration.">
<meta name="author" content="Rocco Augusto">

<!-- Here we set the viewport so the device knows that this page is not one that can
scale/zoom -->
<meta name="viewport" content="width=device-width; initial-scale=1.0; maximum-scale=1.0;
user-scalable=0;" />
<link href="style.css" rel="stylesheet" type="text/css" >

<!-- Here we pull in two fonts from the Google Font API database -->
<link href="http://fonts.googleapis.com/css?family=UnifrakturCook:bold" rel="stylesheet"
type="text/css">
<link href='http://fonts.googleapis.com/css?family=Bevan' rel='stylesheet'
type='text/css'>
```

```
</head>

<!--
    HEADER
    We are adding two different sub headings (h6) to this page.
    One heading will be for the "Smartphone Edition" of the
    page and the second will be for the "Tablet Edition"
    of the page. Both pages are the same but depending on
    the screen size the pages CSS will tell the browser which
    subheading to display.
-->
<header id="mast">
    <hgroup>
        <h1>The Daily Droid</h1>
        <h6>Smartphone Edition</h6>
        <h6>Tablet Edition</h6>
    </hgroup>
    <time datetime="2011-05-29">May 29th, 2011</time>
</header><!-- /HEADER -->
```

As you can see from the code in Listing 5–1, both the Smartphone Edition and Tablet Edition text appear in the HTML. The CSS (discussed in "The Daily Droid CSS" later in this section) will select the correct one to display. In part 2 of the HTML, shown in Listing 5–2, we'll lay out the content and article space, and then finish up the HTML structure.

Listing 5–2. *HTML code for The Daily Droid, part 2*

```
<section id="content">
    <!--
        SECTION: FEATURED ARTICLES
        The featured article would be the main article on the page
        that will be featured. Think of it in this sense as the
        front page story on a newspaper - which makes sense since
        this demo's completed code would be a mock vintage newspaper
        layout.

        The article contains several sections. You have the header
        section which contains the title of the article as well as
        a "figure" or image that would be displayed with the article
        and any caption text that would go along with it.
    -->
    <section id="featured">
        <article>
            <header>
            <h1>Title goes here...</h1>
                <figure>
                    <img src="ww1647-05.jpg" width="100%" alt="" />
                    <figcaption>Figure caption...</figcaption>
                </figure>
            </header>
            <div class="entry">
                <p>Article content goes here...</p>
            </div>
        </article><!-- /ARTICLE -->
    </section><!-- /SECTION: FEATURED ARTICLES -->

    <!--
        SECTION: REGULAR ARTICLES
```

```
        The regular articles on this page will be housed in this
        section of the document. The markup of this section is
        exactly the same as the featured articles section. The only
        difference will come down to how they are displayed based
        off their assigned styles.
    -->
    <section id="regular">
        <article>
            <header>
                <h2>Title...</h2>
            </header>
            <div class="entry">
                <p>Body Content...</p>
            </div>
        </article><!-- /ARTICLE-->
    </section><!-- /SECTION: REGULAR ARTICLES -->

</section><!-- /SECTION: CONTENT -->
<body>
</body>
</html>
```

Now let's turn to the CSS and the visual presentation of The Daily Droid.

The Daily Droid's Semi-magical CSS Code

Now here's the CSS Style Sheet used to set the overall appearance of The Daily Droid.
CSS, as you remember, will take the plain HTML structure explained in the preceding
section and apply various styles to the tags, as we specify. We've broken the CSS into
several parts to help explain what it does. The first part, as shown in Listing 5–3, sets
how the body text and some of the headings should look.

Listing 5–3. *CSS Code for The Daily Droid, part 1*

```
/*
    CSS reset code only for the elements that will be
    used in our code. We could use a more robust CSS reset
    solution, but I am a firm believer that you should not
    riddle your stylesheet with code that you have no
    intention of using in your markup.
*/
html, body, h1, h2, h6, p, article, figure, figcaption header, hgroup, section {
    padding:0;
    margin:0;
}
/*
    General global styles to be used throughout the demo
*/
html, body {
    width:100%;
    overflow-x:hidden;
}
body {
    font-size:14px;
    font-family:"Times New Roman", Times, serif;
    line-height:20px;
```

```
    background:url(bg.png);
    -webkit-box-shadow: inset 0 -5px 300px rgba(153,99,38,1); /* This inset box-shadow
adds gives the page a nice vintage feel to it */
    box-shadow: inset 0 -5px 300px rgba(153,99,38,1);
}
h1, h2 {
    font-weight:normal;
}
h1 {
    font-size:36px;
    line-height:42px;
}
h2 {
    font-size:20px;
}
h6 {
    font-size:16px;
    text-transform:uppercase;
}
p {
    margin:10px 0;
}
/*
    Header/Mast CSS code
*/
#mast {
    padding:20px 0 0 0;
    text-align:center;
    letter-spacing:1px;
}
#mast h1 {
    font-family:'UnifrakturCook', Georgia, "Times New Roman", Times, serif;
    font-size:62px;
    line-height:48px;
}
```

Now that we've got some of the CSS in place, it's time to see the code that switches between the "Tablet" and "Smartphone" edition. By default, we want to display Tablet Edition, so that code is shown in Listing 5–4:

Listing 5–4. *CSS Code for The Daily Droid, part 2*

```
#mast h6 {
    display:none; /* hiding both of the pages subheaders */
}
#mast h6:nth-child(3) {
    display:block; /* displaying the "Tablet Edition" subheader by default */
}
#mast time {
    display:block;
    margin:10px 0;
    border-top:double 6px #000;
    border-bottom:double 6px #000;
    text-transform:uppercase;
    font-size:16px;
    line-height:24px;
}
/*
```

```
    Article/Content styles.
    This section will rely heavily on two new features
    of CSS3: Flexible Box Model and Columns.

    The Flexible Box Model is probably one of my favorite
    new features of CSS3. In a nutshell, it allows one to
    take control of how their page is laid out, using a grid
    of flexible boxes and essentially eliminating the need to
    hack together layouts by improperly using floats in one's
    code.

    CSS3 Columns are another time saving new feature of CSS3
    and allow a designer/developer to take a block of code
    and automatically convert it into a column based layout
    that is just perfect for a newspaper demonstration.
*/
#content {
    padding:0 10px;
    display:-webkit-box; /* here we are using the -webkit-box argument instead of
        plain old "box," so our code will work across newer and
        older Android browsers*'
    */
    -webkit-box-orient: horizontal; /* setting the box orientation to horizontal
        displays the content in this container from
        left to right instead displaying the content
        in the traditional way of top to bottom */
}
#featured {
    max-width:50%; /* our featured article will take up half the width of the display */
    height:100%; /* our featured article will take up all of the available height of the
display */
    box-flex:1; /* tell our child elements to be evenly sized and take up one "box"
space */
    -webkit-box-flex:1;
}
#featured .entry {
    -webkit-column-count: 2; /* this will display our featured content article text in 2
columns */
    -webkit-column-gap: 20px; /* here we add a hearty 20px gap/spacing between our
columns */
    -webkit-column-rule: 1px solid rgba(91,58,21,0.5); /* here we are adding a border to
our columns */
}
#regular {
    margin-left:5px;
    padding-left:10px;
    max-width:49%;
    box-flex:1;
    -webkit-box-flex:1;
    -webkit-column-count: 3;
    -webkit-column-gap: 20px;
    -webkit-column-rule: 1px solid rgba(91,58,21,0.5);
    border-left: 1px solid rgba(91,58,21,0.5);     /* here we are adding a border to the
#regular container to match the rest of the columns' borders */
}
#regular article {
```

```
    display:inline; /* displaying our articles inline prevents our articles from
stacking on top of each other */
}
article h1, article h2 {
    margin-bottom:10px;
    font-family:Bevan, "Times New Roman", Times, serif;
}
article .entry {
    text-align:justify; /* to give the page a more realistic feel we will justify the
column text */
}
article figure {
    width:90%;
    padding:0;
    margin:10px auto 20px auto;
}
article figcaption {
    font-style:italic;
    text-align:right;
}
```

Now we'll set up the Smartphone code (in Listing 5–5) and adjust the layout accordingly.

Listing 5–5. *CSS Code for The Daily Droid, part 3*

```
/*
    Android Smartphone Devices
    Here we will use CSS3 media queries to determine
    the resolution of our screen and present the user with
    a completely different layout if their viewing
    does not meet certain requirements.

    Here we are targeting smartphone devices that will,
    on average, have a width of 320px (portrait) and up
    to 569px (landscape).

    This layout will display the content in a more
    commonly used smartphone style layout, presenting the
    user with a list of articles that they can scroll up
    and down to view.
*/
@media screen and (min-width: 320px) and (max-width: 569px) {
    body {
        -webkit-box-shadow: inset 0 -5px 50px rgba(153,99,38,1); /* lessen the shadow on
the page to adjust to the screen's new dimensions */
        box-shadow: inset 0 -5px 50px rgba(153,99,38,1);
    }
    h1 {
        font-size:20px;  /* lower the size of the header font to accommodate the smaller
screen resolution */
        line-height:24px;
    }
    h6 {
        font-size:12px; /* same as the h1 above it */
    }
    #mast h1 {
        font-family:'UnifrakturCook', Georgia, "Times New Roman", Times, serif;
        font-size:42px;
```

```css
        line-height:42px;
    }
    #mast h6:nth-child(2) {
        display:block; /* since we are dealing with a smaller screen we will show the
"Smartphone Edition" subheader */
    }
    #mast h6:nth-child(3) {
        display:none; /* and hide the "Tablet Edition" subheader */
    }
    #mast time {
        font-size:12px;
        line-height:24px;
    }
    section#content {
        -webkit-box-orient: vertical; /* here we are telling this content to display
vertically instead of horizontally */
        padding-bottom:15px;
    }
    #featured {
        max-width:100%; /* take up the entire width of the screen instead of half of it
*/
    }
    #featured .entry {
        -webkit-column-count: 1; /* only display our text in a single column, which is
more appropriate for our screen real estate */
        -webkit-column-gap: 0; /* remove the 20px padding around columns */
        -webkit-column-rule: none; /* remove the border off our columns */
    }
    #regular {
        margin-left:0px;
        padding-left:0px;
        max-width:100%; /* like our featured article we will now take up the entire
width of the page */
        -webkit-column-count: 1; /* like our featured article we will display a single
column of text */
        -webkit-column-gap: 0;
        -webkit-column-rule: none;
        border-left: none;
    }
    #regular article {
        display:block; /* display our articles as blocks so they appear vertical */
    }
    article .entry p, article figure {
        display:none; /* hide all of our article content so the user is not stuck
scrolling into oblivion */
    }
    article .entry p:first-child {
        display:block; /* display only the first paragraph of an article for the user */
    }
    article {
        margin-bottom:10px;
        border-bottom:2px solid rgba(0,0,0,1);
    }
}
```

This is a lot of code for a simple newspaper; however, the beauty of it is in its versatility: One HTML page and one CSS page to rule all devices—phones, tablets, Android Media players, and whatever else someone puts Android on! Let's take a moment to discuss how this magic happens, using media queries.

Media Queries

When you looked at the preceding code, the first thing that you probably noticed is that the very fluid vintage newspaper layout that was programmed consists of only two relatively small files of code. Five to seven years ago, in a land where web developers had to wear two different hats—web developer hat and Internet Explorer 6 hacker hat—creating a layout such as this would have been a ridiculously cumbersome task that would have most likely consisted of two, if not more, completely different layouts. Each layout would have had to be its own set of HTML and CSS files, displayed to the client by some backend server code that looked up your device's user agent string. Mobile devices would have been served the HTML and CSS templates designed specifically for mobile devices. Desktop computers would have been served desktop equivalent templates. There was no melding or fluidity between the code versions.

Fast forward a few years into the future—where we sit at the dawn of HTML5 and CSS3—and the landscape is completely different. Currently we live in a world where Desktop Internet browsers are being developed and released faster than most users can get around to installing the most recent update. On the mobile front, it is almost equally as progressive, with new versions of the Smartphone's operating systems, and in turn new feature rich versions of their Internet browsers, being released every six to twelve months, if not sooner!

What that means for you, the mobile web developer, is that you are not stuck in the past, coding your sites for browsers that are a decade old if not older. At the most, as a developer targeting the Android user experience, you really only have to worry about developing for the last year and a half of Android releases. The ability to focus on newer devices without worrying about hindering your user's experience by focusing too much on past technologies gives developers a certain freedom that we did not possess before. With that freedom comes innovation and with innovation comes better technology and features—such as CSS3 media queries—the technology that is responsible for letting us create the beautiful "The Daily Droid" demo that we previously built.

Media queries have, in some form or other, been a part of web development since the days of HTML4. During that dark shadowy time of font tags and nested tables, media types made their big claim to fame by controlling styles and style sheets associated with the medium in which the user would be using to view the content (see Figures 5–10 and 5–11). For instance, a developer would assign some styles to the "print" media type to remove all advertisements from printed articles on a blog so their user would not unnecessarily use up their expensive ink when trying to print the blog's content (see Listing 5–6).

Listing 5–6. *Media Query Example 1: Hiding or showing a block based on media type*

```
<style type="text/css" media="screen">
    #advertisements {
        display:block;
    }
</style>

<style type="text/css" media="print">
    #advertisements {
        display:none;
    }
</style>
```

Figure 5–10. *The Android Thoughts homepage viewed in a normal Desktop web browser*

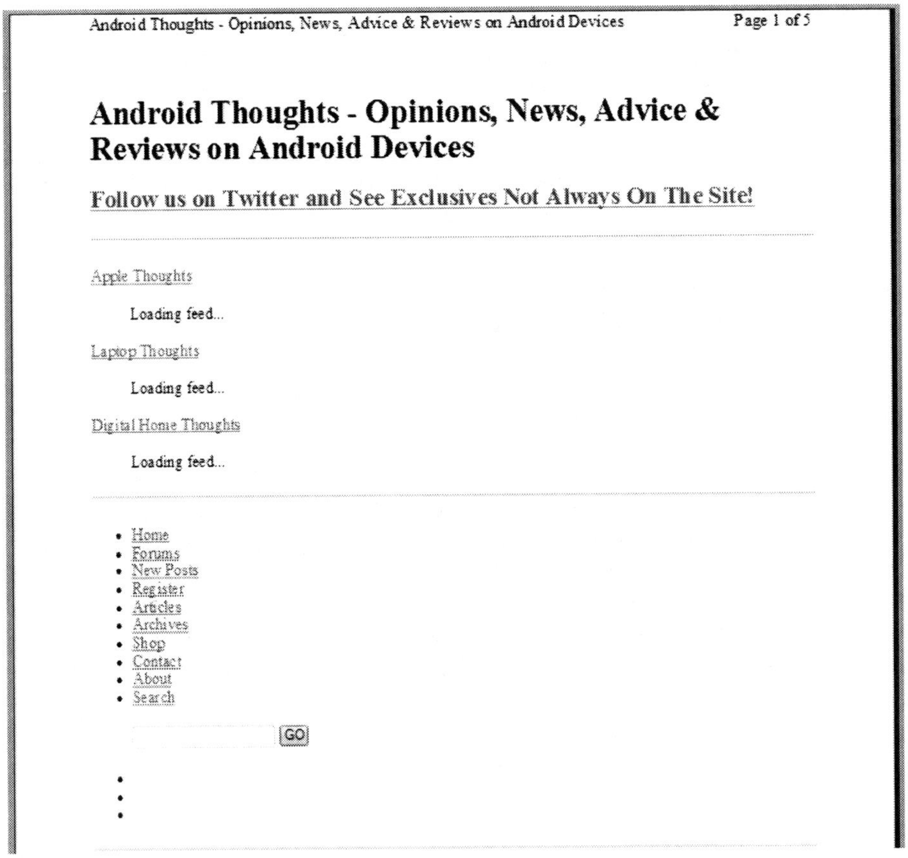

Figure 5–11. *The same Android Thoughts web page viewed when printed*

A developer could also assign styles or style sheets to the "projection" media type, to account for washed out colors in a site's header when viewing a project on a projector in a meeting room (see Listing 5–7).

Listing 5–7. *Media Query Example 2: Changing background color based on media type*

```
<style type="text/css" media="screen">
    #header {
        background: #444444;
    }
</style>

<style type="text/css" media="projection">
    #header {
        background: #111111;
    }
</style>
```

However, with CSS3, the concept of media types has evolved into something much more beautiful and flexible, which gives Cascading Style Sheets the ability not to be just a "dumb" mechanism for adding style to documents and markup made for the web.

Media queries are something that, when used, feel like they should have been a part of CSS from the very beginning. I have heard some friends of mine refer to media queries as "freedom" and have even heard one developer I know—granted, after a very long night of coding—refer to media queries simply as the new "black magic" of the digital age. In reality, they are neither. Media queries serve as a tool that, when mastered, will make your job as a developer easier and at the end of the day will give you a beautifully flexible layout that instantly transforms to your user's viewing medium, right before your eyes!

If you have worked with JavaScript or any other scripting or programming language of the past, then media queries will probably be easy for you to learn. Basically, what one is doing is assigning logic to their style sheets that will let the browser on the client side do all of the heavy lifting when it comes to assigning the right template styles to the right viewing device. The following is a very basic example of using CCS's media queries:

```
<link rel="stylesheet" media="screen and (orientation:portrait)" href="portrait.css" />
```

In this example, we are telling the client's browser to load the "portrait.css" stylesheet when the browser is viewing the application, or website, from a mobile device that is in the vertical position.[2] One is not limited to assigning media queries to the link tag. Media queries can also be added directly to your device's CSS files, as we saw with the preceding example of "The Daily Droid". In fact, one can even go as far as invoking media queries when using the @import rule to call a CSS file for the correct display as in the following example:

```
<style type="text//css">
    @import url(landscape.css) screen and (orientation:landscape);
</style>
```

In the following example, we will have several @import rules importing in many different CSS files for different layout types (see Listing 5–8).

Listing 5–8: *Media Query Example 3*

```
<style type="text//css">
    <!-- Styles for a smartphone landscape display -->
    @import url(landscape.css) handheld and (orientation:landscape) and (max-
width:480px);

    <!-- Styles for a Honeycomb tablet landscape display -->
    @import url(landscape.css) handheld and (orientation:landscape) and (max-
width:648px);

    <!-- Styles for a portrait display -->
    @import url(landscape.css) all and (orientation:portrait);
</style>
```

---

[2] Devices that have sensors to detect movement typically will tell the software if the phone is switched from landscape to portrait view, allowing your web page to reformat automatically based on the styles you define.

I know exactly what you're thinking, "What if I have to code my web application to match a Google TV Android device hooked up to a television or device with a 16x9 display?!" Well don't you fret because the flexible nature of CSS3 media queries has you covered, as it does in the following example:

```
<link rel="stylesheet" media="all and (device-aspect-ratio: 16/9)" href="television.css" />
```

As you can see from these preceding examples, media queries are an incredible tool in any web developer's arsenal in a world that is quickly becoming dominated by HTML5 and CSS3 capable devices and applications. To learn more about the power of Media Queries, check them out on the W3.org website here—www.w3.org/TR/css3-mediaqueries/#media0.

Summary

In this chapter, we've talked a lot about the size of your web pages and how that size can change based on the screen used to view the content. Now that we've got the screen resolution issue out of the way, we'll zoom in a bit and address the best ways to handle different browsers!

Chapter 6

Handling Different Browser Platforms

So far, we've discussed ways to detect the type of device that is accessing your web page or application and to deal with it appropriately. This has involved special CSS files, formatting concerns, and more. Like any good baker will tell you, however, it is not always the wisest of ideas to keep all of your eggs in one basket. That is why, in this chapter, we're going to take a step back and discuss methods that you can use to understand what device is accessing your service and to act appropriately.

The reason for this is simple: Not one solution will fit all problems. For instance, you might need to allow mobile users to access a web application and you might find it possible to format pages that look great on the desktop as well as on a phone. For extremely simple layouts, this is often what developers do. However for more complex systems, one might need to create a completely separate website. The middle ground is to build one HTML document that can look good on the desktop, tablet, or phone. In this chapter, we're going to give you the tools you need to figure out what device is looking at your page, and we'll provide some ideas on how your page can react to each device. After all, just as no two websites are exactly alike—although similar—no two devices will behave exactly alike (but thankfully, as with websites, there are similarities).

META Tags and the Viewport

We've discussed many things about HTML that are hidden to normal users—the different tags that are used, the different sections, such as the head and body, and even how things like CSS and JavaScript can be embedded into an HTML document. However META tags or elements are special in that, while they aren't shown to the user, they do generally impact the user's experience with the how the page is displayed or formatted.

META tags live in the head section of an HTML page, and generally have two elements, the name of the element, and the value. For example, the following value specifies the keywords associated with the particular webpage:

```
<meta name="keywords" content="android, howto, information" >
```

A Little META History

Back when search engines first began indexing the Internet, they used the keywords and description META elements to understand what a given webpage was all about. In the late 1990s, full-text search engines (such as Google) began indexing and using all of the text of a given webpage to determine what the page contained, and these META elements became less important. In fact, an entire industry had sprung up purporting to help web page owners get more traffic by "optimizing" their web pages, which usually included updating the META elements search engines used. This industry of "search engine optimization," or SEO, still exists today and is in fact a very cutthroat type of business, although many search engines look for the older "tricks" used and may penalize pages for using them today. For example, one trick used was known informally as "keyword stuffing", which was what it sounded like—stuffing the META keyword element with many different terms, some of which may score highly to search engines but weren't exactly accurate in regards to the page's actual content. Modern day SEO firms must rely on a number of other techniques to increase a page's search rank, including a number of things we don't normally consider as designers (e.g., what links are on the page, page titles, layout, wording, etc...).

One of the interesting things about META tags is that there are considerably fewer "official" META tags than the total that exist on the web. Various software companies that produce web browsers, such as Microsoft, may decide to build their browser to detect "unofficial" META tags and respond to them.

For example, Microsoft pioneered the use of the MobileOptimized META tag, which told its mobile internet browser (Pocket Internet Explorer or Internet Explorer Mobile) how to specially render a page that used this tag. Some non-Microsoft produced browsers supported the tag, but no guarantee could be made that the tag would help users of rival browsers as much as it did users of Internet Explorer. Similarly, our old friend AvantGo, mentioned earlier, used a tag named HandheldFriendly for much the same purpose, with the same problems associated.

The Viewport Element

All of this confusion, rivalry, and non-conforming led to the introduction and fairly wide acceptance of a new META element known as Viewport that, while still unofficial, is the most current "special" META tag of interest to mobile developers. The Viewport can be thought of as a window on top of a web page. Sometimes the entire web page fits into the window, and other times we want to size the window differently, depending on how we build the page. One reason that the Viewport tag has been a bit more successful than previous attempts is the amount of information one can place in it. For example, a simple Viewport tag might look like this:

```
<meta name="viewport" content="width=320,height=device-height" />
```

This code tells the mobile browser that the content of this page should be 320 pixels wide and as tall as the device's screen. (If you're designing for a Tablet, you would probably adjust this to 800px wide.) To get a better idea of how this would display a page, take a look at Figure 6–1. It shows the "Who's That Tweet?" game we made in Chapter 2 using the preceding viewport setting.

Figure 6–1. *Here we have the "Who's That Tweet?" game with a viewport set*

Notice how the layout of the page is bigger than the available viewing real estate of the handset? This is because while we set the height to be the height of the device, we set the width too wide—320px—and the browser doesn't know anything about the initial scale, as evidenced by the zoom buttons on the bottom of the page. The browser, in this case, zoomed in to show the upper left of the page, and provided the zoom buttons so users can zoom in and out of the page to either view as much or as little of the page as they choose (While there are times when it is nice to be able to zoom content on a page, it would be even better if we could disable that feature on this page so we can guarantee that our layout will appear the way we intended it to). In other words, the browser made an educated guess on how it should display this page, and it failed miserably by pulling it to the upper left. It could have also displayed everything zoomed out, in which case all 320px would have fit, but the text would be really small. We're going to give it more information so it displays it right the first time.

Luckily for us, Viewport tags can also contain information regarding the scaling of the page—including the ability of the user to zoom in and out of the given page. The following—slightly more complex—Viewport tag specifies all of these things:

```
<meta name="viewport" content="width=320, height=device-height, user-scalable=no,
initial-scale=1.0, maximum-scale=1.0, minimum-scale=1.0" />
```

This code tells the browser two things. First, it provides scale values, which allow the browser to know what you consider the largest and smallest scale, and where to set the scale initially. In this example, we're telling the browser that we coded the page so that it's designed to be seen at 100%, and it shouldn't be any larger or smaller. The second item this code adds is the ability to turn off the user's zoom in and out options, as can be seen in the following Figure 6-2. Now we don't have to worry about our design not being seen the way we intended it to be displayed to the user. Personally, I am a fan of always taking away the user's ability to scale the page when building a mobile site or application. I know some people really like the ability to pinch and zoom their way through scaling heaven but, in reality, mobile devices have a very limited amount of screen real estate and I feel, as a designer or a developer, that it is your job to use that limited screen space to your advantage instead of putting the extra burden of having your user pinch and zoom to navigate around your finished product.

Figure 6–2. *Chapter 2's "Who's That Tweet?" game with the user-scalable turned off*

But what if you want the happy medium in the sense that your app should zoom in automatically, but should also allow the user to modify the zoom if they so wish? And what about devices that have a higher pixel count (such as the Google Nexus One, with 480px wide)? We can address this in a few ways. The first is to just remove the user-scalable=no line in the META tag, and adjust the scale values targeted to a certain screen density. This lets the META tag give the initial values, but doesn't constrain the user. To determine if this is the right move, we can conduct a bit of user testing (i.e., surveys to see what people think of our mobile interface) or if we really are curious, we could implement some javascript code to see what users are doing and then write it to a log (This is beyond the scope of this book, although resources do exist, such as the discussion on this page: http://htmldoodads.appspot.com/zoom-level.html). We can also build a page that displays differently depending on the device pixel density— something that we would have to specify in the underlying CSS, using tags for low density (ldpi), medium density (mdpi), and high density (hdpi), and then specifying different CSS formatting for each situation.

Finally, if we have the luxury of developing for simply one platform (i.e., only Android phones), we can look into specific features of the browser. In this case, the Android Webkit browser reduces the size of text elements automatically so they fit on the screen (go view an article in an online newspaper and zoom in on a wide block of text to see this in action). If this is our usage scenario, then no META worries exist for us. While this can be tempting to rely on, you should thoroughly test your page on an Android device. It also doesn't hurt to use the META tags as an extra layer of security to help the built-in browser.

The User Agent

Sometimes specifying what the browser should do with your page isn't enough for your needs. For example, perhaps you know certain information, no matter how it's zoomed or formatted on a mobile device, is just too much for the average user to handle on a small screen. Maybe your page uses a bunch of Flash applets, which don't work on an iOS device such as an iPhone or iPad, and you'd like to redirect those users somewhere else. Maybe there are features and functionality available on your site that are not available across all applications and would need to be disabled for less advanced browsers. Finally, maybe you just want to give out one web address, http://mysite.com, and have it automatically direct mobile phones and tablets to a special optimized version, while showing everyone else the full page. The way most sites accomplish these goals is by reading the user agent string, supplied by the visitor's web browser. Let's first take a look at an example user agent, and then see how we use it in our application.

The Nexus One User Agent

The format of a user agent string is codified by RFC 1945, the HTTP specification, which includes the definition of this string. The string is made up of the product name and version, and an optional comment. While those are the parts of the string required by

RFC 1945, many vendors add additional information such as the operating system, loaded extensions, and platform details. The built-in browser on a Google Nexus One, running Android 2.2 (Froyo) sends the following user agent:

```
Mozilla/5.0 (Linux; U; Android 2.2; en-us; Nexus One Build/FRF91) AppleWebKit/533.1
(KHTML, like Gecko) Version/4.0 Mobile Safari/533.1
```

This string, broken down, translates to:

- Mozilla 5.0 browser

- Running on a Linux operating system, specifically Android 2.2

- Using the language English—US (en-us)

- On a Nexus One phone, running build FRF91 of the operating system.

- Which (the comment instructs) is like an AppleWebKit browser (version 533.1).

A lot of information is available to our web page or application (and if you look at the RFC, more information might even be available in terms of the engine or the level of security the current browser offers). Using this, we can direct users of specific phones, browsers, operating system, and languages to specially formatted pages we've created for them or display features specific to that browser which we are targeting.

However, there is one caveat to consider with user agent detection: User Agent Spoofing. Many third-party browsers, such as the popular Dolphin HD browser on Android, allow users to set their own user agent. There are multiple reasons for this, including:

- The user wants to see the desktop version of a page, no matter how horribly formatted it might look.

- The user wants to access pages that are specifically built for another operating system or browser (i.e., perhaps the web developer hasn't built an optimized Android version yet, but has an optimized iOS version.)

- The user just wants to appear to the website's logs as a desktop system, for some reason or another! One that comes to mind is a restriction placed by the developer (i.e., only show a special offer to a desktop user) that the mobile user wishes to view.

There isn't much one can do about user agent spoofing. After all, the setup of the entire system revolves around the user agent being reported accurately. If this is a concern of yours, you may want to use alternatives in addition to user agent detection to deliver the correct page to your user, despite what they want. This typically would take the form of scripts that could test for capabilities of a browser—however, one would need to know which minute capabilities mobile browsers have and which only desktops would have— which is well beyond our scope here.

Now that you have a basic understanding of what the user agent string is used for, let's take a look at a few examples where we detect a user agent string of our end user.

PHP User Agent Detection

Listing 6–1 shows a PHP example in which we are going to detect the user agent string and display it to the user. If the user is using an Android web browser, then they will be presented with the always pleasant smiley face (see Figure 6–3), but if they try viewing the script on a non-Android powered device, then they will be accosted with the ever unpopular frowny face (see Figure 6–4).

Listing 6–1. *PHP User Detection Code*

```php
<?php
$userAgent = strtolower($_SERVER['HTTP_USER_AGENT']);
if(stripos($userAgent,'android') !== false) {
    echo 'You are using an Android web browser! :)';
}
else {
    echo 'You are not using an Android web browser! :(';
}
?>
```

To understand how this code is working, we are going to pick it apart, line by line. First, we define the variable $userAgent, which grabs the user agent string of the browser requesting the page. Then we use the PHP striposfunction—which searches a string for the occurrence of a string—to parse the user agent for our supplied value. If the value, in this case android,is not found within the string, then the user is presented one message. If it is found, another message is presented.

This is just a small example of how you can use PHP to detect a user agent string, but there are many more situations where this technique might save you from ripping your own hair out. For example, using detection in PHP may allow you to block content before it is even sent (something JavaScript detection won't do, generally). Also, if the bulk of your application is written in PHP, you may be more comfortable recording user agents in this manner, rather than through JavaScript.

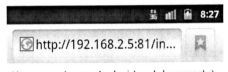

You are using an Android web browser! :)

Figure 6–3. *Using PHP, we are taking the user agent string and using that to decide which content is showed to the end user*

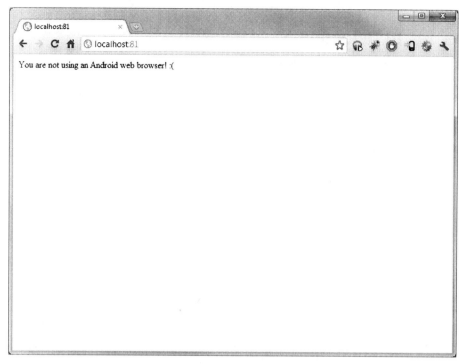

Figure 6–4: *Drat! Looks like this person isn't using an Android browser!*

JavaScript User Agent Detection

While PHP is great for detecting the user agent string on the server's side, there might be times when a developer would need to detect the User String on the client side. As an example, let's say you are working on a site or application that gives you the ability to export information into either a text file or binary format file on the user's computer for viewing later. On an Android device, the text is no problem but if your user chooses the binary format, they might be confused when it can't be opened. Thus, we may just want to hide that option, leaving the other available. Luckily, using JavaScript for this task is just as easy as it was using PHP.

Introducing the JavaScript Agent Detection Code

The JavaScript code shown in Listing 6–2 gives us a quick taste of how simple detection in JavaScript can be; it is similar to PHP. The only major difference in this code, when compared to the last, is that instead of writing our message to the page like we did with PHP, we are instead opting to show our users a popup **alert** dialog (see Figures 6–5 and 6–6).

Listing 6–2. *Javascript User Detection Code*

```
<script type="text/javascript">
var ua = navigator.userAgent.toLowerCase();
window.onload = function() {
    if(navigator.userAgent.match(/android/i)) {
        alert('Android Rocks!');
    }
    else {
        alert('Yawn, I guess your boring Desktop browser is okay');
    }
}
</script>
```

Figure 6–5. *Alert dialog box on the Android 2.3 Gingerbread device*

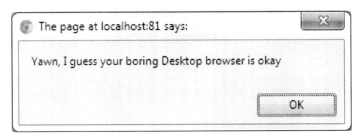

Figure 6–6. *Boring alert dialog box on Google's Chrome web browser*

Using JavaScript Agent Detection to Show Different Content to Different Platforms

One natural progression of a single-platform developer (i.e., someone who writes applications for Android, or iOS, or just one operating system) is to jump to different platforms. Web apps are great for this, in that they largely can be coded once and 'ported' over to other similar architectures with ease. However, to avoid derivative versions that can become a nightmare (i.e., an Android and an iOS version, requiring you to make additions separately to both versions), it might be easier just to have one piece of code that can change based on where it's being run. In this example, we'll show you how to implement the JavaScript code from Listing 6–2 in the preceding section into a Web App that will show different content depending on where it is running.

We'll also give you a taste of something you'll see quite a lot of in the next chapter, jQuery Mobile, by using it as the 'framework' for this application. If you like the look of the next few screens, then you'll enjoy reading Chapter 7!

Let's first start by discussing our overall goal: To display the appropriate link to download an application. In Android, we want the link to go to the Android Market (or perhaps to one of the new Android app stores that have opened, such as Amazon's). In iOS, we want the link to go to the Apple App Store. We'd also like to show the appropriate graphic. Let's start by building a simple page that shows the Android link. We first need to grab the graphic (Available on the Android Branding page, (www.android.com/branding.html), as well as the Apple App Store graphic (www.apple.com/itunes/affiliates/resources/documentation/identity-guidelines.html), and place both of them in the same directory as Listing 6–3.

Listing 6–3. *Download our App HTML Page*

```
<!DOCTYPE HTML>
<html>

<head>
<meta charset="utf-8">
<meta name="viewport" content="width=device-width, initial-scale=1">
<title>Download our App</title>
<link rel="stylesheet" href="//code.jquery.com/mobile/1.0.1/jquery.mobile-1.0.1.min.css"
/>
<script src="http://code.jquery.com/jquery-1.6.4.min.js"></script>
<script src="//code.jquery.com/mobile/1.0.1/jquery.mobile-1.0.1.min.js"></script>

<script type="text/javascript">

$( '#aboutPage' ).live( 'pageinit',function(event){

    if (navigator.userAgent.match(/android/i)) {
        document.getElementById("androiddiv").style.display = "block";
    }

    if (navigator.userAgent.match(/iPhone/i)) {
        document.getElementById("applediv").style.display = "block";
    }
});
```

```
</script>

</head>

<body>

<div data-role="page" id="aboutPage">

<div data-role="header">
<h1>Our App!</h1>
</div><!-- /header -->

<div data-role="content">
<div id="androiddiv" style="display: none">
<p>We have an application you can download in the Android Marketplace!</p>
<p align="center"><img src="45_avail_market_logo1.png"></p>
</div>
<div id="applediv" style="display: none">
<p>We have an application you can download in the Apple App Store!</p>
<p align="center"><img src="app-store.png"></p>
</div>
</div><!-- /content -->

<div data-role="footer">
<h4>bugjr.com</h4>
</div><!-- /footer -->

</div><!-- /page -->

</body>
</html>
```

You'll notice that this page is fairly simple. If you look at the content of the page, you'll see we have two blocks of content: The first, named `androiddiv`, shows the Android Marketplace text and image. The second, `applediv`, shows the Apple App Store text and image. Both blocks are set to `"display: none"` in their div tag, which means that, by default, neither is shown. At the top of the page is a very simple JavaScript function, which tests to see which user agent is detected, and toggles on the appropriate block of text (by setting the display to `"block"`). If we load this page in the Android web browser, we will see Figure 6–7:

Figure 6–7. *Loading the Download App HTML page in the Android Browser*

If, however, we load this page in Safari on the iPhone, we will see Figure 6–8:

Figure 6–8. *The Download App HTML Page in Safari*

Now we have a simple way to route our user to the correct download, without requiring them to tap on one icon or the other! As you can imagine, we could use this same detection for other purposes—showing different text to different users, displaying different advertisements, etc... The best part is that it's all in HTML and JavaScript, meaning that if you elect to use a product to turn your Web App into a native app (something we'll discuss in Chapter 13, using tools such as PhoneGap or Titanium Mobile), you can use this trick to provide a greater level of customization for the user!

Now that we've talked about detecting the User Agent in both PHP and JavaScript, we'll finish by discussing how we can use the Apache Web Server to do the detection for us.

.htaccess User Agent Detection

These types of files are configuration files commonly associated with Apache web servers. Also referred to as a distributed configuration file, the .htaccess file can set a series of rules and configurations to a web application on a per-directory basis. The .htaccess file can be used to control rewriting the URLs to something much cleaner and easier to read by humans by using the mod_rewrite module if the server supports it. Another fun use for the .htaccess file is to use it to detect the user agent string and direct the user to a different site or sub-domain, if needed. See Listing 6–4.

Listing 6–4. *an example .htaccess file*

```
<IfModule mod_rewrite.c>
RewriteEngine On
RewriteBase /
RewriteCond %{HTTP_USER_AGENT} ^.*Android.*$
RewriteRule ^(.*)$ http://android.yoursitesurl.com [R=301]
</IfModule>
```

The preceding code first checks to see if your Apache server supports the rewrite code, then it turns on the rewrite engine and sets up a condition and a rule. The condition checks for Android in the user agent, and if found, the rule tells the web browser to redirect the request to `http://android.yoursiteurl.com` instead of your usual `http://yoursiteurl.com` (or whatever else the user typed in).

This type of detection is very powerful, and one that can annoy some users. While users can disable JavaScript detection by turning off JavaScript, .htaccess and PHP user agent detection can only be 'tricked' by changing the user agent, something that not all browsers support. (It's worth noting that the Dolphin HD Browser, which is free, allows one to switch their user agent easily between Android, iOS, and Desktop, making it useful for testing and tricking!) Furthermore, it's possible that users may want to view the full web page in their Android browser, and while the PHP method allows you to provide some sort of toggle code-wise (i.e., a link the user could click that would set a PHP Session variable telling your code not to show the mobile site), the .htaccess user agent detection does not allow this. However, in simple situations, the .htaccess solution is the easiest to configure. Choose your detection method wisely!

Summary

Congratulations! You have made it through yet another chapter, and with your newfound knowledge Viewports and user agent strings, you will be better equipped to handle certain pesky user interface problems that might crop up from time to time. Even though this book is mostly focusing on building web applications for Android devices, it would just be foolish to think that you will never run into a situation where you will need to develop something that works across all platforms. Using what we've talked about there, you can custom tailor a solution for your app that is efficient and elegant!

Chapter **7**

Building an Impressive User Experience with jQuery Mobile

Believe it or not, I do not possess too much artistic talent for someone whose mother had a scholarship to art school and whose father was in advertising for a number of years. Most of my programming endeavors focus on function over style... with mixed results. On one hand, many people praise this minimalist design—for example, one app of mine named *Fast Food Calorie Lookup* is little more than two drop down boxes and a few buttons. With over 1000 reviews, it has a 4.3 out of 5 rating on the Android Market.However, for every person that raves "SOOO much easily-navigated, handy information!" (actual review), I get people who don't understand why it doesn't look prettier.

Thankfully, in the web application space, there are options that make design 'slobs' like me look like we paid some very high-priced designer to make things look gorgeous. In reality, tools are available to accomplish this goal for free, and in this chapter we're going to take a deep look at one of them: jQuery Mobile (http://jquerymobile.com). It is by no means the only option you have.Others that come to mind are: The Wink Toolkit (www.winktoolkit.org/), Sencha Touch (www.sencha.com/products/touch/), Zepto.js (http://zeptojs.com), Jo (http://joapp.com/), xui.js (http://xuijs.com/), and JQTouch (www.jqtouch.com/). However, for our purposes, jQuery Mobile offers the biggest bang for the proverbial buck in terms of features and ease of configuration. So—let's jump in and explore!

The Basics

If you are familiar with the jQuery UI toolkit for desktop browsers, then you should pick up jQuery Mobilepretty quickly! jQuery Mobile is one of those frameworks that try to take a lot of the tedious tasks that come with developing a mobile application out of the hands of developers and place all that grunt work into the hands of the framework, so you can spend more time focusing on other items and features that might be more important to your application. Creating a series of touch-optimized widgets and user interface elements, jQuery Mobile is quickly shaping up to be one of the top contenders in the mobile javascript framework space.

One of the best features of jQuery Mobile, however, is its very simple and easy to modify templating structure. With a little bit of CSS knowhow, a developer can easily modify the styles of their jQuery Mobile theme to look however they want. This is great for people like me who like to get their hands dirty and muck around through the innards of any piece of code they touch. On the other hand, as we'll see shortly, creating a custom theme is by no means difficult—in fact, we don't have to touch the CSS at all if we don't want to!

On top of all of this, jQuery Mobile is an incredibly easy framework to get up and running. All one needs to do to get started is to include the jQuery Mobile source files in the header of their documents and then use special data attributes in their HTML markup. Data attributes are a fun addition to HTML5. In XML, and previous versions of HTML, formally defined attributes were used within tags to describe data or the formatting of data. While it was always possible in previous versions of HTML to add custom attributes to your HTML code, it was always frowned upon.And, more often than not, if your code was run through a validation program,it would end up spitting up errors left and right.Listing 7–1 shows an invalid custom "mood" attribute, and Listing 7–2 shows how a valid "data-mood" attribute can be used in HTML5.

Listing 7–1. *An example of an invalid custom attribute in HTML*

```
<div class="post" mood="awesome">
<h1>Today was an awesome day!</h1>
<p>Suspendisse consectetur consequat risus non viverra. Phasellus ligula urna, egestas
porttitor facilisis vel, euismod sit...</p>
</div>
```

Listing 7–2. *An example of a valid custom attribute in HTML5*

```
<div class="post" data-mood="awesome">
<h1>Today was an awesome day!</h1>
<p>Suspendisse consectetur consequat risus non viverra. Phasellus ligula urna, egestas
porttitor facilisis vel, euismod sit...</p>
</div>
```

Let's take a look at the preceding code example. In the first attempt at writing the code, we are creating a div container with an invalid custom attribute attached to it, to indicate the mood of the individual creating this blog entry. While there is nothing stopping us from using this whimsically created mood attribute, the code would not validate with popular validation engines such as the W3c Markup Validation Service (http://validator.w3.org/). The reason for this is because mood is not an approved attribute of the HTML spec. After years of complaining from developers left and right, the Powers That Be decided to take a little bit of pity on us developers and gave us the ability to finally create custom attributes to attach to our code. These new data attributes could be used by a developer to add any sort of data to their markup code that could be used for whatever purposes we can imagine. In our second example (Listing 7–2), we are using the `data-mood` attribute to record our mood in a way that will please validators, while still allowing us to use those data in our scripts as needed! As long as we put the prefix "data-"in front of the string of data we'd like to store, it is valid HTML5 code. We can use these as small data containers, as in the following example."

Now that you have an understanding of how data attributes work, and how they can be used to enrich our mobile applications, let us take a look at some jQuery Mobile code and dissect how it is all working.

In Listing 7–3, we're going to display a very simple page using the jQuery Mobile framework. You'll notice that it uses a number of data-role attributes.

Listing 7–3. *The HTML markup from the default jQuery Mobile boilerplate example*

```
<!DOCTYPE HTML>
<html>
<head>
<title>Our Super Rad Demo Page</title>
<link rel="stylesheet" href="http://code.jquery.com/mobile/1.0a1/jquery.mobile-
1.0a1.min.css" />
<script src="http://code.jquery.com/jquery-1.4.3.min.js"></script>
<script src="http://code.jquery.com/mobile/1.0a1/jquery.mobile-1.0a1.min.js"></script>
</head>
<body>
<!-- page -->
<div data-role="page">
<!--header -->
<div data-role="header">
<h1>Well Then, Soldier...</h1>
</div>
<!-- /header -->
<!-- content -->
<div data-role="content">
<p>How goes the day?</p>
</div>
<!-- /content -->
<!-- footer -->
<div data-role="footer">
<h4>&copy 2011 Dodo Men Ply, Inc.</h4>
</div>
<!-- /footer -->
</div>
<!-- /page -->
</body>
</html>
```

With just the few lines of the preceding code, one can create a very native mobile application look and feel using just a regular old web browser. This page happens to be pretty simple. For starters, we have our main container with the data-attribute value of "page," which is a wrapper for our content. As would be expected, after that we have our "header," which would usually house the Title of the page and any navigation elements one would decide to put there. After we pass the header, we start to journey towards the meat of the page, also known as the "content" data-attribute, which is shortly followed by our "footer."

As I said before, there is not a whole lot of stuff going on with this markup. Most of the magic happens behind the scenes, within the inner workings of the jQuery Mobile application. Over the next few examples, we'll explore what one can do with jQuery Mobile, starting from the simple to the more complex, and then into custom theming!Let's fire up our trusty web browser and see how this page looks on our mobile devices (see Figure 7–1)!

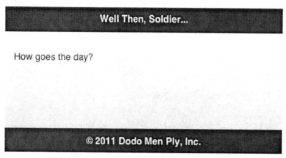

Figure 7–1. *A very native looking user interface created by jQuery Mobile and displayed on an Android 2.3.4 handset*

You see how easy that was? The best part is that we were just barely scratching the surface of what jQuery Mobile is capable of. With a little time, one could easily put together a full-featured mobile web application complete with fancy user interface elements, modal windows, dialog boxes, page transitions, navigational toolbars, and a whole lot of other stuff too! Let's dig a bit deeper.

Adding Multiple Pages

Typically, applications consist of more than one page! In Listing 7–4, we'll create a more advanced jQuery Mobile document that contains three pages: a Home page, an About page, and a Contact page. Along the way, we'll comment a little heavier than usual, so that you see which part of the code creates which element (displayed in Figures 7–2, 7–3, and 7–4). This way, you'll see exactly what you'll need to modify if you would like to customize certain elements.

Listing 7–4. *All UI elements on the page are created by the jQuery Mobile application*

```
<!DOCTYPEHTML>
<html>
<head>
<title>Our Super Rad Demo Page</title>
<link rel="stylesheet" href="http://code.jquery.com/mobile/1.0a1/jquery.mobile-
1.0a1.min.css" />
<script src="http://code.jquery.com/jquery-1.4.3.min.js"></script>
<script src="http://code.jquery.com/mobile/1.0a1/jquery.mobile-1.0a1.min.js"></script>
</head>
<body>
<!-- home -->
<div data-role="page" id="home">
<div data-role="header"><h1>Hello World</h1>
```

In the header, we'll specify the test we want to see in the black bar at the top of the page. I could include more than just one line of text if I like, and the black bar will continue to increase. However, this may be a bit distracting for the user.

Listing 7–4 Cont. *The content of the main page*

```
</div>
<div data-role="content">
<ul data-role="list-view" class="ui-listview">
<li data-theme="b" class="ui-btn ui-btn-icon-right ui-li ui-btn-up-c">
<div class="ui-btn-inner ui-li">
<div class="ui-btn-text">Pellentesque habitant morbi tristique senectud    </div>
</div>
</li>
<li data-theme="b" class="ui-btn ui-btn-icon-right ui-li ui-btn-up-c">
<div class="ui-btn-inner ui-li">
<div class="ui-btn-text">Morbi ultrices dignissim erat id blandit    </div>
</div>
</li>
<li data-theme="b" class="ui-btn ui-btn-icon-right ui-li ui-btn-up-c">
<div class="ui-btn-inner ui-li">
<div class="ui-btn-text">Etiam massa quam, tempus quis    </div>
</div>
</li>
<li data-theme="b" class="ui-btn ui-btn-icon-right ui-li ui-btn-up-c">
<div class="ui-btn-inner ui-li">
<div class="ui-btn-text">Nam laoreet congue aliquet    </div>
</div>
</li>
<li data-theme="b" class="ui-btn ui-btn-icon-right ui-li ui-btn-up-c">
<div class="ui-btn-inner ui-li">
<div class="ui-btn-text">Morbi et ligula vel ligula lobortis pharetra ut eu massa
</div>
</div>
</li>
<li data-theme="b" class="ui-btn ui-btn-icon-right ui-li ui-btn-up-c">
<div class="ui-btn-inner ui-li">
<div class="ui-btn-text">Nam commodo erat orci.    </div>
</div>
</li>
</ul>
</div>
```

If you're coding along at home, you'll notice that each of those items appears in a button-like list. You might be wondering if we could make these lists a little more interesting. Indeed we could—jQuery Mobile supports several types of lists (http://jquerymobile.com/demos/1.0.1/docs/lists/index.html) has a complete list and examples). We're using a read-only list here, as we aren't linking the list items to any particular page or action. However, other link options are available, such as:

- A nested list (see Figure 7–2), where one list item, when tapped, slides away to reveal several more list items.

Figure 7–2. *A nested list*

■ Count bubble lists (see Figure 7–3), where the ends of each list item can have a number displayed, inset into the item. This is useful for displaying counts for numbers of new items, notifications, news stories, etc...

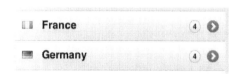

Figure 7–3. *A count bubble list*

■ Thumbnail (Figure 7–4)and icon (Figure 7–5) lists, which display either a thumbnail graphic or an icon to the left of the list text. This is useful for displaying small photos and descriptive icons of the action the item is used for, or just for decoration.

Figure 7–4: *A thumbnail list*

Figure 7–5. *An icon list.*

■ Several options to create inset search fields (Figure 7–6), normally a list item at the top that lets one filter later list items.

Figure 7–6. *A search filter box at the top of a list*

▩   Finally, one can create a list with forms (Figure 7–7), allowing you to create a nicely ordered form page inside a list view. Useful for checkout pages, settings pages, and similar situations.

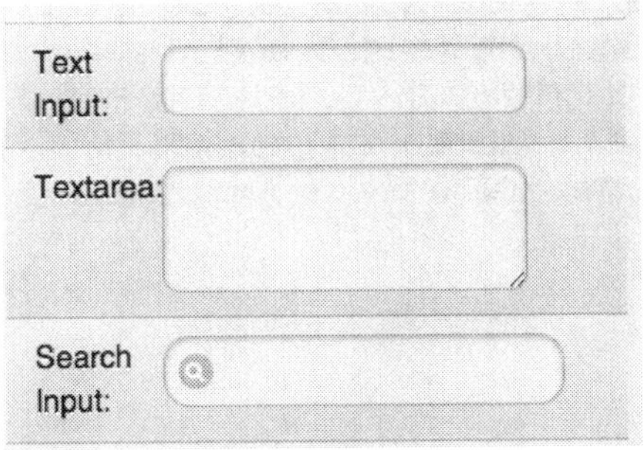

Figure 7–7. *Form elements within a list*

The sky is the limit in terms of what you can do with lists! Now, back to the code…

Listing 7–4 Cont.: *The footer of the main page.*

```
<div data-role="footer" class="ui-bar">
<a href="#about" data-transition="flip" data-role="button" data-theme="b">About</a>
<a href="#contact" data-transition="pop" data-role="button" data-theme="b">Contact</a>
</div>
</div>
<!-- /home -->
```

You'll notice that, at the bottom of the main page, we've created a footer section (which looks like another black bar), and we've added two buttons. Creating buttons in jQuery Mobile is very simple—fundamentally, it's just adding `data-role="button"` to any regular HTML link.

The second two attributes—transition and theme—refer to how the page transition should occur, and the color and styling of the button. We'll cover both of these in detail in the next few chapters. We can also manually add a bit more styling to buttons by specifying an icon. Where it makes sense, jQuery Mobile automatically adds icons to buttons (i.e., by adding an X icon to a dialog close button). However, we can do this manually if we like. For example, changing the preceding "Contact" link to read

```
<a href="#contact" data-transition="pop" data-role="button" data-theme="b"
data-icon="plus">Contact</a>
```

would add a nice + icon to the button. The full list of icons can be found on jQuery Mobile's website (http://jquerymobile.com/demos/1.0.1/docs/buttons/buttons-icons.html). By default, icons appear on the left side of a button; however, we can use data-iconpos="right" or "top" or "bottom" to move it. We can also use data-iconpos="notext" to show the icon and nothing else!

What if you want to use your own icon? Well, that's possible as well. You'll need to add some custom CSS to do this, as well as create a properly formatted icon file (both of which are explained at the link provided previously).

Finally, one can format buttons to appear as part of the same group by surrounding a series of buttons with the <div data-role="controlgroup"> and </div> tags. This will let you visually cluster buttons with similar meaning (i.e., a "Yes," "No," or "Cancel" group). This usually means that only the corners of the top and bottom buttons are rounded (if using the default theme) and there is little to no space between the buttons. This is very useful to give the user a subtle prompt about the related nature of the groupedbuttons. Now that the first page is all done, header to footer, we'll define another two pages in the same HTML document!

Listing 7–4 Cont.: *The about and contact pages.*

```
<!-- about -->
<div data-role="page" id="about">
<div data-role="header">
<h1>About Us</h1>
</div>
<div data-role="content">
<p>Vivamus sit amet nulla vitae odio ultricies fringilla quis at felis. Integer sagittis
eleifend leo, et tempor elit adipiscing in. Pellentesque commodo condimentum pulvinar.
Integer vitae tellus ac sapien molestie euismod. Sed a enim ut leo fermentum lobortis ac
eget velit. Mauris commodo porta felis id fermentum. Aenean eleifend justo eu sem
consectetur auctor. Quisque convallis ullamcorper elementum. Integer hendrerit vehicula
nisi eu congue. Integer aliquet quam a arcu cursus ac consequat est pretium. Nam nec
pharetra lorem. Maecenas lacinia facilisis eros quis tempor.</p>
</div>
<div data-role="footer" class="ui-bar">
<a href="#home" data-transition="flip" data-role="button" data-theme="b">Home</a>
<a href="#contact" data-transition="pop" data-role="button" data-theme="b">Contact</a>
</div>
</div>
<!-- /about -->

<!-- contact -->
<div data-role="page" id="contact">
<div data-role="header">
<h1>Send Us Mail!</h1>
</div>
<div data-role="content">
<form action="#" method="get">
<div data-role="fieldcontain">
<label for="name">Name:</label>
<input type="text" name="name" id="name" value="" />
<label for="email">Email:</label>
<input type="email" name="email" id="email" value="" />
</div>
```

```
<div data-role="fieldcontain">
<label for="message">Message:</label>
<textarea id="message"></textarea>
</div>
<div class="ui-body ui-body-b">
<fieldset class="ui-grid-a">
<div class="ui-block-a">
<button type="submit" data-theme="d">Cancel</button>
</div>
<div class="ui-block-b">
<button type="submit" data-theme="a">Send</button>
</div>
</fieldset>
</div>
</form>
</div>
</div>
<!-- /contact -->

</body>
</html>
```

Now that we've discussed how the code works, let's see how the main page looks in Figure 7–8.

Figure 7–8. *Our jQuery Mobile Home Page being viewed on a Android 2.3.4 mobile device*

We'll jump quickly over our About page as there is not a lot of action going on here. There is one little tidbit of tasty goodness that we are going to cover, though. I'm sure that you, looking at this page, are probably asking yourself, "Hey, why didn't he create some sort of visual cue that could be used to navigate back to the previous page we were on?!" (Even if you didn't think of this already, you are now) Well, don't you worry about that! If you load this page we just created in your web browser and view the About page you will notice that jQuery Mobile was nice enough to include a back button in your page for you (see Figure 7–9), even including the correct icon as I mentioned it would!

Figure 7–9. *Our jQuery Mobile About Page being viewed on a Android 2.3.4 mobile device. Notice the back button that jQuery Mobile automatically included in the user interface?*

Finally, here on our Contact page is where we really start to have fun with some of the features that jQuery Mobile provides (see Figure 7–10). Looking at our code, you will see there are two div containers with the data-roles of "fieldcontain" on this page. As I am sure you already guessed by now, these containers are used to house and separate form input fields that do not necessarily have to be bunched up together. Basically, it is used for aesthetics for those of us that are graphic design impaired. After separating our form fields, we have yet another div container that is holding our Cancel and Submit buttons. These buttons are positioned in a grid-like format on the page by assigning the fieldset element the CSS class of ui-grid-a ("a" in this case stands for the theme that will be used to style the grid container). Finally, it's worth noting that our code here sends the email form to nothing (#) as it's written now. Later in this chapter, we'll see how we can use JavaScript to process forms, or one could write a simple PHP script to accept the form data and process it.

As you can see, jQuery Mobile allows you to create a very nice looking user interface in a very short amount of time!

Figure 7–10. *Our jQuery Mobile Contact Page neatly formatted and viewed on a Android 2.3.4 mobile device*

So – About Those Transitions

If you've been coding along, you'll notice that the buttons in the previous example transition differently depending on what we want to do. Animation is a key element in mobile design as it lets the small screen give the user a sense of three dimensions, which can help them understand what they're doing. By default, the jQuery mobile framework will implement a right to left slide transition, which gives the user the feeling of turning a page. The framework is also nice enough that when the 'back' button is pressed, it will reverse the transition it initially used, so in this case, turning to a previous page. In Listing 7–5, I've created a simple page that shows off all of the transition types, moving from Page One to Page Two.

Listing 7–5. *transition demo HTML*

```
<!DOCTYPE HTML>
<html>
<head>
<title>This is jQuery's Base Template, Showing off The Transitions</title>
<meta name="viewport" content="width=device-width, initial-scale=1">
```

```
<link rel="stylesheet" href="http://code.jquery.com/mobile/1.0/jquery.mobile-
1.0.min.css" />
<script type="text/javascript" src="http://code.jquery.com/jquery-
1.6.4.min.js"></script>
<script type="text/javascript" src="http://code.jquery.com/mobile/1.0/jquery.mobile-
1.0.min.js"></script>
</head>
<body>

<div data-role="page" id="one" data-title="First Page">

<div data-role="header">
<h1>The Title</h1>
</div><!-- /header -->

<div data-role="content">
<p>This is where we put what we want to talk about on this page, it's going to be
great</p>
<a href="#two" data-transition="pop">Pop Page 2</A><br>
<a href="#two" data-transition="slide">Slide Page 2</A><br>
<a href="#two" data-transition="slideup">Slideup Page 2</A><br>
<a href="#two" data-transition="slidedown">Slidedown Page 2</A><br>
<a href="#two" data-transition="fade">Fade Page 2</A><br>
<a href="#two" data-transition="flip">Flip Page 2</A><br>
</div><!-- /content -->

</div><!-- /page -->

<div data-role="page" id="two" data-title="Second Page">

<div data-role="header">
<h1>The Title of Page 2</h1>
</div><!-- /header -->

<div data-role="content">
<p>This is where we put what we want to talk about on this page, it's going to be
great</p>
<a href="#" data-rel="back">Back to page 1</A>
</div><!-- /content -->

</div><!-- /page -->

</body>
</html>
```

When rendered, the page looks like Figure 7–11, with several text links that will show the appropriate transition as needed.

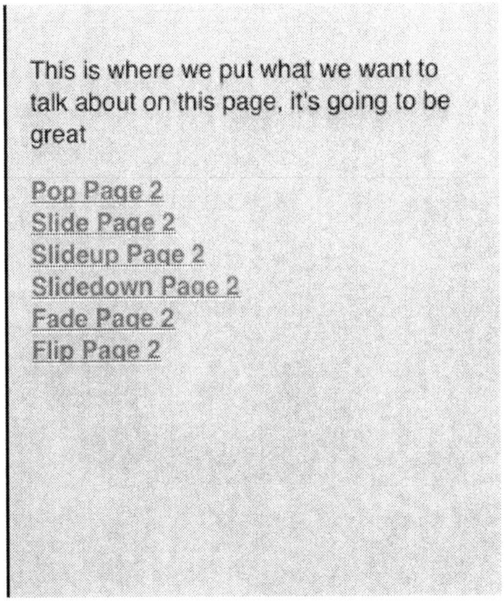

This is where we put what we want to talk about on this page, it's going to be great

Pop Page 2
Slide Page 2
Slideup Page 2
Slidedown Page 2
Fade Page 2
Flip Page 2

Figure 7–11. *The transition demo page*

Press on each link to see the appropriate transition, and then use the back button on Page 2 to see the inverse. We specify the transition we want in the HTML HREF link in Listing 7–4, and you're able to play with them as much as you want. Remember, however, when working with transitions, one should probably decide what each transition means in advance, to keep the user from getting confused. If entering something into a database causes a fade transition, while a slide up indicates a message or error, switching those around freely might make the user second-guess the action they took. Also note that the Flip and Pop transitions might not render properly on some versions of the Android stock browser, so one might want to avoid them. Speaking of showing messages to the user...

Let's Have a Dialog

Dialog boxes have been around for a long time in terms of computers. We've already shown some very simple ones earlier in this book; however, jQuery Mobile has a very nice built-in way to show these dialogs, which we'll show off using the following Listing 7–6.

Listing 7–6. *Dialog example*

```
<!DOCTYPE HTML>
<html>
<head>
<title>This is jQuery's Base Template, Showing off The Dialogs</title>
<meta name="viewport" content="width=device-width, initial-scale=1">
<link rel="stylesheet" href="http://code.jquery.com/mobile/1.0/jquery.mobile-
1.0.min.css" />
<script type="text/javascript" src="http://code.jquery.com/jquery-
1.6.4.min.js"></script>
<script type="text/javascript" src="http://code.jquery.com/mobile/1.0/jquery.mobile-
1.0.min.js"></script>
```

```
</head>
<body>

<div data-role="page" id="one" data-title="First Page">

<div data-role="header">
<h1>The Title</h1>
</div><!-- /header -->

<div data-role="content">
<p>This is where we put what we want to talk about on this page, it's going to be
great</p>
<a href="#two" data-rel="dialog" data-role="button">Open Dialog</A><br>
<a href="#two" data-rel="dialog" data-role="button" data-transition="slidedown">Slide
Down Dialog</A><br>
<a href="#two" data-rel="dialog" data-role="button" data-transition="flip">Flip
Dialog</A><br>
<a href="#two" data-rel="dialog" data-role="button" data-transition="Pop">Pop
Dialog</A><br>
</div><!-- /content -->

</div><!-- /page -->

<div data-role="page" id="two" data-title="Second Page">

<div data-role="header">
<h1>The Title of Page 2</h1>
</div><!-- /header -->

<div data-role="content">
<p>This is a dialog box</p>
<a href="#" data-rel="back">Back to page 1</A>
</div><!-- /content -->

</div><!-- /page -->

</body>
</html>
```

When we load Listing 7–6, we get a page with a series of 3 buttons (Figure 7–12) which we can press to see Page Two (the same page from our transitions demo) pop up (or slide, or flip). In the dialog, once open, we also get a little black X button in the upper right to dismiss the message, without any extra coding required.

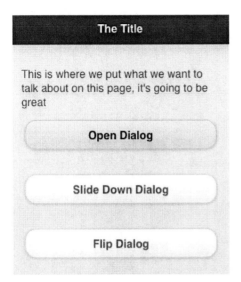

Figure 7–12. *The Dialog Demo page, dialogs.html*

Dialogs are useful when you need to get the user's attention and don't want to give the impression that they are moving to a new page. Properly used, they'll give your user a nice, polished experience.

Now that you've added some personal touches with transitions and dialogs, let's revisit a topic I mentioned earlier: A custom theme.

Rolling Your Own Theme with ThemeRoller

Let's face it: creating a theme is not an easy proposition. There are a lot of things to consider, and while Apple has done a lot to make a somewhat standard look to mobile pages, you don't want our Android applications looking exactly like iPhone clones, do you? (Actually, maybe you do, but hey—it's always nice to have options!) Thankfully, the jQuery Mobile team has created an awesome web application of their own called ThemeRoller (Figure 7–13), which lets you create a theme quickly and painlessly.

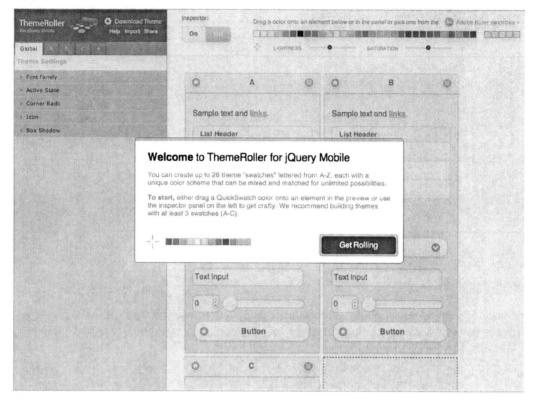

Figure 7–13. *The main start up screen for ThemeRoller*

ThemeRoller lets you tweak each and every element of the stock jQuery Mobile themes. In the right hand side of the screen, one will see three themes (A, B, & C)—each can be customized and one can even add more themes if desired. Once created, we can specify which theme we want on a given page by using the data-theme attribute (examples of which can be seen in earlier listings, such as Listing 7–4).

Once you dismiss the "Get Rolling" screen, you can begin expanding the options on the left side of the screen, as I've done in Figure 7–14.

Figure 7–14. *Customizing options on the left side of the ThemeRoller screen*

I can make changes globally, to all of my themes, or I can change things specifically on theme A, B, or C. In this case, all of the defaults provide a very iPhone-y look to things. I'm going to change them around to create the configuration shown in Figure 7–15.

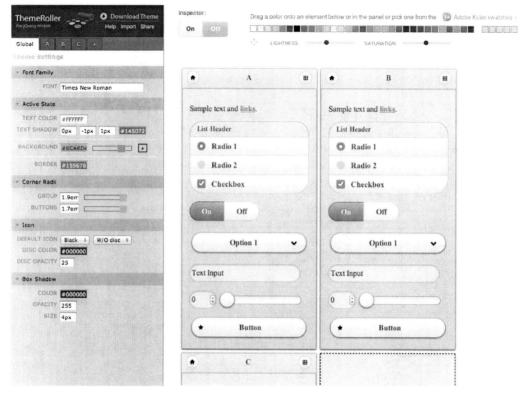

Figure 7–15. *Changing the options updates the preview on the right*

You can see that I've changed quite a lot of the settings, which has made the interface very different. I haven't changed colors yet, although I can do that very easily. In fact, ThemeRoller will even give me a collection of Adobe kuler swatches (Figure 7–16; collections of colors that go well with each other– (www.adobe.com/products/kuler/) to help me pick a set of colors that will be pleasing to my users.

Figure 7–16. *Adobe kuler swatches help me find exactly the sort of color scheme I'm looking for*

After a few minutes (or hours) of customizing, I can download my theme by entering a few options, as shown in Figure 7–17. This provides me with a ZIP file containing a themes directory, a sample index.html that correctly embeds my theme, the images needed, and two CSS files for my theme, which I could then edit by hand if I wanted.

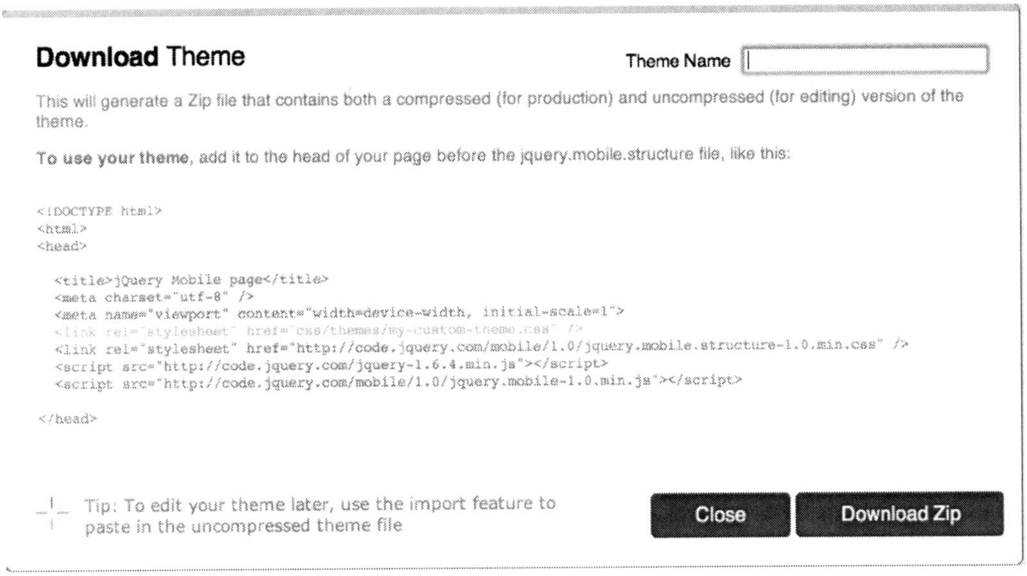

Download Theme   Theme Name [   ]

This will generate a Zip file that contains both a compressed (for production) and uncompressed (for editing) version of the theme.

To use your theme, add it to the head of your page before the jquery.mobile.structure file, like this:

```
<!DOCTYPE html>
<html>
<head>

  <title>jQuery Mobile page</title>
  <meta charset="utf-8" />
  <meta name="viewport" content="width=device-width, initial-scale=1">
  <link rel="stylesheet" href="css/themes/my-custom-theme.css" />
  <link rel="stylesheet" href="http://code.jquery.com/mobile/1.0/jquery.mobile.structure-1.0.min.css" />
  <script src="http://code.jquery.com/jquery-1.6.4.min.js"></script>
  <script src="http://code.jquery.com/mobile/1.0/jquery.mobile-1.0.min.js"></script>

</head>
```

_!_ Tip: To edit your theme later, use the import feature to
 | paste in the uncompressed theme file   [Close]   [Download Zip]

Figure 7–17. *The download theme window with instructions*

If I ever need to make changes to my theme, I can use the "Import" option in ThemeRoller to bring it back into the web app and play around once more. I can then export my new theme the same way as I did the first one. Imagine: you can create custom themes (like the one I created previously, shown in the example index file in Figure 7–18), and then modify them for 'sister' applications—without ever touching the CSS directly!

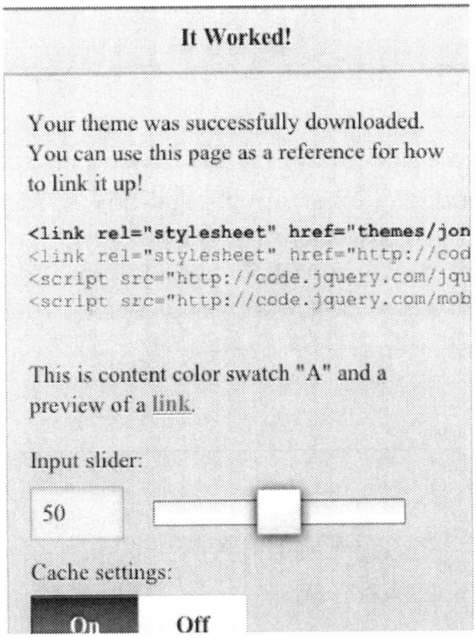

It Worked!

Your theme was successfully downloaded. You can use this page as a reference for how to link it up!

```
<link rel="stylesheet" href="themes/jon
<link rel="stylesheet" href="http://cod
<script src="http://code.jquery.com/jqu
<script src="http://code.jquery.com/mob
```

This is content color swatch "A" and a preview of a link.

Input slider:

[50]   [=========O===================]

Cache settings:

[On]   Off

Figure 7–18. *My custom theme applied to the example index file provided by ThemeRoller*

Now I've got my application looking the way I want, and I know how to build additional pages, transitions, and dialogs. I'm well on my way to creating not only a killer application in terms of functionality, but one that looks nice too!

Rolling it All Together: Simple Calc

Now that we've built a few example pages in jQuery Mobile, let's build something useful: A simple calculator. We'll build a very simple calculator that will take two numbers and perform some operation on them, returning the result. I'm also going to create a custom theme to use. The end result looks like Figure 7–19:

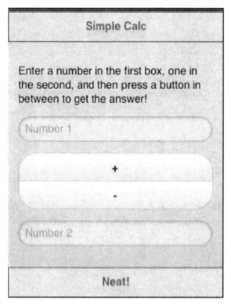

Figure 7–19. *The Simple Calc jQuery Mobile App*

Simple Calc is an extremely simple calculator. You put a number into the first box, a number into the second box below the buttons, and then hit the + or –. A small JavaScript alert pops up, telling you what the answer is. It's simple, for sure, but useful for showing how to add a bit of interactivity into a jQuery Mobile page using JavaScript. Let's look at the code in Listing 7–7.

Listing 7–7. *The code for Simple Calc*

```
<!DOCTYPE HTML>
<html>
<head>
<title>Simple Calc</title>
<link rel="stylesheet" href="http://code.jquery.com/mobile/1.0a1/jquery.mobile-
1.0a1.min.css" />
<script src="http://code.jquery.com/jquery-1.4.3.min.js"></script>
<link rel="stylesheet" href="themes/simplecalc.css" />
<script src="http://code.jquery.com/mobile/1.0a1/jquery.mobile-1.0a1.min.js"></script>
```

```
<script type="text/javascript">
function addnums() {
var num1 = document.calc.number1.value;
var num2 = document.calc.number2.value;
var num3 = num1 + num2;
alert(num3);
}

function subnums() {
var num1 = document.calc.number1.value;
var num2 = document.calc.number2.value;
var num3 = num1 - num2;
alert(num3);
}
</script>
</head>
<body>
<!-- page -->
<div data-role="page" id="aboutPage">

<!--header -->
<div data-role="header">
<h1>Simple Calc</h1>
</div>
<!-- /header -->

<!-- content -->
<div data-role="content">
<form action="#" name="calc" method="post">
<p>Enter a number in the first box, one in the second, and then press a button in
between to get the answer!</p>
<p><input type="number" name="number1" id="number1" placeholder="Number 1">
<p><div data-role="controlgroup"><a href="#" data-role="button"
onclick="addnums()">+</A><a href="#" data-role="button" onclick="subnums()">-</A></div>
<p><input type="number" name="number2" id="number2" placeholder="Number 2">
</form>
</div>
<!-- /content -->

<!-- footer -->
<div data-role="footer">
<h4>Neat!</h4>
</div>
<!-- /footer -->
</div>
<!-- /page -->

</body>
</html>
```

Let's walk through this code. First, we begin by adding in our usual HTML headers and links to jQuery Mobile. You'll notice that my custom theme is also included on line 7 (simplecalc.css). I built this using the ThemeRoller we discussed in the last section!

Next comes a custom set of JavaScript functions, addnums() and subnums(). These functions access the two number boxes (declaring them num1 and num2 respectively) and do the desired operation. They then pop up a standard JavaScript alert box with the result. If you're looking to flex your JavaScript muscle, you could combine these two functions into one!

A bit further down, we see the actual content laid out. We've put in two inputs, number1 and number2, and between them, our two buttons. We've made use of a controlgroup, so that the buttons group together, rather than separately. You'll notice that each button has an onclick= reference to the JavaScript function it corresponds to. This is where the magic happens—and why we didn't actually have to build a form action page— JavaScript takes care of all of the calculating.

There you have it—a simple calculator!

Summary

Using jQuery Mobile, one can quickly take a bare-bones application and make it look like it was professionally designed. You can also make quick and pretty "informational" applications (i.e., an application that serves as the program for a conference or a tour guide for a building or event). We've covered the basics of jQuery Mobile, but there are still some advanced topics and nuances left for you to explore on your own if you need them—your imagination is the only limit!

Chapter **8**

Building Visually Rich Internet Applications

Now that we have a better grasp of what JavaScript and the various mobile oriented JavaScript frameworks can do to enhance our user experience, it is time to dive in and get our hands messy with a bit of digital finger painting. Building awesome web applications isn't just about programming and logic. A fair amount of web development takes a lot of cues from the design realm. Take CSS, for instance. One of the main reasons why it drives developers crazy is because CSS is a design tool and not really a development tool. Sure, we have to write code to make everything look pretty, but really what we are doing is meticulously setting margins, padding, colors, typefaces, etc.

Keeping that in mind, in this chapter we will explore all of those fun aspects of development that deal more with design. We will take a look at resources for Creative Commons icons and graphics, resources for web fonts, CSS frameworks, and even a nice bitmap and vector graphic editor targeted toward web developers and web designers called Adobe Fireworks (`www.adobe.com/products/fireworks.html`).

Finding and Using Icons and Stock Photography

One of the easiest ways to make a website look more attractive is to add some icons or inviting stock photography to your project. There are plenty of resources out there where artists gladly offer up their sets of icons they created or the majestic looking photos they shot, free to use with no questions asked.

In this section, we will take a look at some of the more popular sites that cater to designers, developers, and all other lovers of things that are attractive and fun to look at.

Iconfinder

Iconfinder (`www.iconfinder.com/`, see Figure 8–1) is a personal favorite of mine, found in the Creative Commons space for open source icons. This search engine allows you to sort through over 150,000 different icons that are just waiting to be used on your next project.

With icons and graphics ranging from 12 pixels to a whopping 512 pixels, this search engine is almost guaranteed to have something that you can use to visually lift up any project you are working on.

While the icons in this search engine are free to use, not all of the icons that are available on commercial web sites (i.e., a site built for a for-profit group, versus a non-profit) are free to use, so please make sure to read the licensing on any icon you find that you might want to use. We've mentioned the Creative Commons license a few times so far, so it makes sense to take a moment and consider it and other licenses. First and foremost, you must remember that whoever originally designed a piece of artwork (whether an icon, photo, etc...) retains copyright to that artwork. It's tempting to think "Hey, it's on the Internet; it must be free." However, that sort of thinking can quickly land you in trouble if the owner finds out. Many artists and designers who do not wish to create a unique license for their content decide to go with one of the Creative Commons licenses (`http://creativecommons.org`). These licenses allow artists to allow their work to be used freely, with or without certain restrictions. You can't merely assume that something licensed under Creative Commons is free to use—it may have a restriction against commercial use (NC is the shorthand used by the Creative Commons team), or it may require attribution in your app (crediting the icon or image to the owner, BY is the shorthand used here). In addition, the owner may specify other options which one should be aware of.

All in all, if you are unsure of whether you can use an icon, don't be afraid to reach out to the author and ask. The worst that will happen is that they will just say no!

Figure 8–1. *Iconfinder search engine home page. Over 158,184 icons strong, and growing!*

Find Icons

Find Icons (Figure 8–2) is another search engine that caters to developers and designers who need a little pick-me-up for their website. The features and layout are similar to Icon Finder, so if you are familiar with one search engine you can easily adapt to using the other search engine.

I have found that it is always good to use both sites when searching for an icon since each site has collections of icons that are not available on the other. You can browse the Find Icons search engine at http://findicons.com/

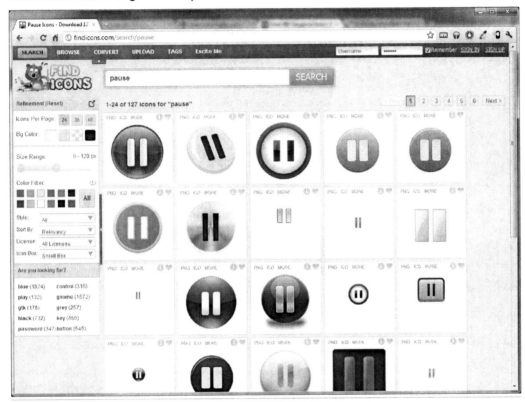

Figure 8–2. *Searching for a "pause" icon on the Find Icons website*

Using an Icon

Assuming that you've found an icon that you like, or you've created one using a service such as favicon.ico Generator (www.favicon.cc/), you can easily specify this icon for your web app by putting the following HTML code in the HTML Header section:

```
<link rel="shortcut icon"  href="http://yourdomain.com/app.ico" />
```

This line tells all modern browsers that your application's icon lives at `http://yourdomain.com/app.ico` (you could put the icon anywhere you choose). This causes the browser to show your icon (instead of the stock 'bookmark' icon) whenever a user bookmarks your page or (in some browsers) browses to it. Figures 8–3 and 8–4 show the URL bar of the Mozilla Firefox browser when viewing a site with a favicon versus one without, respectively.

Figure 8–3. *Firefox displays a website URL with a favicon specified*

Figure 8–4. *Firefox displays a website URL without a favicon*

You might also want to include one additional line:

```
<link rel="apple-touch-icon" href="/image.png" />
```

This line specifically tells mobile browsers (such as Apple's Safari and Android's Browser) that the reference image file (typically either a 57x57 pixel image or a 114x114 image file (for newer system) should be used in functions that pin a shortcut to a home screen. For a web app, this can give a polished appearance to users, bringing them closer to a native application experience.

Now that we've got an icon picked out and in use, let's talk about making our application a bit more image friendly, by finding and using stock photography. We'll begin with one of the oldest image search tools, deviantART.

deviantART

It seems as though deviantART (`www.deviantart.com/`, see Figure 8–5) has been around forever, and in technology terms, it has. This ancient relic of the year 2000 has stood the test of Internet time and is a shining pillar of the creativity of amateur and professional artists and graphic designers alike.

Add to this some social media features that allow users to comment on or share works or arts with other users and you have an addicting user experience that offers up a ton of great resources... and sometimes not so great resources.

Make sure to check out their photography sections for a slew of free stock photography that can be manipulated and used in one of your upcoming projects. Also be sure to check out the licensing agreements of the stock photography being offered. Some of the artists might have special requirements that will have to be met before you can take advantage of their work. These requirements may be fairly mundane (i.e., no commercial use) to very specific (i.e., must be used in a public service announcement or for a charity).

Figure 8–5. *Viewing the stock photography section of deviantART*

iStockphoto

Another more professional—and expensive—solution to getting great stock photography for your web application is iStockphoto (www.istockphoto.com/). This is a service that I have used for years to purchase royalty-free images for client projects.

While, unlike deviantART, this resource is not free to use, the images you will be purchasing have come from professionals and will tend to be better quality then the amateur stuff you would find elsewhere.

Add to that a large archive of images that can be easily searched to find what you are looking for and you have a resource that should always be kept on hand! You never know when, one day, one of your clients might call you up and say "Hey, I've decided we really want to add a big giant pink telephone to our website" and even though that sounds crazy and ridiculous, chances are you will be able to find an image of a giant pink telephone on iStockphoto.

In addition to iStockphoto and deviantART, one can also find images at Shutterstock (www.shutterstock.com) and Flickr (www.flickr.com). Flickr, in particular, has a very nice advanced search function (www.flickr.com/search/advanced/?), which allows you to specify that you only want Creative Commons licensed content (and further, that you only want CC licensed content that is free to use commercially and can be adapted). This is a simple way to get a very nice user-submitted photograph for your application.

Before we finish discussing photographs, it is probably useful to discuss when you should and shouldn't elect to use one. It can be tempting to use images in many different spaces to promote your application and/or make it shine; however, there is a fine line that must be walked.

Guidance on Using Photos in Web Apps

Upon finding the services we've discussed in the preceding sections, it may be very tempting to jump in and find a photo for each and every part of your application. For example, you might have large navigation buttons on your app's main screen, and wouldn't those large squares look great with photos in them, versus words or simple icons? Perhaps… However, we'd suggest you first consider the following:

- **How much load time am I adding with each photo?** Recall that when we are testing, our application normally lives on our computer. This leaves the argument of load times largely moot—we simply don't know how our app might load given certain circumstances. With that in mind, pretty photos can sometimes cause an app to load sluggishly. We'd suggest using photos of appropriate size (e.g., resize them if necessary; do not simply specify a height and width that will make them render smaller but not actually be smaller in file size—less than 10 kilobytes if possible), and testing both photo and non-photo versions of pages under a variety of conditions (e.g., served from a production web server, to a device on both WiFi and a cellular data connection).

- **Do my images distract my user?** Yes, while a picture is worth 1000 words, some pictures are worth much more in the debate they cause among users. A photograph of a STOP sign may be easy to interpret to the user in some circumstances, but be confusing in others (e.g., in a game—does the STOP sign mean end of round? Exit the game? Stop my little man from walking?). Images should only help the user find things more quickly, not confuse the user by being distracting, confusing, or of poor quality.

- **Will using an image invoke a user stereotype?** Images can be powerful, but in some cases they can be associated with both traditional stereotypes we're well aware of, and some you might not consider. For example, using the tried-and-true "man with a business suit" and "woman using a laptop" might seem appropriate for your app; however, users generally will have seen these stock images before and may assume your web app will be just as uninspired as others who have used the same images. This is why many sites now tend toward a minimalist design trend—it's less predictable than "hard working executive" or "soccer mom."

Assuming you've thought through the issues discussed in the preceding list, using photos can be a wonderful way to reinforce your application's appeal. Just be mindful of your use! Now we'll look at a more subtle image manipulation: using custom fonts in our web app.

Web Fonts

You might have remembered that we briefly touched base on working with web fonts in Chapter 2 when building our "Who's That Tweet?" application. Over the past year and a half, all of the most popular Desktop browsers have rolled out updates and can now use web fonts in their markup. Almost all of Android's mobile browsers can use them as well.

Adding web fonts to your web site or application is easy as pie, as seen in Listing 8–1.

Listing 8–1. *Loading the Droid Sans font into our web browser with a little CSS magic.*

```
<style type="text/css">
@font-face {
    font-family: 'Droid Sans';
    font-style: normal;
    font-weight: normal;
    src: local('Droid Sans'), local('DroidSans'), url('droidsans.woff') format('woff');
}

body {
    font-family:'Droid Sans', Arial, Helvetica, sans-serif;
}
</style>
```

Let's take a quick look at the code in Listing 8–1 so you can understand what we are doing here. The first property we are going to define in our @font-face code is the font-family property. Here we can name the font anything we want. We are using the font's real name here, Droid Sans, but I could have called it "Turtle Wax" if I really wanted to. Using a custom name may be helpful if you want to use an internal naming structure, although it might be confusing if you want to use the same font for two different products.

Next, we are going to define the font-style of our new font. This is important because we can have different variants of our Droid Sans font load depending on what the font-style is. This is the area where you, as a developer, will want to be careful to make sure you don't go overboard and load 10 different variants of a font when they're not needed. Not only does this clutter up your code, it also loads resources unnecessarily, which bogs down the user experience. In this case, we simply want to use the default or 'normal' look for this font; i.e., we do not want italics.

After our font-style we have our font-weight. This, just like the property before it, can be used to load different versions of a font, such as Droid Sans Bold.

Last, but not least, we have our src, which is used to tell your computer where to find our font on the server as well as what the font might be called on the user's computer. If the font is on the user's machine, this could end up saving us some bandwidth by not having to download a file we already own. While local loading is preferable much of the time, you might run into situations where you want the font loaded from another location, such as when you are testing a variety of font styles to determine the best fit.

Google Web Fonts

You might remember when we grabbed the Droid Sans font from Google Web Fonts in one of our earlier chapters. At the time, we did not go into much detail about Google Web Fonts and just how incredible a resource it is for designers and developers alike.

One of the most intriguing aspects of using Google Web Fonts (shown in Figure 8–6) with your next project is that all of the fonts are open source and can be used by anyone without the fear violating a license and owing someone money.

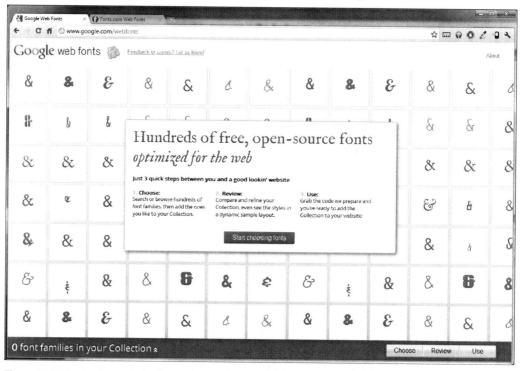

Figure 8–6. *The landing page for the newly designed Google Web Fonts site*

One of the biggest complaints I hear about developers who are against using web fonts is that fonts can tend to be a little bulky in weight, which does increase loading times. While this can be annoying on a mobile device due to limited bandwidth, Google has taken this into account and created an easy method to shrink the size of the font file that is loaded into your user's browser.

Take a quick look at Listing 8–2. Here we have the basic HTML markup needed to add the Chivo Google Web Font to our web application.

Listing 8–2. *Loading a non-optimized version of the Chivo font into our user's browser.*

```
<link href='http://fonts.googleapis.com/css?family=Chivo' rel='stylesheet'
type='text/css'>
```

Now, if you take a look at Listing 8–3, you can see how we are optimizing the size of the font by only loading the letters we need to make up the words "Hello World." This is perfect if you need to load a font into your site that is only going to be used once, such as for the logo, and that will only use a few letters.

Listing 8–3. *Loading an optimized version of the Chivo font that only loads the letters we need from the font*

```
<link href='http://fonts.googleapis.com/css?family=Chivo&text=Hello%20World'
rel='stylesheet' type='text/css'>
```

On top of allowing you to optimize your fonts, Google continues to add new fonts to the Google Web Font directory on a regular basis. It is hands down one of my favorite places to browse when I'm bored because you never know when you are going to find that one magical font that inspires you to sit down and start coding something new.

Font Issues to Consider

Just as in using photographs, there are a few caveats to using different fonts and text styling that one will want to consider and plan for:

- **What do different styles mean?** We noted previously that we could specify stylistic changes to a font, such as making text italic or bold, or even using different variants of a font, such as one that uses block lettering. While these variants provide a great amount of flexibility, they can also confuse the user if not applied consistently. You should consider if you want block text to refer to actions (e.g., the PLAY button of a video or audio clip) or if you'd rather have that be in italics (although italics can be hard to read on a mobile screen if the text isn't large enough). However, if the actions are in italics, how should captions below photos be displayed? Bold might seem too strong there, or might imply that the text is a link. See how this can become a bit complex? Creating an informal 'style guide' for your app can work wonders toward producing a consistent and beautiful output and effective use of fonts.

- **Is the style worth the fluency trade off?** Researchers in cognitive psychology — or the psychology of how the brain interprets information — use the term 'fluency' to refer to the ease of processing information. A font with just enough weight to keep its lines separate, as well as one devoid of serifs, is highly fluent, meaning that readers can easily parse it quickly and understand what you're saying. On the other hand, a wavy script font of 'elegant' handwriting or a very boxy block font (Where letters begin to run into one another) is very disfluent. This means that users will take longer to read those sections. In some cases, this is a good thing — we might want to draw attention to a certain part of the app and make sure users spend an adequate amount of time considering it (e.g., the notification that all data is about to be erased might be a good candidate for block lettering, assuming it's not so disfluent as to cause people to bypass it out of frustration!). However, in other cases, we might want to focus on speed over style.

■ **Colors Can Mean More Than Fonts**. While it is tempting to use different fonts to create different looks inside your application, one should consider if simply changing the color of text may be sufficient. Use of colors that fit nicely together in a scheme (perhaps using a reference such as Color Combos (www.colorcombos.com/)) can do more in terms of creating a rich appearance than can changing fonts. The same rules discussed previously apply to color (i.e., color should consistently convey to the reader the same message—is this a warning, an action, a description?); however, the cost is less than the cost of using fonts in terms of loading and configuration.

Now that we've discussed using fonts, images, and icons to create a look you would like to have, we'll move into a broader context—that of CSS frameworks, where we can get an entire 'skin' of CSS to wrap around our app, with far-reaching effects and consequences!

CSS Frameworks

Love them or hate them, over the past few years, CSS grid frameworks have become increasingly popular with newbie web designers and developers alike. I blame it all on Blueprint, a CSS framework that became really popular around 2008. Blueprint was created to reduce development time and to stop developers from ripping out chunks of their hair[1] in frustration when they forget what the difference between margin and padding is. That last part might be a little jest on my part, but it isn't too far from the truth.

As we discussed at the beginning on the chapter, a tool like Cascading Style Sheets is widely used by developers, but is really intended as a tool to be used by designers. Developers might not be comfortable with CSS—somewhat akin to asking a carpenter to run the electrical lines in a home. He may know enough to do it, but then again, he might make a bigger mess of it than if he hadn't ever started.

While that might sound a little ridiculous, there has been many a time that I have taken on a project for a client that dealt with styling already coded by a developer or engineer and it was painfully apparent that they had approached the whole method of writing their CSS in the same way they would write logic in their code. Think of CSS as design standards, not rules laid down in code.

If you sound like one of those people that just don't seem to "get" CSS, then you might want to take a look at some of the frameworks out there that have been created to make your life easier. In the long run, they will save you time and money by quickly helping you solve a lot of those common problems that developers have when trying to style their

---

[1] For Rocco, this isn't much of a problem. For Jon, he needs all of the chunks of hair he can get!

content into grids. They are also wonderful tools to pick apart to voraciously learn how they work.

Who knows, after playing around with CSS frameworks for a bit and learning how they operate, you might end up developing a real passion for the style sheet language and end up writing your own CSS faster by hand than you would implement an already made solution!

In the following, we've highlighted three frameworks, starting with the simplest, which takes care of many of the desktop/mobile CSS headaches for you—the *1140px Grid*. Second is *Less Framework 4*, which provides some support but has more room for modification. Finally, we discuss *320 and Up*, a version of Less Framework 4 that allows you to quickly get up and running without a massive amount of tweaking!

1140px Grid

The 1140px Grid is another CSS framework currently running around on the Internet with a pretty big following. The framework itself is released under the Creative Commons license and is free to use, copy, distribute, and manipulate to your heart's content.

This framework was created to accommodate recent changes in screen resolution, specifically the current prominence of 1280 x 800 computer screens, while also scaling fluidly for smaller displays. Up until very recently, most sites were designed around the idea that the common user's browser would have a resolution of around 1024 pixels in width and 800 pixels in height. However, over the course of the past few years, a lot of developers have noticed that ever so slowly the average user screen resolution has been shifting higher.

Keeping this in mind, 1140px Grid was designed to take advantage of that now more common screen resolution and to scale down from there in a fluid manner using responsive web design, as discussed in Chapter 5 of this book. What that means for you as a developer is that if you were designing and building a web application for a desktop user experience, you would only have to design the application once for a larger monitor. The framework then intelligently scales the application down for you for any browsers with a lower resolution.

However, this isn't always a set-it-and-forget-it process and sometimes it does require you to get in there and muck around with the CSS a bit, to get it looking exactly how you want it to look. For example, the grid will allow you to use a number of columns; however, if you intend for your application to be both appealing on the desktop and on a small browser (similar to what we discussed earlier in the book, when discussing dedicated mobile versions as opposed to one page to serve both), you may wish to limit yourself to one grid. All in all, though, if you have to build big before you build small, you can make your life a little easier by checking out 1140px Grid framework at http://cssgrid.net/

Less Framework 4

The Less Framework (http://lessframework.com/, Figure 8–7) is another one of those CSS grid systems making the rounds. Containing three different typography presets and four different types of layouts, Less Framework is a little more robust then some of the competition out there. Unlike the 1140px Grid framework, this framework is built with the idea of tablets and smartphones in mind. If you are building an application or page that only has to display on phones or tablets, Less Framework 4 is a better choice than 1140px Grid. While this framework is developed with iPad and iPhone users in mind, it still works really well on Android Webkit based browsers.

The Less Framework, however, is not a do-everything-for-you framework like some of the other options out there. To get the best use out of this framework, it is recommended that you have a comfortable relationship with both HTML and CSS. The three of you don't have to be best friends and invite each other over for Christmas dinner, but it wouldn't hurt to make small talk at the water cooler and see how the kids are doing every once in a while.

For an example of what we mean: Consider that Less Framework 4 has two mobile layouts: a normal and a wide. The wide layout is intended for mobile phones in landscape orientation. Given that your user might switch their phone's orientation at various times for various reasons, you might want to take steps in your JavaScript or HTML to re-render or re-organize material based on orientation. An app that looks good in wide may look horrible in normal—something you should determine, test, and debug.

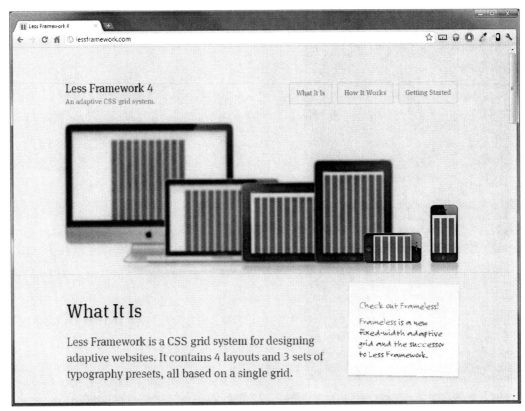

Figure 8–7. *Less Framework 4 homepage as seen in a Google Chrome Desktop browser*

320 and Up

Another Creative Commons licensed framework, 320 and Up
(http://stuffandnonsense.co.uk/projects/320andup/) was created from the get-go
with smaller viewing portals in mind. As the 320 and Up website says, this framework is
"tiny screen first." Created by Andy Clarke and Keith Clark and based off Less
Framework 4, this collection of CSS styles comes with preset typography styles and a
few extra JavaScript goodies to resize images and improve the all around performance
of the site in older browsers. As you can see in Figures 8–8, 8–9, and 8–10, it scales
nicely to the different common orientations and screens in use today on Android
devices.

320 and Up is a good choice when you want to avoid any overlap between your desktop
and mobile versions of an app, and when responsiveness is your primary goal. 320 and
Up also includes with more customizations than Less Framework 4, such as built-in
JavaScript libraries for resizing photos, and applying appropriately optimized CSS. If the
customization of Less Framework 4 appears daunting to you, you may want to start with
320 and Up and see if you really need to dig any deeper!

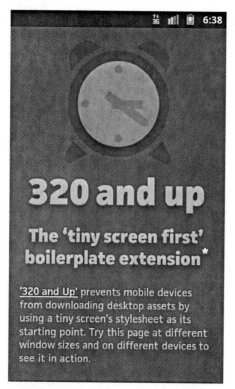

Figure 8–8. *360 and Up website viewed on an Android 2.3.4 Gingerbread handset in portrait mode*

Figure 8–9. *360 and Up website viewed on an Android 2.3.4 Gingerbread handset in landscape mode*

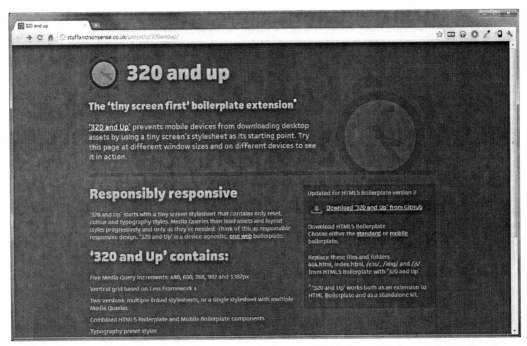

Figure 8–10. *360 and Up website viewed in Google Chrome in a Desktop browser. Notice how this and the figures before it all showed the same markup code but the page looks different depending on the user's browser resolution.*

Comparing Frameworks: About Jon!!

Choosing the right framework can be hard, so in this example, we're going to take the same content and render it in all three frameworks. The material is my (Jon's) biosketch from my personal website. Presumably, this would be a page in my mobile Jon application. First, let's look at the original page, rendered in a desktop web browser (see Figure 8–11)—this is what we're trying to emulate to some extent in the mobile version.

About Jon Westfall

Jonathan E. Westfall, PhD, born 1982, is a researcher and technologist working in New York City at Columbia Business School. His current research focuses on the variables individuals use when making economic and consumer finance decisions, specifically strength of handedness, a variable correlated with a number of decision-making and cognitive psychology tasks and measures. Dr. Westfall also conducts research on consumer financial decision making, and applications to both marketing and public policy. His current appointment is as the Associate Director for Research and Technology at the Center for Decision Sciences, a center within Columbia Business School at Columbia University in New York City. Additionally, he holds an appointment as a Lecturer in the Columbia University Psychology department, periodically teaching a course in Judgment and Decision Making.

Figure 8–11. *Jon's Biosketch rendered on the desktop.*

First, we'll render this in the 1140px Grid. Recall that the strength of this framework was that we could get something similar from Desktop to Mobile. First, the view in Mobile (Figure 8–12):

Jonathan E. Westfall, PhD, born 1982, is a researcher and technologist working in New York City at Columbia Business School. His current research focuses on the variables individuals use when making economic and consumer finance decisions,

Figure 8–12. *Jon's Biosketch rendered on mobile using 1140px Grid*

Now, let's look at the view in the desktop browser (Figure 8–13):

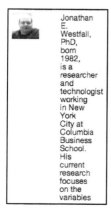

Jonathan E. Westfall, PhD, born 1982, is a researcher and technologist working in New York City at Columbia Business School. His current research focuses on the variables

Figure 8–13. *Jon's Biosketch rendered on the desktop using 1140px Grid*

This is not exactly ideal—the two one-column layouts are stacked in Mobile. However, in Desktop view, they're shown side by side, and extremely 'squished'. By tweaking the HTML code, we can alleviate this and make the Desktop version look nicer (see Figure 8–14) while also maintaining the mobile version. In this case, the problem was simply that we were using two 'onecol' boxes instead of a onecol on the left, and an elevencol on the right (filling up the rest of the screen). The 1140px Grid requires that you know how many columns you would like to fill from the start, and use the appropriate div statements. There are 12 columns, so whatever combination you use, it should add up to 12 (i.e., in this case, 1 onecol and 1 elevencol). You'll also note that the last column has the word 'last' on its div statement (see Listing 8–2), it lets 1140px Grid know that it is the last column in the row and thus should fill the rest of the page.

 Jonathan E. Westfall, PhD, born 1982, is a researcher and technologist v research focuses on the variables individuals use when making econom a variable correlated with a number of decision-making and cognitive ps consumer financial decision making, and applications to both marketing for Research and Technology at the Center for Decision Sciences, a cer City. Additionally, he holds an appointment as a Lecturer in the Columbi Judgment and Decision Making

Figure 8–14. *A snippet of the desktop view of Jon's Biosketch, fixed*

The code for the 1140px example can be seen in Listing 8–2:

Listing 8–2. *Jon's biosketch using the 1140px grid.*

```
<!DOCTYPE HTML>
<html lang="en">

<head>
    <meta charset="utf-8" />
    <title>The 1140px Grid &middot; Fluid down to mobile</title>
    <meta name="viewport" content="width=device-width, initial-scale=1.0" />
    <link rel="stylesheet" href="css/1140.css" type="text/css" media="screen" />
    <script type="text/javascript" src="js/css3-mediaqueries.js"></script>
    <style type="text/css">

    body {
    font-family: "Helvetica Neue", Helvetica, Arial, sans-serif;
    }

    .container p {
    color: #000;
    line-height: 16px;
    background: #FFF;
    text-align: left;
    margin: 20px 0 0 0;
    }

    </style>

</head>


<body>

<div class="container">
    <div class="row">
        <div class="onecol">
            <p><img src=http://jonwestfall.com/wp-content/uploads/2010/03/jon-
website.jpg></p>
        </div>
        <div class="elevencol last">
            <p>Jonathan E. Westfall, PhD, born 1982, is a researcher and technologist
working in New York City at Columbia Business School. His current research focuses on
```

the variables individuals use when making economic and consumer finance decisions, specifically strength of handedness, a variable correlated with a number of decision-making and cognitive psychology tasks and measures. Dr. Westfall also conducts research on consumer financial decision making, and applications to both marketing and public policy. His current appointment is as the Associate Director for Research and Technology at the Center for Decision Sciences, a center within Columbia Business School at Columbia University in New York City. Additionally, he holds an appointment as a Lecturer in the Columbia University Psychology department, periodically teaching a course in Judgment and Decision Making</p>
        </div>

    </div>
</div>

</body>

</html>

Now, let's look at this in Less Framework 4. First, you'll notice that Less Framework took the liberty of applying some basic font formats, something that 1140px lets us do manually, or not at all if we'd like. This might help you get up and running quicker if you want that 'mobile' feel, as seen in Figure 8–15.

Figure 8–15. *Jon's biosketch using the Less Framework 4 Framework*

The code is quite a bit simpler to implement as well, mostly because we're not worrying about a desktop version. Listing 8–3 gives us the entirety of the code, referencing the CSS provided in the Less Framework 4 package.

Listing 8–3. *Jon's biosketch using the Less Framework 4 Framework*

```
<!DOCTYPE HTML>
<html>

    <head>
        <meta charset="utf-8"/>
```

```
        <title></title>

        <link rel="stylesheet" href="main-16px.css"/>
        <meta name="viewport" content="width=device-width, initial-scale=1"/>
        <p><img src=http://jonwestfall.com/wp-content/uploads/2010/03/jon-website.jpg
height=220px width=240px></p>
        <p>Jonathan E. Westfall, PhD, born 1982, is a researcher and technologist
working in New York City at Columbia Business School. His current research focuses on
the variables individuals use when making economic and consumer finance decisions,
specifically strength of handedness, a variable correlated with a number of decision-
making and cognitive psychology tasks and measures. Dr. Westfall also conducts research
on consumer financial decision making, and applications to both marketing and public
policy. His current appointment is as the Associate Director for Research and Technology
at the Center for Decision Sciences, a center within Columbia Business School at
Columbia University in New York City. Additionally, he holds an appointment as a
Lecturer in the Columbia University Psychology department, periodically teaching a
course in Judgment and Decision Making</p>
        </head>

        <body>

        </body>

</html>
```

Finally, we'll take a look at my biosketch with 320 and Up. It applies further formatting, with a background image and custom font, as you can see in Figure 8–16.

Figure 8–16. *Jon's biosketch using the 320 and Up Framework*

The code, again, is on the simpler side compared to 1140px Grid, since we do not care about desktop rendering. See Listing 8–4.

Listing 8–4. *Jon's biosketch using the 320 and Up Framework*

```
<!DOCTYPE HTML>
<head>
<meta charset="utf-8">

<title>320 and Up Version</title>
<!-- http://t.co/dKP3o1e -->
<meta name="HandheldFriendly" content="True">
<meta name="MobileOptimized" content="320">
<meta name="viewport" content="width=device-width, target-densitydpi=160dpi, initial-
scale=1.0">

<!-- For all browsers -->
<link rel="stylesheet" href="css/style.css">

</head>

<body class="clearfix">
<div role="main">
     <p><img src=http://jonwestfall.com/wp-content/uploads/2010/03/jon-website.jpg
height=220px width=240px></p>
        <p>Jonathan E. Westfall, PhD, born 1982, is a researcher and technologist
working in New York City at Columbia Business School. His current research focuses on
the variables individuals use when making economic and consumer finance decisions,
specifically strength of handedness, a variable correlated with a number of decision-
making and cognitive psychology tasks and measures. Dr. Westfall also conducts research
on consumer financial decision making, and applications to both marketing and public
policy. His current appointment is as the Associate Director for Research and Technology
at the Center for Decision Sciences, a center within Columbia Business School at
Columbia University in New York City. Additionally, he holds an appointment as a
Lecturer in the Columbia University Psychology department, periodically teaching a
course in Judgment and Decision Making</p>

<!-- Scripts -->
<script src="js/libs/jquery-1.6.2.min.js"></script>
<script src="js/plugins.js"></script>
<script src="js/script.js"></script>
<script src="js/mylibs/helper.js"></script>
</div>
</body>
</html>
```

As you can see, each framework formats in slightly different ways, allowing you to pick which one you would like to use. While Less Framework 4 and 320 and Up look very 'mobile' in their appearance, they lack any cross-functionality with the desktop version. 1140px Grid, on the other hand, isn't very 'mobile' in its style, which means you would need to add that in manually. However, as a plus, you get a desktop and mobile version in one file.

Choosing the right CSS Framework for you can be difficult; however, given the frameworks we've covered here, it should give you a starting point to choosing the right one for your app!

Adobe Fireworks

Adobe Fireworks, shown in Figure 8–17, is probably the second most used tool in my Web Development utility belt, and for good reason. This very easy to use vector and bitmap editing program is perfect for touching up or compressing graphics, as well as for mocking up designs and prototyping new projects.

Originally created and owned by Macromedia and later acquired by Adobe in 2009, this wonder application for Web Designers everywhere hasn't received as much attention as Adobe's flagship photo editing program, Photoshop, but that is all right because it has plenty of fantastic features that easily make it a no-brainer for a program that should be included in your arsenal. In fact, for many of the tasks web developers and designers tackle, Fireworks is the better product for the job.

Just like Adobe Photoshop, Fireworks is also littered with keyboard shortcuts accommodating the needs of power users, while at the same time keeping a sparse UI with easy to find tools, options, and properties to make it easy for any new user of Adobe Fireworks to easily find their way around the application.

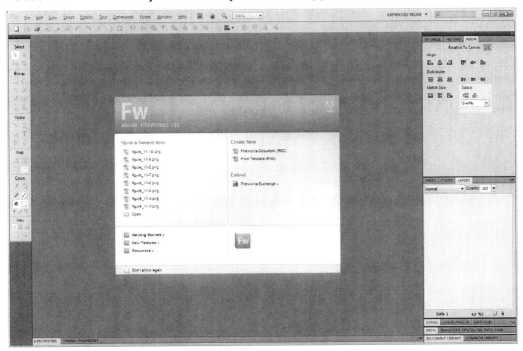

Figure 8–17. *Adobe Fireworks CS5 running on a Windows 7 PC*

One of the coolest features of Adobe Fireworks is its ability to create Pages within its specially formatted PNG file type, which would allow designers to very neatly create beautiful layouts to be passed on down to their local developer. The pages work by essentially giving you a new canvas to work on whenever you need a new page. You can easily access your pages by pressing the F5 key from within Fireworks.

When viewing your Pages, as seen in Figure 8–18, you can select which page you are viewing and working on with a simple click of your mouse. Once you are on your newly selected page, you can hop on over to the Layers tab and see all the layers related to just the current selected page instead of dealing with the layers of five or more pages within a single canvas.

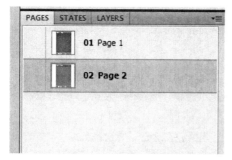

Figure 8–18. *A close up of the Adobe Fireworks Pages panel*

Keeping your designs cleaner will help you when it finally becomes time to start writing your code. The less time you have to spend scrolling through endless amounts of layers, trying to find the right resource to extract from your mockups to use in your site, the better!

On top of that, when it comes time to present your prototypes to your clients, it is always a good idea to give them the impression that you're neat and organized (as in Figure 8–19 and Figure 8–20) and that you will put that same care and consideration you spent in your mockups and prototypes into building their site or application.

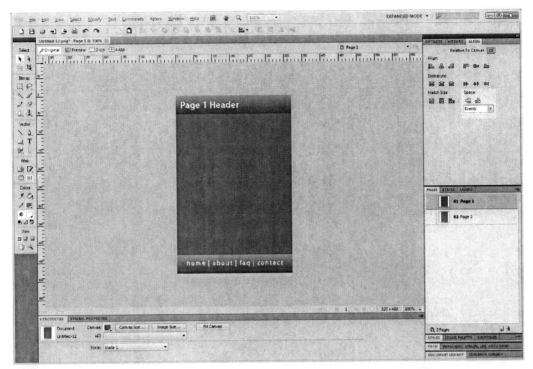

Figure 8–19. *Adobe Fireworks CS5 viewing Page 1 of a design comp on a Windows 7 machine*

Figure 8–20. *Adobe Fireworks CS5 viewing Page 1 of a design comp on a Windows 7 machine*

Summary

Hey, look at that! It looks like we are another chapter down and you have even more knowledge and other tasty tidbits floating around your cranium. Now you have a better idea of where to go and what to use to make your mobile web applications sprout jazz hands and dance around the room.

In a world where our fashion designers can make even homeless attire look fashionable, and where everywhere you look someone is raving about how "pretty" their new gadget is, it is becoming less and less acceptable for applications and websites to have that "newly engineered" look and smell to them. Even Google has cleaned up its act of designing ugly but highly functional products with the release of Google+ and the rollout of the new Google+ theme across the myriad of products they offer! However, as with all of the concepts we've discussed so far, with great power comes great... accountability. By using these tools in a consistent manner, you can produce a visually stunning and useful application!

Chapter 9

HTML5 Location-Based Applications

One of the biggest opportunities presented to mobile developers is the wealth of options opened up by the very nature of Android devices like phones and tablets: They are mobile! While the location of a user of a traditional desktop application can be interesting, it's rare for someone to pick up a desktop machine and move about with it all day. But mobile devices move, and their location (and, by implication, the location of the device user) can influence everything from games, to searching for products and information, to nuances and options for things as diverse as language settings and device behavior.

In this chapter, we'll explore geolocation in HTML5, CSS, and JavaScript for Android devices. We'll explore a simple location-enabled app, and see how the features and functions of HTML5 can be leveraged. So, let's get moving!

The Mechanics of Geolocation

In order to make your geolocation ideas a reality, it's important to understand the capabilities of all the moving parts (sorry, we couldn't resist that joke). In any Android-targeted geolocation web application, two sets of capabilities are important. First, what capabilities does a given Android device present to any web-based location-focused application? Second, what features of HTML5 (and to a lesser extent, CSS3 and JavaScript) provide location capabilities? Ultimately, the combination of what a device can say about its location, and what a web application can do with that information, will set the boundaries for what you can achieve. Let's look at the background for both.

Understanding Device Capabilities

No matter what kind of device you have, it can rely on a surprising range of technologies to provide location-based data. Even for devices that lack dedicated hardware, options exist. The devices you work with (and the examples we'll use) typically have access to one or more of the following capabilities:

- **Global Positioning System (GPS)**—hardware in the device that receives and decodes GPS satellite signals (or similar competing services like Galileo or Glonass). Accuracy can be as fine-grained as 1 meter, although this can degrade with caching and other effects.

- **WiFi triangulation**—your device uses WiFi for network connectivity, but it can also use a combination of known SSID names for WiFi networks, together with signal strength in dBm, to triangulate location. This tends to be cruder than GPS, and suffers in less built-up areas or areas with many transient hot-spots. Note that your users may disable WiFi for power consumption or conservation reasons.

- **Cell Tower triangulation**—similar to the WiFi technique, your device knows with which cell it has registered at any given time, and also knows what other cells are detectable (along with signal strengths and related timing information). Even with only one cell tower nearby, your device's location can still be known to the coarse level of that tower's service area.

- **IP Address allocation**—While your device most likely receives a dynamic IP address when connecting to WiFi or mobile networks, your provider usually has a known set of IP address blocks, and known patterns of distribution in various geographic areas. While this won't locate your device to the nearest meter, it can do a pretty good job of determining whether you're in Kansas or Kathmandu.

As you can see, multiple methods are available that support the actual mechanics of determining your device's location. Regardless of the methods supported by the device, you don't have to concern yourself with selecting a given mechanism when writing your web applications. What you do have to consider are the other two governing constraints on your geolocation application.

The first such constraint is the user's choice of settings for device-wide location features. Quite literally, has the user enabled or disabled use of GPS, and for that matter, have they allowed or prohibited other location-determining mechanisms from pinpointing the device? Figure 9–1 shows the normal settings over which the user has control

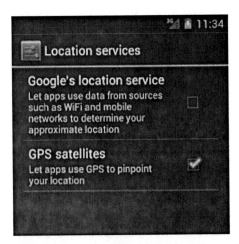

Figure 9–1. *Android Device location services settings in Android 4.0*

These settings are pretty obvious in their function. Turn off GPS satellites, and it won't be available to any service, including the location-related features of browsers. This is where our second constraint comes in. Just because the HTML5 specification outlines the API for geolocation, it doesn't mean the user's browser has implemented all (or any!) of the features.

Understanding HTML5 Capabilities

It's all fine and dandy for a given device to have a range of location capabilities, but how do these tie in to your actual web application? The answer comes from the changes made to the Document Object Model (DOM) with HTML5, which now incorporates an API to support a range of DOM events specifically for location-related activities. This is a fairly important subtlety. HTML5 does not implement the location-aware features, per se. Rather, it incorporates an API specification for how a web browser and a web server or application can work with location data. This affects you as a developer, as you need to consider not only what the HTML5 specification says should happen for geolocation activities, but how each browser has been implemented to actually support these features. Without getting too far ahead of ourselves, an example would be to understand what third-party geolocation services a given browser might use if a web application asks for location.

Detecting Browser Geolocation Support

The basis for pretty much all geolocation activity within a browser is the `navigator.geolocation` object. We can use this foundation as a neat shorthand to determine if the browser has implemented at least the basics of the HTML5 geolocation specification. Listing 9–1 shows our first code example: a bare-bones HTML and JavaScript example that determines if a given browser understands a `navigator.geolocation` object.

Listing 9–1. *Simple geolocation support check*

```
<html>
    <head>
        <title>Android Web Application Development-Geolocation example 1</title>
    </head>
    <body>
        <script type="text/javascript">
            if (navigator.geolocation) {
                alert("Congratulations, your browser supports geolocation");
            } else {
                alert('Sorry, your browser does not support geolocation');
            }
        </script>
    </body>
</html>
```

You can find this code in the file `ch09-example01.html`. Simply place this under the control of the web server of your choice, and then point your browser (desktop or mobile) to it to see the results.

> **NOTE:** This example, and the others in this chapter, typically should be run from a web server, rather than opened as a file straight from a desktop or mobile browser. This is because most contemporary browsers prevent any `file://` based URL from accessing the geolocation API. Put simply, any attempt to access a `navigator.geolocation` object, its methods, or data members will silently fail. This is due principally to security concerns, which could fill a chapter on their own. Choose a web server with which you are comfortable, such as Apache or Nginx, and you won't see any issues.

Figures 9–2 and 9–3 show the results you should see when running our first example in a desktop browser and mobile browser, respectively.

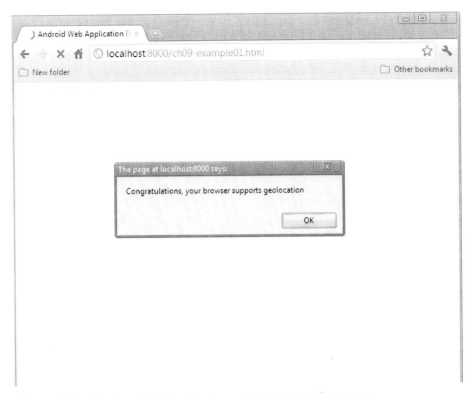

Figure 9–2. *Results of our simple desktop browser test for geolocation support*

Figure 9–3. *Results of our simple mobile browser test for geolocation support*

There are two things to note about our first piece of code that tests for geolocation support. First, it really is that simple to determine a given browser's support (although see the section "What Could Possibly Go Wrong?" later in this chapter for some more nuanced analysis of when a device with support for geolocation does not actually cooperate). The second is that using the JavaScript alert function is annoying most of the time in desktop applications, and it gets even more annoying on a small-screen mobile device. The experienced general web developers among you will know this, while for the novices, this is a good time to consider pushing your working code into a function that you can easily reuse without annoying your good users. Listing 9–2 refactors our detection example to create a separate geoSupport() function that we can re-use as we see fit.

Listing 9–2. *Simple geolocation support check revised*

```html
<html>
    <head>
        <title>Android Web Application Development-Geolocation example 2</title>
        <script type="text/javascript">
            function supportsGeo () {
                var geosupport = "Sorry, your browser does not support geolocation";
                if (navigator.geolocation) {
                    geosupport = "Congratulations, your browser supports geolocation";
                }
                return geosupport;
            }
        </script>
    </head>
    <body>
        <script type="text/javascript">
            document.write(supportsGeo());
        </script>
    </body>
</html>
```

You could, of course, take this further and push this function into a separately loaded JavaScript source file. You're free to do that and adapt the later code in this chapter, if you wish.

Exploring Our Sample Application

It's time to introduce our sample application. Unless you've been living under a rock, you're likely aware of the range of popular "check in" style applications that have flourished along with the explosion of mobile devices. Whether it's Foursquare, Latitude, TripIt, or other similar apps, these all allow you to announce your position to the wide world—presumably so your fans and the paparazzi can track your famous movements. Many of these applications are implemented as native applications for a given device, but there's nothing that stops us from developing the same style of application as a web application available within the browser of any device.

Our application is fully self-contained in ch09-example03.html, which you can run from your chosen web browser. Let's take a look from the users' perspective first, to see what it (apparently) does. Pointing our browser to the page brings up the very simple, but functional, home page of our new location-based check-in style application, which you can see in Figure 9–4.

Figure 9–4. *Our example application prior to invoking geolocation*

At the moment, it's not exactly a graphic design tour-de-force, but we'll get to that. For now, let's see what happens when we click the "Geolocation Check-In!" button. Figure 9–5 shows our page dynamically updated with what looks like a set of latitude and longitude coordinates. It looks like that because that is exactly what it is—and they are from the very location this test was run.

Figure 9–5. *Our location revealed thanks to our sample application.*

Building Our Basic Geolocation Application

At this point, you might be wondering exactly how much logic and code was required to get this apparently simple application working. Let's take a look at Listing 9–3, where we'll see the entire set of code for the ch09–example03.html file.

Listing 9–3. *Geolocation checkin example*

```
<html>
    <head>
        <title>Android Web Application Development-Geolocation example 3</title>
        <script type="text/javascript">
            function supportsGeo () {
                if (navigator.geolocation) {
                    return true;
                } else {
                    return false;
                }
            }

            function changeDiv (name, data) {
                var div = document.getElementById(name);
                if(div)
                {
                div.innerHTML = data;
                }
            }

            function checkIn () {
                var geoData = "";
                if (supportsGeo()) {
                    navigator.geolocation.getCurrentPosition(function(position) {
            geoData = position.coords.latitude + ", " +
                        position.coords.longitude;
                    });
                    <!-- alert("Confirm geolocation access before clicking OK"); -->
                } else {
                    geoData = "Your browser does not support HTML5 geolocation";
                }
                changeDiv ("myCheckIn",geoData);
            }
        </script>
    </head>
    <body>
    <h1>
        <div id="myCheckIn">
            <!-- This is where your check-in will display -->
            <p>Ready to check in...</p>
        </div>

        <form name="checkInFrm">
            <input type="button" name="checkInBtn" value="Geolocation Check-In!"
            onClick="checkIn()">
    </h1>
    </body>
</html>
```

Let's break this down into four parts, so you can digest what's happening, and also tinker and change the code yourself so you can explore possibilities as we go.

Testing for Geolocation Support, Redux

The `supportsGeo()` function we introduced earlier in the chapter has been tweaked to return a Boolean value, so we can use its result in-line in other expressions:

```
function supportsGeo () {
    if (navigator.geolocation) {
        return true;
    } else {
        return false;
    }
}
```

This provides a little more utility than the previous version that returned a string value.

Creating a Utility Function for Dynamic Page Changes

Next, we've introduced a simple utility function to control dynamic HTML behavior for `<div>` elements anywhere in our code. The `changeDiv()` function takes the name of a `<div>` element, and the desired textual change, and performs the necessary changes:

```
function changeDiv (name, data) {
    var div = document.getElementById(name);
    if(div)
    {
        div.innerHTML = data;
    }
}
```

This isn't strictly related to geolocation, but we think you'll agree this will make the rest of our code examples clearer, by removing the mechanics of these changes from the main logic.

Reviewing the Basic HTML

Our HTML code is almost the innocent bystander in our example. It provides a named `<div>` element, myCheckIn, on which our functions will work their geolocation magic.

```
<h1>
    <div id="myCheckIn">
        <!-- This is where your check-in will display -->
        <p>Ready to check in...</p>
    </div>

    <form name="checkInFrm">
        <input type="button" name="checkInBtn" value="Geolocation Check-In!"
        onClick="checkIn()">
</h1>
```

The form and input button invokes our central function, `checkIn()`, that will perform the actual geolocation work.

Delving into the Coordinates

OK, enough dancing around the edges! The checkIn() function performs the key tasks in our little example.

```
function checkIn () {
    var geoData = "";
    if (supportsGeo()) {
        navigator.geolocation.getCurrentPosition(function(position) {
            geoData = position.coords.latitude + ", " + position.coords.longitude;
        });
        <!-- alert("Confirm geolocation access before clicking OK"); -->
    } else {
        geoData = "Your browser does not support HTML5 geolocation";
    }
    changeDiv ("myCheckIn",geoData);
}
```

The geoData variable eventually holds our resulting latitude and longitude. We invoke our supportsGeo() function to ensure our browser can support our intentions. Then we get down to business by calling the navigator.geolocation.getCurrentPosition() function. This is one of the core HTML geolocation functions, and has pages and pages of overloaded definitions at http:// http://dev.w3.org/geo/api/spec-source.html.

For now, what you need to know is that navigator.geolocation.getCurrentPosition() is an asynchronous function, which in the form used here passes a call-back function to be invoked once the browser and underlying hardware have responded to the request for the caller's current location. Our position call-back assigns our geoData variable with two data members: the position.coords.latitude and position.coords.longitude values, which equate to the caller's latitude and longitude.

All that remains is for us to call the utility changeDiv() function to update our HTML page, and voila! Of course, we also ensure that browsers that don't support geolocation are targeted with the appropriate message indicating no support for our geolocation work.

> **NOTE:** You might observe that we have a commented-out call to an alert(), asking the user to confirm geolocation access before continuing. If you haven't allowed web pages to freely ask for your location (and there's no reason you should), then you'll need to confirm access when asked by your browser. But even the fastest human will not be able to do this before the call to navigator.geolocation.getCurrentPosition() returns, even though it's asynchronous. At this point, the call-back will return an error that our code currently doesn't catch (but see the section "What Could Possibly Go Wrong" later in this chapter), and our example will silently fail. Uncomment this alert in your testing to give yourself better control over the asynchronous behavior of navigator.geolocation.getCurrentPosition().

Dealing with the Four Corners of Android's Geolocation World

Our initial sample application introduces some of the key building blocks of almost all web applications that utilize geolocation. To round out the world of geolocation, we need to address the four questions of *Where am I?*, *What am I?*, *What could possibly go wrong?*, and *Where am I going?*

Where Am I?

We've already touched on the fundamentals of determining where a device happens to be, with our use of the `position.coords.latitude` and `position.coords.longitude` data members in our earlier example. You might be thinking that there's not much more to determining location than that, but there are a few additional data points you should consider.

While latitude and longitude can tell you if you're in Hawaii or The Himalayas, you'll probably agree that there's another dimension you care about in both of those locations: altitude! The HTML5 specification includes a `position.coords.altitude` data member to provide an elevation above notional sea level. Note that support for this is quite patchy, such that even the Android emulator and its browser fail to support it in many releases of the Android Development Tools (ADT).

Along with latitude, longitude, and altitude, you might be concerned with how accurate a reading you've been given. We introduced four possible location mechanisms at the start of the chapter, and each of these has varying levels of accuracy. Two additional data members are available, `position.coords.accuracy` and `position.coords.altitudeAccuracy`, to provide the margin of error for any geolocation data provided.

Interestingly, there's no direct method by which you can determine which location mechanism was used to provide your coordinates. You can infer that it was GPS if you interrogate another data value, `position.coords.satellites`, which, if supported by your browser and device, will return the number of satellites used to provide a GPS fix. The only problem with this is that if your device lacks GPS support, or fails to get a GPS fix, both situations will return NULL. So you'll be left in an ambiguous state as to what determined the lack of satellite count.

What Am I?

We've already largely dealt with the best way of answering the *What am I?* question. The HTML5 geolocation specification doesn't provide exhaustive ways of determining what particular hardware exists on a device. The best way to approach the question is using the `supportsGeo()` function, or one like it, that we introduced in the preceding section. This turns our question into one of: *What am I? A device and browser combination that supports geolocation or not?*

What Could Possibly Go Wrong?

Imagine you write your great check-in application, to take on the likes of Foursquare and company. Your users are happy, and all is good with the world. Nothing could possibly go wrong, right? Well, perhaps we spoke to soon.

On any device, at any time, you can find yourself having to deal with a range of issues that prevent your geolocation code from returning an accurate value, or even any value at all. It could be the weather, the alignment of the sun and the planets (actually, that's less of a joke than you might think), or even user intervention. Whatever the cause, there are well-defined error states that you should handle in your code.

The four main error conditions that can exhibit under the HTML5 specification are:

- **TIMEOUT**: No location mechanism responded within the allowed time with location data.

- **POSITION_UNAVAILABLE**: Your device has one or more valid location mechanisms (such as GPSor WiFi), but none of them could provide valid location data.

- **PERMISSION_DENIED**: The browser was prevented from accessing the HTML5 geolocation API by reason of permissions. Either the user blocked access when prompted, or the browser is configured explicitly to block access.

- **UNKNOWN_ERROR**: For reasons unknown, location data was not available.

It's all well and good to know what the error conditions are, but how does one make use of them? You'll remember we said the getCurrentPosition() function had a myriad of overloaded versions. A significant subset of these include a common pattern of accepting a callback function for reporting position as the first parameter, and a callback function for error handling as the second parameter. Take a look at the next iteration of our sample application, in the file ch09–example03.html. The key change is to our checkIn() JavaScript function, which now looks like this.

```
function checkIn () {
    var geoData = "";
    if (supportsGeo()) {
        navigator.geolocation.getCurrentPosition(
            function(position) {
                geoData = position.coords.latitude + ", " + position.coords.longitude;
            },
            function(error) {
                switch(error.code) {
                    case error.TIMEOUT:
                        alert ('Geolocation returned a timeout error');
                        break;
                    case error.POSITION_UNAVAILABLE:
                        alert ('Geolocation returned a position unavailable error');
                        break;
```

```
                case error.PERMISSION_DENIED:
                    alert ('Geolocation returned permission denied (did you deny
access?)');
                    break;
                case error.UNKNOWN_ERROR:
                    alert ('Geolocation encountered an unknown error');
                    break;
            }
        }
    );
    <! -- alert("Confirm geolocation access before clicking OK"); -->
    } else {
        geoData = "Your browser does not support HTML5 geolocation";
    }
    changeDiv ("myCheckIn",geoData);
}
```

In the bolded text, you'll see we've changed the method signature (overloaded version) of the getCurrentPosition() function to register our error callback, and alert the user should any error condition be returned. We're in the fortunate position (OK, we're being sarcastic here) that the Android emulator is notoriously slow and temperamental when it comes to responding to geolocation requests. For this reason, it's always good practice to test your code on real devices, as well as the emulator. The authors managed to trigger a POSITION_UNAVAILABLE error without really trying, on our first attempt. You can see the results in Figure 9–6.

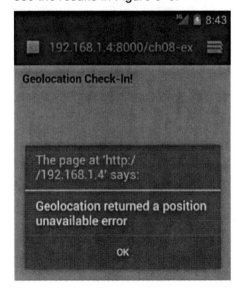

Figure 9–6. *A geolocation attempt returns a POSITION_UNAVAILABLE error*

As we did with our supportsGeo() function, you should turn this style of error checking into a utility function for use throughout your code, rather than bombard the user with alert-style errors—although, in this case, it might be warranted.

Where Am I Going?

To round out the capabilities we're exploring, we can ask ourselves—or more accurately the device—*Where am I going?* There are two approaches that are worth covering. First, our trusty geolocation data members include two more useful values, `position.coords.speed` and `position.coords.heading`. These indicate the last known speed of the device, and the last known directional heading. These values sound great for tasks like plotting movement on a map, and, in theory, that's exactly what they're designed to provide. In practice, however, a disturbingly large number of devices either don't report data for these values, or use such simplistic GPS chipsets as to not support collecting it in the first place.

This brings us to an alternative approach. To date, we've been showing off the `getCurrentPosition()` method of `navigator.geolocation`. This method has a peer method that is a little more sophisticated and useful when it comes to determining location over time, and the movement that goes with it. This is the `watchPosition()` method.

The `watchPosition()` method, in its various overloaded forms, has fairly similar behavior to our `getCurrentPosition()` method. It registers a callback function to use for normal positioning, and another callback function for error handling, but it also accepts a range of options, including a timer option for how frequently it should sleep and wake itself and *keep calling* your callbacks. The `watchPosition()` will continue to operate until halted by a call to `clearWatch()`, or its parent process terminates. Listing 9–4 shows the next iteration of our ongoing example application, from ch09–example05.html.

Listing 9–4. *Geolocation tracking over time(and movement!)*

```
<html>
    <head>
        <title>Android Web Application Development-Geolocation example 5</title>
        <script type="text/javascript">
            function supportsGeo () {
                if (navigator.geolocation) {
                    return true;
                } else {
                    return false;
                }
            }

            function changeDiv (name, data) {
                var div = document.getElementById(name);
                if(div)
                {
                    div.innerHTML = data;
                }
            }

            function startWatch () {
                var geoData = "";
                var watchOptions = { frequency: 5000 };
                if (supportsGeo()) {
```

```
                    geoData = navigator.geolocation.watchPosition(onWatchSuccess,
                                     onWatchError, watchOptions);
                } else {
                                        geoData = "Your browser does not support HTML5
geolocation";
                    changeDiv ("myCheckIn",geoData);
                }
            }

            function onWatchSuccess(position) {
                var currentLocation = "";
                currentLocation = 'Latitude: ' + position.coords.latitude + ',
Longitude: ' +
                                    position.coords.longitude;
                changeDiv("myLocationWatch",currentLocation);
            }

            function onWatchError(error) {
                var currentError = "";
                currentError = 'Error code: ' + error.code + ', Error message: ' +
error.message;
                changeDiv("myLocationWatch",currentError);
            }
        </script>
    </head>
    <body>
    <h1>
        <div id="myLocationWatch">
            <!-- This is where your check-in will display -->
            <p>Ready to check in...</p>
        </div>

        <form name="watchFrm">
            <input type="button" name="watchBtn" value="Start Watching"
            onClick="startWatch()">
    </h1>
    </body>
</html>
```

Our utility functions supportsGeo() and changeDiv() are the same, and the HTML layout
is only cosmetically changed. The key is that the button now calls our startWatch()
function, which itself ultimately calls watchPosition(). We pass it to our regular and
error callbacks- onWatchSuccess() and onWatchError()—and an options construct. In
this case, our options look like this

```
var watchOptions = { frequency: 5000 };
```

This effectively is used to pass a 5 second refresh frequency to the watchPosition()
function. If you run the code yourself, and choose the Start Watching button you see,
your browser should update approximately every five seconds with your location. This is
a little hard to show in static screen shots, so you'll have to try it for yourself. Don't
worry if you aren't actually moving around: you should still see updates to the
coordinates, because the accuracy of each reading will be slightly different depending

on number of GPS satellites used for the fix, varying local interference, etc. You should see small changes to the least significant digits even if you are relaxing on your sofa!

Expanding Your Horizons with Maps

By now you will almost certainly agree that our example application is not exactly a work of art. So let's add a bit of pizzazz, and introduce the near-ubiquitous accompaniment to geolocation: maps!

Adding a Map to Our Application

Our latest example is from file ch09–example06.html, which uses Google Maps to take our earlier check-in example to the next level. Instead of just reporting numeric co-ordinates, it uses them with the Google Maps API hosted at http://maps.googleapis.com/ to load a map, and place a marker on it highlighting your location. Listing 9–5 is our modified JavaScript, CSS and HTML5.

Listing 9–5. *Geolocation and Maps working together*

```
<html>
    <head>
        <title>Android Web Application Development-Geolocation example 6</title>
        <meta name="viewport" content="initial-scale=1.0, user-scalable=no" />
        <style type="text/css">
            html { height: 100% }
            body { height: 100%; margin: 0; padding: 0 }
            #mapContainer { height: 100% }
        </style>
        <script type="text/javascript"
src="http://maps.googleapis.com/maps/api/js?key=AIzaSyBpoxnQbCGPTIcpIJ8YPO3pTNcJX3zbc4c&
sensor=false">
        </script>
        <script type="text/javascript">
            function supportsGeo () {
                if (navigator.geolocation) {
                    return true;
                } else {
                    return false;
                }
            }

            function changeDiv (name, data) {
                var div = document.getElementById(name);
                if(div)
                {
                    div.innerHTML = data;
                }
            }

            function mapMe(thisLat, thisLong) {
                var myLatlong = new google.maps.LatLng(thisLat, thisLong);
                var myOptions = {
                    center: new google.maps.LatLng(thisLat, thisLong),
```

```
                zoom: 12,
                mapTypeId: google.maps.MapTypeId.ROADMAP
            };
            var map = new google.maps.Map(document.getElementById("mapContainer"),
                                           myOptions);
            var marker = new google.maps.Marker({
                        position: myLatlong,
                        map: map,
                        title:"Hello World!"
            });
        }

        function initialize() {
            if (supportsGeo()) {
                myLatitude = "";
                myLongitude = "";
                navigator.geolocation.getCurrentPosition(
                    function(position) {
                        myLatitude = position.coords.latitude;
                        myLongitude = position.coords.longitude;
                    },
                    function(error) {
                        switch(error.code) {
                            case error.TIMEOUT:
                                alert ('Geolocation returned a timeout error');
                                break;
                            case error.POSITION_UNAVAILABLE:
                                alert ('Geolocation returned a position unavailable
                                        error');
                                break;
                            case error.PERMISSION_DENIED:
                                alert ('Geolocation returned permission denied (did
                                        you deny access?)');
                                break;
                            case error.UNKNOWN_ERROR:
                                alert ('Geolocation encountered an unknown error');
                                break;
                        }
                    }
                );
                alert("Confirm geolocation access before clicking OK");
            }
            mapMe(myLatitude, myLongitude);
        }
    </script>
</head>
<body>
<h1>
<body onload="initialize()">
    <div id="mapContainer" style="width:100%; height:100%">
        <!-- Your map goes here! -->
    </div>
</body>
</html>
```

You'll note that our code starts with some CSS, and ends with very simple HTML that
invokes our new initialize() method as soon as the page loads. The CSS is

boilerplate stuff from Google to allow a div to act as a container for map objects. Following this, you'll see the JavaScript reference to the Google Maps API (the following line has the formatting massaged to better fit this page):

```
<script type="text/javascript"
  src="http://maps.googleapis.com/maps/api/js?
    key=AIzaSyBpoxnQbCGPTIcpIJ8YPO3pTNcJX3zbc4c&sensor=false">
</script>
```

This invokes the Maps API with a particular API key. This is Google's technique for uniquely identifying users of its API, and also rate-limiting how many calls to various APIs can be made. You should definitely sign up for your own API key so that you can control your own API access, monitor usage, etc.

> **TIP:** At the time of printing, the free Google Maps API is throttled to 25000 invocations per day. To get your own Maps API key, visit http://developer.google.com/ and follow the instructions.

Our initialize() function is very similar to our old checkIn() function, so we won't rehash that here. The key differences are it populates two local variables for latitude and longitude, and then calls our new function, mapMe(), to do all the hard mapping work.

```
function mapMe(thisLat, thisLong) {
    var myLatlong = new google.maps.LatLng(thisLat, thisLong);
    var myOptions = {
        center: new google.maps.LatLng(thisLat, thisLong),
        zoom: 12,
        mapTypeId: google.maps.MapTypeId.ROADMAP
    };
    var map = new google.maps.Map(document.getElementById("mapContainer"), myOptions);
    var marker = new google.maps.Marker({
                    position: myLatlong,
                    map: map,
                    title:"Hello World!"
    });
}
```

Within mapMe(), we complete four main actions to present our map and location marker. First, we create a google.maps.LatLng object using the latitude and longitude we received from our HTML5 geolocation calls. Next, we construct an options object named myOptions, which consists of a center object which will be used to choose the center of the map presented in the browser. The zoom value dictates the starting zoom setting in the map—this is very important on mobile devices, as the default zoom is at far too high a scale, leaving the user to zoom in several times with imprecise pinch and zoom techniques.

We then get to the meat of our mapping. We create a new google.maps.Map object, and pass the element that will hold the map ("mapContainer" is the ID of our <div> in our HTML), and the options object we constructed. This actually creates and displays the map in the user's browser. Following its creation, we create a google.maps.Marker object at the same coordinates on our map, and give it a meaningful label. The results in Figure 9–7 speak for themselves.

Figure 9–7. *Our HTML geolocation application adapted to use Google Maps*

Other Location-based Services

We've looked at one of the popular mapping services, but it's worth considering broadening your horizons to other providers of both basic geolocation services, as well as providers of things like map tiles (the graphic "tiles" that actually display).

There are a handful of reasons you might consider hedging your bets, and at least ensuring you can perform equivalent actions with other services:

- **Free services, scaling and cost**: Many services, like Google, Yahoo, Bing, MapQuest, Nokia/Ovi etc. offer some level of free service. The usual terms dictate that you and your users can consume a set number of map impressions per day before being throttled, and/or asked to pay.

- **Different strengths and weaknesses**: Some services, like Google, offer useful things like directions in some locations, details of public transport, etc. But in other places, services like Open Street Map provide significantly more detail, more recent data, and for some services like OpenCycleMap, the entire map rendering and data is focused on specialist uses: in this case, cyclists.

▓ **Separation of duties**: While it's convenient to use a single service to do everything, you may find that you want to separate the aspects of retrieving raw map data around a given location, and the rendering of a relevant image (map tile) for that location. Abstracting your mapping means you can mix and match to suit your needs.

Possibly the most important reason to abstract your map data and image provider(s) is that the field is rapidly evolving and changing, and good software engineering should lead you to isolate all of your other code from such volatile dependencies where you are able. This volatility can also be the result of version upgrades and changes by the providers themselves.

Here are some useful data providers, map tile providers, all-in-one services, and even ready-made mapping abstraction JavaScript libraries, that you might also like to consider along with the usual suspects:

▓ Open Street Map (openstreetmap.org)—one of the original open data providers, now also providing other services on top of the crowd-sourced base geolocation data

▓ CloudMade (cloudmade.com)—a map tile provider for use with Open Street Map data. Also the providers of Leaflet, an open source tile set service.

▓ Mapnik (mapnik.org)—a map renderer that is often found in other tools (including some of the others listed here).

▓ CartoDB (cartodb.com)—a cloud based geospatial database

▓ Mapstraction (mapstraction.com)—a ready-to-use JavaScript library that provides abstraction of mapping services and data providers.

▓ Wax (mapbox.com/wax)—another ready-to-use abstraction layer. And from the same company, TileMill for tile generation.

This list could fill pages, but you get the idea. Even more exciting is the realization that dozens of such companies and service providers are cropping up every week.

Gaming Your Location

Even though you're developing a mobile app, don't forget the tools available to you to help test and refine your geolocation code. For instance, DDMS in the Android Developer Tools plug-in for Eclipse provides you with the ability to set arbitrary coordinates/location data for your emulator device. With a running project in your emulator, you can switch to DDMS mode, and open the Emulator Console tab. You'll see the ability to set raw coordinates, or provide GMX or KML data directly, as shown in Figure 9–8, which your emulator browser can then use.

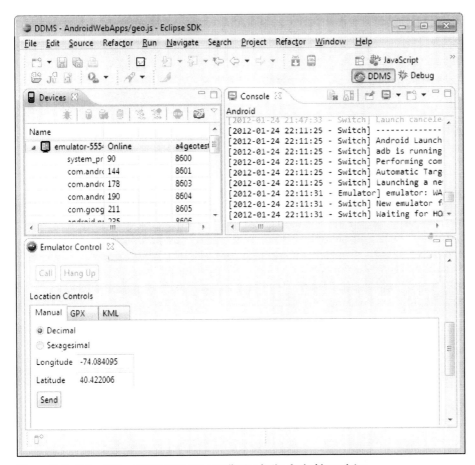

Figure 9–8. *Using ADT and Eclipse to set coordinates in the Android emulator*

If running Eclipse is not your preferred way of development, you can also use Android's adb tool to issue the geo fix command to provide latitude, longitude, and altitude. Finally, if you're debugging an application on a device that's not attached to your computer, you can use the free application Fake GPS location (https://market.android.com/details?id=com.lexa.fakegps) to set your location.

Gaming Your Location–for Fun!

One of the great ways to explore web application geolocation capabilities is to make a game out of it—literally! Using the simple building blocks from the preceding section, you can build games and activities including treasure hunts, orienteering events, and even driving, racing, and sailing games. You should find it very straightforward to combine our startWatch() example with our Google Maps example, to create a "Map Tracks" style application that plots your movements in real-time on a map, and depending on the game or competition, could also show the movements and locations of other players, and even where entire other games are taking place.

An interesting use of geolocation features, such as the ones we've shown here, can be found in the popular "geocaching" movement. Do a search through your preferred search engine for more details, or carry on to chapter 10 and use your own search interface to do the searching!

The sky really is the limit (and, in fact, your geolocation data should happily work from your favorite hot-air balloon too!).

Summary

In this chapter, we've explored the location based features available to you as a mobile web developer. Our sample application has demonstrated how to use many of the core geolocation features at your disposal, including where you are, what capabilities your users' devices might have, and how to deal with constant location changes. We'll explore more on geolocation application development, and also cover other online services and APIs, in Chapter 10.

Using Cloud Services: A Transport Application

Mastering the basics of geolocation is all well and good, and as we learned in Chapter 9, we can have fun working with our coordinates. A huge range of possibilities opens up once we know where we are, and what other services are available to mix our location information with other data. In this chapter, we're going to take our geolocation know-how, and mix in some local searching capabilities, to build a personalized transit application.

Our example transit application will find where you are, and then search for your nearest transit options, be it a bus stop, a subway or train station, or even an airport. With the basics in place, you'll be able to extend our transit application to pretty much any search-plus-location problem.

As a developer, you have many options for how much or how little work you want to do when blending web- or cloud-based services with your own applications. You have a choice of building your own services using publicly available data feeds, using a full service, or building a hybrid. Using a full service would give us nothing to talk about in this chapter, so we have opted for a hybrid approach, where we'll then use our geolocation know-how to use a standard search service to provide useful transit information.

Before we dive into code, examples, and explanations, consider for a minute the various building blocks you probably already use, but may not actively think about. When building any kind of transport or transit application, we want to combine knowledge and data then to present some useful options to the user. These would include:

- **Who am I ?** In a way, it can be useful to think of "who" is using your application as a combination of the actual user, and the device they are using along with its capabilities. We'll be reusing the detection code we covered in Chapter 9 to determine if a device supports geolocation.

■ **Where am I?** From Chapter 9, we learned how to determine your user's location from the geolocation capabilities of their Android device and their browser. We'll take that fundamental starting point to drive other options.

■ **Where do I want to go?** This is always a nuanced question. Does the application user have a location in mind, or a type of transport in mind, or in fact any preference for how to travel between points. The two key points to remember here are not to prematurely limit the options you make available in your application, and that when you do limit options, you do so deliberately and take the user with you. For instance, let them know that other routes or transit methods are available.

■ **What do online services know about me and my location?** This is a big area, and covers many generic services. Given a location, and some kind of desired journey or destination, think about what help is available to you as a developer, so that you don't need to do all the work yourself. For example, APIs for general web searching from companies like Google, Yahoo, and Microsoft can cope with many types of transit search, including finding transit stops, measuring distances, and calculating transit times. Use these so you don't have to do this yourself (unless, of course, you're aiming to compete in that space).

■ **What specialized services know about my location?** The biggest area to consider, but don't be daunted. Specialized APIs and services exist for a bewildering array of transit and transport types. A very large number of public transport agencies around the world make available scheduling and routing data, which we'll discuss later in this chapter. However, many also provide a direct API to answer queries for the next service, nearest service, and so on. Aggregators exist to provide pan-provider services. An example is Kayak for airline transit searches. You can take specialized APIs even further, by thinking about (and asking) why your user wants to make a specific trip. If it's to visit the cinema, eat at a restaurant, or partake in some other event, services like Yelp, TripAdvisor, and others provide APIs to search for specific venues and events. As an application developer, you can create useful applications that combine all of these to target your users.

■ **What can I usefully conclude with this knowledge?** Take the data your application gathers about where the user is, where they want to go, and what they want to do when they get there, and you start to picture the flow and the features of your application. Focus on using the building blocks described in the preceding paragraphs, rather than reinventing them, and you'll build compelling applications that stand out from the crowd. As an example, imagine if you know that users want to travel by boat from Manhattan to Brooklyn to visit a particular restaurant. You could take the experience to the next level, and use the OpenTable online service to check availability, and note that the user's restaurant is booked out, and instead suggest a dinner cruise on the Hudson. You save them a disappointing trip, and give them a great experience instead.

So now we have the big picture about what we want to build, and why a user would want to use such an application. Let's get started!

Introducing the "Move Me" Example Application

Our sample application is called "Move Me." We'll use it to explore how we can find nearby transport options from any location. Of course, we'll detect our location using the techniques we covered in chapter 9. Namely, we'll use the geolocation capabilities of our Android device to determine our latitude and longitude, and then use those data to drive a search service to find our preferred mode of transport.

Examining the Code

Listing 10–1 shows the code for the first version of Move Me. Don't be daunted by its length: we'll break this down and cover the various components to give you an understanding of its workings, and inspiration to take this example further and expand it to your own ideas.

Listing 10–1. *The Move Me application source code, version 1*

```
<!--
  Licensed under the Apache License, Version 2.0: http://www.apache.org/licenses/LICENSE-
2.0
  -->
<html>
    <head>
        <title>Move Me! - Transit Search Example
        </title>
        <link href="./ch10-example01.css" rel="stylesheet" type="text/css"/>
        <script
            src="http://www.google.com/jsapi?key=AIzaSyBU-TWQkYc-
                ynkeYIrd_aPOUFdyRieCyRO"
            type="text/javascript">
        </script>
        <script type="text/javascript">
            google.load('maps' , '3', {"other_params":"sensor=false"});
            google.load('search', '1');

            var myLatLong;
            var myTransitMap;
            var myLocalSearch;
            var searchResults = [];

            var resultMarker = new google.maps.MarkerImage(
                "Red_Train_Marker.png",
                new google.maps.Size(20, 34),
                new google.maps.Point(0, 0),
                new google.maps.Point(10, 34));
```

```
var youMarker = new google.maps.MarkerImage(
    "You_Marker.png",
    new google.maps.Size(20, 34),
    new google.maps.Point(0, 0),
    new google.maps.Point(10, 34));

function supportsGeo () {
    if (navigator.geolocation) {
        return true;
    } else {
        return false;
    }
}

function changeDiv (name, data) {
    var div = document.getElementById(name);
    if(div)
    {
        div.innerHTML = data;
    }
}

function getLocation() {
    if (supportsGeo()) {
        myLatitude = "";
        myLongitude = "";
        navigator.geolocation.getCurrentPosition(
        function(position) {
            myLatitude = position.coords.latitude;
            myLongitude = position.coords.longitude;
        },
        function(error) {
            switch(error.code) {
                case error.TIMEOUT:
                    alert ('Geolocation returned a timeout error');
                    break;
                case error.POSITION_UNAVAILABLE:
                    alert ('Geolocation returned a position unavailable
                            error');
                    break;
                case error.PERMISSION_DENIED:
                    alert ('Geolocation returned permission denied (did you
                            deny access?)');
                    break;
                case error.UNKNOWN_ERROR:
                    alert ('Geolocation encountered an unknown error');
                    break;
            }
        }
        );
        alert("Confirm geolocation access before clicking OK");
    }
    myLatLong = new google.maps.LatLng(myLatitude, myLongitude);
}

function prepareMap() {
```

```
    // Union Square test
    myLatLong = new google.maps.LatLng(37.788056, -122.4075);
    //getLocation();

    myTransitMap = new google.maps.Map(document.getElementById("map"), {
        center: myLatLong,
        zoom: 14,
        mapTypeId: google.maps.MapTypeId.ROADMAP
    });

    var yourMarker = new google.maps.Marker({
        position: myLatLong,
        map: myTransitMap,
        icon: youMarker,
        title:"You!"
    });

    myLocalSearch = new GlocalSearch();
    myLocalSearch.setSearchCompleteCallback(null,
                                        processLocalSearchResults);
}

function execSearch() {
    var searchText = document.getElementById("searchtext").value;
    myLocalSearch.execute(searchText);
}

function processLocalSearchResults() {
    for (var i = 0; i < myLocalSearch.results.length; i++) {
        searchResults.push(new LocalResult(myLocalSearch.results[i]));
    }
}

// Google's common example LocalResult object
function LocalResult(result) {
    var me = this;
    me.result_ = result;
    me.resultNode_ = me.node();
    me.marker_ = me.marker();
    document.getElementById("resultlist").appendChild(me.resultNode_);
}

LocalResult.prototype.node = function() {
    if (this.resultNode_) return this.resultNode_;
    return this.html();
};

LocalResult.prototype.marker = function() {
    var me = this;
    if (me.marker_) return me.marker_;
    var marker = me.marker_ = new google.maps.Marker({
        position: new google.maps.LatLng(parseFloat(me.result_.lat),
                              parseFloat(me.result_.lng)),
        icon: resultMarker,
        map: myTransitMap});
    return marker;
};
```

```
        LocalResult.prototype.html = function() {
            var me = this;
            var container = document.createElement("div");
            container.className = "unselected";
            container.appendChild(me.result_.html.cloneNode(true));
            return container;
        }

        GSearch.setOnLoadCallback(prepareMap);
    </script>
</head>
<body>
    <p>Move Me! Transit Search Example</p>
    <div style="width: 330px;">
        <input type="text" id="searchtext" style="width: 240px;"/>
        <input type="button" value="Find" onclick="execSearch()"/>
        <div style="position: absolute; left: 440px;">
            <div id="resultlist">
            </div>
        </div>
        <div id="map" style="height: 450px;"></div>
    </div>
</body>
</html>
```

First, let's get the easy stuff out of the way. You should already recognize several JavaScript functions from our geolocation introduction in chapter 9. Our old friends `supportsGeo()` and `changeDiv()` are present, performing the same geolocation support detection functions, and `<div>` content changing functions respectively.

Our example code slightly changes the way we're invoking some of the publicly available services we're consuming. In this case, because we've elected to use Google's Maps API and its Search API, we've refactored loading Google's JavaScript libraries to first load the base framework as follows

```
<script
    src="http://www.google.com/jsapi?key=AIzaSyBU-TWQkYc-ynkeYIrd_aPOUFdyRieCyRO"
    type="text/javascript">
</script>
```

Then, in our own JavaScript, we use Google's `google.load()` function to additionally load the Maps API and Search API. If you choose another service or set of services such as Bing, Yahoo, Baidu, or something else, loading APIs would change to match the appropriate invocation for those services. For our example, the code is very simple:

```
google.load('maps' , '3', {"other_params":"sensor=false"});
google.load('search', '1');
```

> **NOTE:** You can revert to using the Google Maps version 2 API should you be more familiar with it, but you'll see repeated warnings that it is deprecated when you use websites relying on that version of the API.

Dealing with Global State

Next, we set up some global state variables that give you a good idea of what we're going to do to make our transit application work.

```
var myLatLong;
var myTransitMap;
var myLocalSearch;
var searchResults = [];
```

The variable names are hopefully descriptive of their purpose, but in case there's any doubt, we'll use myLatLong to hold the user's coordinates; myTransitMap represents the map of the user's location and eventually will also include the nearby transport options; myLocalSearch is the search object, which will house our criteria for finding relevant transport options; and finally the searchResults array will hold the results returned from our myLocalSearch search.

Customizing Location Markers

If you've ever used an online map service (of any kind) you're probably familiar with the virtual "Map Pins" that are used to pinpoint locations. In our example, as we're using Google maps, we use the google.maps.Marker object to denote specific locations on our maps. Rather than use the vanilla red map marker icon that comes by default with Google Maps, we've crafted some custom markers for our Move Me application. The code for our custom google.map.MarkerImage graphics is as follows.

```
var resultMarker = new google.maps.MarkerImage(
    "Red_Train_Marker.png",
    new google.maps.Size(20, 34),
    new google.maps.Point(0, 0),
    new google.maps.Point(10, 34));
var youMarker = new google.maps.MarkerImage(
    "You_Marker.png",
    new google.maps.Size(20, 34),
    new google.maps.Point(0, 0),
    new google.maps.Point(10, 34));
```

The two .png image files referenced are included in the source code with this book. The first, Red_Train_Marker.png, is styled on the normal red pin used by Google Maps, with the addition of the letter T, for transit or transport. The You_Marker.png map pin is a blue marker with the word "You" superimposed. We've specified the normal size for our map pins, to aid the user when they want to tap the marker to see the "info bubble" for more details on a given point. This makes the pins look somewhat larger on small phone screens, but keeping the normal size is important in order to make it less likely that the user will miss touching the pin when they press the screen.

You will note that both MarkerImage objects have two calls to google.map.Point(). The first sets the origin point for the image to be used as an overlay. In our preceding examples, we're not changing what would be the default. The second call to google.map.Point() sets the anchor for the image. By default, when a google.map.Marker is overlaid on a map, any associated MarkerImage rendered with the top left of the image at the anchor point. We actually want the pointy end of our pin image to appear to point visually to our location of interest, so we want the middle, bottom edge of our MarkerImage to line up with our location result. To achieve this, you'll see we've offset the anchor by half the width of the pin image—10 pixels—and the complete height of the pin image - 34 pixels.

Preparing Our Map

With those preparations made, we plunge into the main function used to drive our transit application, the prepareMap() function.

```
function prepareMap() {
    getLocation();

    myTransitMap = new google.maps.Map(document.getElementById("map"), {
        center: myLatLong,
        zoom: 14,
        mapTypeId: google.maps.MapTypeId.ROADMAP
    });

    var yourMarker = new google.maps.Marker({
        position: myLatLong,
        map: myTransitMap,
        icon: youMarker,
        title:"You!"
    });

    myLocalSearch = new GlocalSearch();
    myLocalSearch.setSearchCompleteCallback(null, processLocalSearchResults);
}
```

The prepareMap() function is easily understood, broken down into its four main actions. First, we invoke our getLocation() function, which is mostly a rebadged version of the code we showed in the initialize() function in chapter 9 in listing 9-5. Here it is again for the sake of completeness:

```
function getLocation() {
    if (supportsGeo()) {
        myLatitude = "";
        myLongitude = "";
        navigator.geolocation.getCurrentPosition(
            function(position) {
                myLatitude = position.coords.latitude;
                myLongitude = position.coords.longitude;
            },
            function(error) {
                switch(error.code) {
                    case error.TIMEOUT:
                        alert ('Geolocation returned a timeout error');
                        break;
                    case error.POSITION_UNAVAILABLE:
                        alert ('Geolocation returned a position unavailable error');
                        break;
```

```
                    case error.PERMISSION_DENIED:
                        alert ('Geolocation returned permission denied (did you deny
                               access?)');
                        break;
                    case error.UNKNOWN_ERROR:
                        alert ('Geolocation encountered an unknown error');
                        break;
                }
            }
        );
    }
    myLatLong = new google.maps.LatLng(myLatitude, myLongitude);
}
```

As in the earlier chapter, this uses the navigator.geolocation object of the browser to determine your latitude and longitude. We'll omit repeating the near-identical code here to save some space.

We then create a new google.maps.Map object called myTransitMap, placing the center of the map on our detected location. We set the zoom level to 14 as this is a good scale for a human on foot, though you can change this to any desired zoom setting. We also choose the standard road map style of map, rather than satellite view.

> **TIP:** Here are some handy values for zoom level settings to keep in mind when rendering maps for your users.
>
> **Zoom level 12:** Suitable for highway-level driving, and showing major routes over tens of miles or kilometers.
>
> **Zoom level 14:** Good for inner city driving, and walking directions in general when the distance is more than a few dozen yards or meters
>
> **Zoom level 15:** Best for detailed walking, showing building outlines, and driving directions showing one-way streets and other impediments.

On to our myTransitMap object, we place a marker at the same latitude and longitude detected for the handset or device. We use our custom blue "You" marker, described previously, and even provide some hover text to reinforce that this pin places you on the map.

Lastly, we construct a new local search object, myLocalSearch, and then register the callback function, processLocalSearchResults(). This will be called when this search object completes execution of a search. The mechanics of the callback are shown a little later in this chapter. With the prepareMap() function complete, we can actually see what our application looks like when the user initially runs it on their device, as shown in Figure 10–1.

Figure 10–1. *The initial screen of the Move Me example application*

We have taken a few liberties with the starting example, having set our coordinates in the Android emulator to a reasonably famous location: Union Square in San Francisco. This isn't quite as contrived as it might sound. Picture yourself as a tourist in San Francisco. You've seen the sights and sounds of the city, and find yourself in Union Square, and want to find a train, bus, or ferry to your hotel or other destination. That's where the rest of the functionality in our example application comes in to play.

Performing Local Transport Searches

The next two functions in our example perform the tasks of executing our chosen local search, and processing the results.

```
function execSearch() {
    var searchText = document.getElementById("searchtext").value;
    myLocalSearch.execute(searchText);
}
```

The execSearch() function simply reads the content of the searchtext field on our HTML form, seen at the top of Figure 10–1, and calls the execute method on our myLocalSearch() object with that text. We registered the processLocalSearchResults() method as the callback function for when myLocalSearch() reports a completed execution.

```
function processLocalSearchResults() {
    for (var i = 0; i < myLocalSearch.results.length; i++) {
        searchResults.push(new LocalResult(myLocalSearch.results[i]));
    }
}
```

The `processLocalSearchResults()` function iterates over our results, instantiates a `LocalResult` object, and adds them to the `searchResults` array. The `LocalResult` object is a common example object Google uses in many of its API examples, which we've copied here. We're using it mainly for the ease with which we can then access the coordinates of a local search result. It does similar work to our previous code, as it places a marker on our map, and it also creates a textual result list. In our current example, we've created CSS to hide the text list, but we'll cover options for this shortly.

Lastly, as far as our JavaScript is concerned, we register our `prepareMap()` function as the callback to invoke once the Google Search API has finished loading.

```
GSearch.setOnLoadCallback(prepareMap);
```

All that remains is the actual HTML code that controls the size of our map, the search field and Find button, and relevant `<div>` names and nesting. We've deliberately chosen explicit pixel sizing for the overall display, and the map object housed within it, to suit vertical display on a phone handset, and horizontal display on a tablet while also showing the text results which we'll cover later in the chapter.

```
<body>
    <p>Move Me! Transit Search Example</p>
    <div style="width: 330px;">
        <input type="text" id="searchtext" style="width: 240px;"/>
        <input type="button" value="Find" onclick="execSearch()"/>
        <div style="position: absolute; left: 440px;">
            <div id="resultlist">
            </div>
        </div>
        <div id="map" style="height: 450px;">
        </div>
    </div>
</body>
```

Our HTML displays the simple form you saw in Figure 10-1.

Running Our Code

So what happens when we actually search for a transport option? In our example so far, our candidate user is a tourist who has found themselves in Union Square, and is looking for the nearest transport option. If you were to find yourself in San Francisco, you might think of using the Bay Area Transit System, or BART. So let's use that as our criterion to display what actually happens when we invoke `execSearch()`. Figure 10-2 shows the results returned via our local search invocation, plotted on our map using the `LocalResult` objects.

Figure 10–2. *Our Move Me application displaying nearby transit options*

Lo and behold, we have found the four nearest BART stations, from the Civic Center to Embarcadero. You can also see the final rendering of the custom transit `MarkerImage` and `Marker` object we described way back at the start of the chapter.

Perhaps, as a tourist, you're really after a great view of the San Francisco Bay, and what better way is there to do this than to find the nearest ferry terminal to seek out a cruise of one of the world's great waterways? Figure 10–3 shows our application finding the nearest ferry terminal.

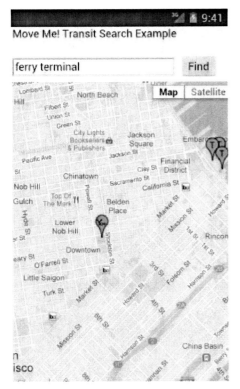

Figure 10–3. *Finding ferry transport with Move Me*

Once again, we've found the transit options we sought. In this instance, you'll notice several markers overlapping one location. This is Google's search returning the several different ferry companies and ferry options that operate from that location, not a mistake in the HTML or JavaScript we're using.

Improving the "Move Me" Example Application

By now, you will have noticed that the simplicity of our form actually becomes a little cumbersome. Sure, your users could enter anything they like in their local search, but maybe you'd like to save them the effort of typing on tiny soft-keyboards. The second version of our example code, in the file ch10-example02.html, revamps the form code to provide simple buttons for popular transit types, and invokes our modified execSearch() function. Our new form is coded as follows.

```
<div style="width: 330px;">
    <input type="button" value="Subway" onclick="execSearch('BART station')"/>
    <input type="button" value="Train" onclick="execSearch('train station')"/>
    <input type="button" value="Bus" onclick="execSearch('bus stop')"/>
    <input type="button" value="Ferry" onclick="execSearch('ferry terminal')"/>
<div style="position: absolute; left: 440px;">
```

Our modified execSearch() function no longer needs to read from a text field, largely because we've removed it! Instead, it takes as a parameter the text we pass in when we call the function, such as "train station" or "ferry terminal," and invokes execution of the relevant search.

```
function execSearch(searchText) {
  myLocalSearch.execute(searchText);
}
```

Our application now looks a little more instantly usable, with relevant buttons for Subway, Train, Bus, and so forth, as shown in Figure 10–4.

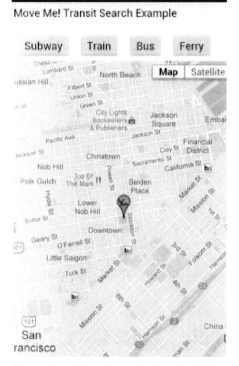

Figure 10–4. *Move Me application with dedicated transit buttons*

From here, pressing a button produces results as before, obviously tailored to match the criteria coded for each of those buttons.

Dealing with Other Transport Possibilities

There are countless ways you could take this example further. One obvious example is to expand the number of buttons for transit options. You could include taxis, airports, trams, and more. There are other nuances to consider as well. The subway in San Francisco can mean the BART system, but much of the Muni system is also considered a subway. In other cities, the subway has other names, such as "Underground" in

London, or "Metro" in Paris. The code could be expanded to re-use your coordinates to determine in which city the user is currently located, and the search text could be localized accordingly.

Limitations to our Approach

Our examples so far are good for finding ourselves or local transport stops or stations. This definitely helps with working out possible transit options from any given location, but like an unfinished journey, it leaves us just short of where we truly want to be. We might know there's a bus stop just around the corner, or a train station just down the street, but do we know what services operate from those points, and to where they're headed? Do we know when the next service is scheduled to arrive? Do we even know if there are any scheduled services at that stop at all?

If only there were some way to find matching transit schedule data for the transit stops we've discovered!

Introducing Transit Data Resources

So far, we've explored how to find ourselves and possible transport options around us, and plot the results on a map. But as any traveler can tell you, knowing *when* transport options operate is just as important as knowing from where they operate. Wouldn't it be great if there were ways of using bus timetables, train timetables, and other transport schedules to expand the possibilities of our transit application? Well, there is a way!

Making Use of Transport Schedules and Timetables

The history of trying to work with a transport agency's data is long and tortuous. To spare you the pain that developers before you had to endure, we'll cut our story short: we'll focus on "then" and "now." Before 1995, dealing with various government or bureaucratic agencies to access their transit data was an exercise in costly masochism. Undocumented proprietary formats, obstructionist public officials, and perverted notions of ownership clouded any attempt to use "public" transit data.

In 1995, an employee of the TriMet transit agency in Portland - the major city of Oregon state in the USA - was frustrated at the proprietary mapping and transit data systems and sources available to her. She wrote to many of the leading mapping and geolocation services at the time, to ask what plans they had to incorporate public transport data into their services. Only one company responded: Google.

From a developer's perspective at the time, dealing with the erratic—and even at times capricious—attitudes of agencies that held custody of the data was immensely frustrating and complex. But TriMet's probing question opened up the idea that frustrated developers who wanted access to the data were matched by frustrated data custodians and public officials who wanted to see the data better used to serve their communities.

This sparked the rise of the General Transit Feed Specification (GTFS), which sought to provide a consistent protocol for the format of transit data. Any historian of this time will observe that the GTFS format is almost exactly the format used by TriMet in Portland for its transit data. As is often the case, the first mover in a given sphere of technology is *de facto* the standard setter. Soon, many more government and transport agencies had the foresight to release the data they held in this format, and it has become the standard for sharing transit schedules, routes and related data.

Almost everyone has, at one time or another, caught a bus, train, plane, or ferry, and so we can jump past the basics of what a GTFS feed is. Instead, let's look at the specification from the point of view of an Android developer.

Reviewing GTFS Components

A GTFS feed is simply a bunch of textual data in comma-separated format, split into several text files, and then packaged as a single zip file for easy handling. As a developer of either web applications or native Android applications, you can source a GTFS feed's zip file and then work with it to incorporate transit locations, schedule information, and so forth into your code. A typical GTFS zip file is composed of (and requires) the following text files:

- **Agency.txt** The agencies and organizations that provided the data in this GTFS package.

- **Calendar.txt** The dates for various services based on a weekly roster. This includes details of start and end dates for services, and days when they are, and are not, available.

- **Routes.txt** The set of stops a given service makes, and the path taken between them. This matches what most people think of as a single bus route, train journey, etc.

- **Stops.txt** The distinct locations where services stop to allow passengers to board and alight, including terminals or end-points.

- **Stop_times.txt** The times at which a given vehicle arrives at, and leaves a stop. This also allows for the calculation of "dwell time," which is the period a service remains at a stop.

- **Trips.txt** Trips for a given route, where a given vehicle makes sequential stops.

In addition to the preceding list of mandatory files , a given GTFS feed can also include some or all of the following optional additional data in the respective text files

- **Calendar_dates.txt** Lists the exceptions to the service details of standard scheduling in the calendar.txt file.

- **Fare_attributes.txt** The details on what it actually costs to use a given service, as charged by the agency running the service.

- **Fare_rules.txt** Rules for applying the fares specified in fare_attributes.txt. This can include things like peak and off-peak rules, concessions for students, seniors, and so forth.

- **Feed_info.txt** Additional information about this GTFS feed, such as version number and dates of applicability.

- **Frequencies.txt** Timing information for services that don't run to a regular frequency.

- **Shapes.txt** Details to help render graphics of routes, such as how to represent differences in outbound and return paths, points of return, etc.

- **Transfers.txt** Details of any rules regarding transferring from one service to another.

Details of the individual file fields, formatting requirements, and other rules can be found on any of the many GTFS-related sites, such as `https://developers.google.com/transit/`.

Many transport agencies around the world make use of a central clearing house for GTFS data, at `www.gtfs-data-exchange.com/`. This site not only acts as a central repository of GTFS feeds, but also includes basic data on the specification, and details on how to contribute new GTFS data sets.

If this all sounds fantastic—nigh on utopian—there is one small wrinkle that always affects the ideal of transport schedules and routes, and the reality for the commuter or tourist. What happens when a service doesn't run on time, or at all? Enter the GTFS-Realtime standard.

Dealing with Timetable Realities

GTFS-Realtime time is a relatively new addition to the core of GTFS, released by a group of interested parties in August 2011. It aims to solve the eternal problem of "when theory meets practice," in the form of providing real-time updates to transport service schedules. It provides the following kinds of updates in real time to anyone subscribing to the data.

- **Trip Updates:** Any changed routing, timing or cancellations for a scheduled service

- **Service Alerts:** Changes at the service level, such as stops that have moved, are closed, or even problems with the entire network like power failures or switching problems.

- **Vehicle Positions:** The location of vehicles in the transport system, and where available, the information on local congestion provided by the vehicles themselves or related traffic infrastructure.

Google was a key participant in the evolution of GTFS-Realtime, which is evident in the choice of data format selected. Instead of keeping with the comma-separated formats of the base GTFS standard, GTFS-Realtime adopted Google's protocol buffer format. This is just another data format created with the ideals of efficient platform-neutral serialization and deserialization in mind—basically a terse parallel to XML. In practice, this just means one needs to refer to a protocol buffer definition to determine field lengths and attributes within the text/data.

Exploring GTFS Examples

Our chapter is already getting long in the tooth, and introducing and exploring even a small GTFS example will run to many hundreds of lines of JavaScript, HTML, and CSS. This isn't because the examples are difficult or complex, but rather, because they need to deal with all of the geolocation and map rendering style code we've already worked with in this chapter, as well as a fair chunk of text processing code and I/O code to deal with sourcing and processing the GTFS data.

There'd be enough material for a separate book in its own right, so rather than swamp our book with such a large detour, we'll instead call out some excellent publicly available examples online, that you can download and explore to your heart's content to discover more about GTFS and its possibilities.

Some of the notable, and very useful, open source examples of GTFS available online include:

- **Google's Transit Developers Page** As an active member of the GTFS community, Google has a wealth of examples available online. Point your browser at `https://developers.google.com/transit/gtfs/examples/display-to-users` for a wealth of examples and background information.

- **The One Busway Project** Originally founded by developers in Puget Sound, `http://developer.onebusaway.org` is the home of the One Busway Project that has expanded to a global initiative for GTFS developers.

- **Community Projects** like UlmApi.de's Live Map, the result of a hackathon that built a fully functional GTFS-based transit app in just a few hours. Full project details are available at `https://github.com/UlmApi/livemap`

In Figure 10–5, you can see the complete transport system in early morning Ulm, as rendered by the UlmApi.de web application for Android.

Figure 10–5. *The UlmApi.de hackathon GTFS application in Android's browser*

In the true spirit of transit and transport based applications, we invite you to go exploring these and other GTFS sites, and see where the ride takes you!

Summary

In this chapter, we've explored further development of location-based web applications for Android. Our example has covered using popular local search web services from Google to demonstrate finding trains, subways, ferries, and other transit options for the fleet-footed tourist. We've only scratched the surface of what can be done with transit data feeds systems like GTFS, but you now know enough to explore the many online options available to you We hope that our sample application has shown how easy it is to merge phone-based location features with cloud-based services to create useful mashups and very easy-to-develop features.

Chapter 11

Pushing the Limits with Audio and Video

Audio and video are two of the most difficult topics to cover in the mobile web. While each one individually can do a lot to enhance the visual and audible appeal of a site or application, more often than not both technologies end up being abused by mobile content creators. For example, one form of abuse I have noticed becoming more common in the mobile world is audio based advertisements targeted toward mobile browsers. While both audio and video technologies can be used incorrectly or just in a regular plain old annoying manner, they do serve wonderful purposes when used correctly.

Let's say, for instance, that we're working on a mobile gaming application and we want to add some relaxing loop of background music to enhance our user's experience. We can use the built-in HTML5 capabilities of the Android operating system's browser to do this fairly easily, with only a few lines of code, when using the audio tag. On top of that, we can even use a little bit of JavaScript to manipulate that audio element as well. We can do things such as play, stop, or pause the audio on the press of a button.

We also have the ability, though Android's Browser program, to make use of the HTML5 video tag as well to enhance our web applications with video formatted in h.264, MPEG-4, and WebM format. Both of these tags—the audio and video tag—when used properly, can create some top-notch user experiences to enhance the applications they are featured in and make them ooze with excellence.

Throughout this chapter we will take a look at each of these elements, their APIs, and the pros and cons of using each of these new HTML5 tags in our budding applications.

Audio for Mobile Web Apps

Until a few years ago, if you, as a developer, wanted to include audio in your web application, your choices were pretty slim to none. Almost every solution out there involved using an Adobe Flash and would use Flash as a middleman to pipe the audio to the users' audio input device. While it was possible to add audio to your user experience via the embed and object tags, more often than not you were left with a pretty limiting and unacceptable user experience that left your end users—and developers—wishing for more.

The rise in HTML5 adoption rates, has made working with audio (while still a pain on some rare instances) generally smooth in Android implementation of the HTML5 audio tag. There are plenty of examples out there of mobile web applications and games making use of the audio element to bring background music and sound effects to their projects, which can help create more engaging scenarios for users to explore.

Unfortunately, like most things in the Web Development world, not all audio codec's are created equal. This is especially true when focusing on the mobile world. Google's Android operating system has been making use of the HTML5 audio tag since Android 2.0 first came out in the middle of 2010, yet it only makes use of two of the more popular audio codec choices—MP3 and the AAC audio format.

Utilizing the HTML5 audio Tag

Using the HTML5 audio tag is really simple. Take a look at this example in Listing 11–1 where we add a repeating audio loop to a user's page.

Listing 11–1. *Basic use of the HTML5 audio element*

```
<audio autoplay="autoplay" controls="controls">
    <source src="audio/stairwell.ogg" type="audio/ogg" />
    <source src="audio/stairwell.mp3" type="audio/mpeg" />
    "Sorry, your browser does not support the audio element."
</audio>
```

The basic usage of the audio tag is very similar to other tags in the HTML space. When declaring the HTML audio element, we could invoke several attributes in our document. Let us take a look at some of those attributes below:

- autoplay—If called this attribute will play your audio element the moment it is ready and available

- controls—Determines whether or not the controls for this audio element are displayed to the user.

- loop—If set, this attribute tells the audio to loop itself indefinitely. Just like the song that never ends!

- preload—This determines whether or not the audio element will be preloaded into the page on document load.

- src—The URL to the audio file.

Looking at Listing 11–1, we can also notice that the audio tag contains two other source tags as well. These source tags each have src attributes that point to the URL of the file on the server.

The reason for the multiple tags is actually an ingenious method of writing one HTML document that works across many browsers. Your browser, if it supports the HTML5 audio tag, will look through each of those source codec's until it finds one that works for your browser. If it succeeds in finding an appropriate file (i.e., you provide a version of the file that can be played on the users' system), it will play it. If it doesn't, it will do nothing at all. If for some reason you are viewing this page from an older Android device that does not display the audio tag, then the browser will ignore the element all together and display the preset error message of "*Sorry. Your browser does not support the audio image*" as shown in Figure 11–1.

Figure 11–1. *The HTML5 audio element on an Android Gingerbread 2.3 device with the 'controls' the attributes set*

Integrating Audio into Who's That Tweet?

In the first application we used in this book, we asked people to guess which Twitter account produced a given tweet. Now imagine we want to put in a bit of audio to soothe the savage mind of those playing our game. We could easily do so with the Audio tag, using the code in the following Listing 11–2.

Listing 11-2. *HTML Code for Who's That Tweet? with Audio*

```
<!DOCTYPE HTML>
<html>
<head>
<meta charset="utf-8">
<title>Who's That Tweet?</title>
<link href='http://fonts.googleapis.com/css?family=Droid+Sans&v1' rel='stylesheet'
type='text/css'>
<link rel="stylesheet" type="text/css" href="css/style.css">
<script type="text/javascript" src="js/jquery-1.6.1.min.js"></script>
<script type="text/javascript" src="js/main.js"></script>
</head>
<body>
<audio autoplay="autoplay" loop="loop">
    <source src="audio/themesong.ogg" type="audio/ogg" />
</audio>

  <header>
    <div class="score"><strong>Score:</strong> <span>0</span></div>
    <h2>Player 1</h2>
  </header>
  <section>
    <div id="tweet">
      <div class="avatar"></div>
      <div class="content"></div>
    </div>
    <ul></ul>
  </section>
</body>
</html>
```

In this case, we've started playing our theme song, and we've set the loop attribute so that it will simply loop repetitiously until the end of time. We don't specify controls, and we aren't showing any message if the audio can't be loaded. Now we just need to find a good theme song that won't annoy our users too much!

Working with Audio Codecs

If you are building your application for an Android device, you are going to want to stick to one of the three following codecs that are available throughout the platform: MPEG-2 Audio Layer III (MP3), Advanced Audio Coding (AAC), and the open source fan favorite Ogg. While each one has its own benefits, most developers out there usually just stick to MP3 and Ogg as there are plenty of free open source tools available to convert your audio to those formats.

MP3

The MP3 audio format is what is referred to as a lossy compression audio format. Lossy compression formats are very popular in multimedia and if you have ever worked with a graphic design program before such as Adobe Fireworks, Gimp, or Adobe Photoshop, then chances are you are loosely (no pun intended) familiar with lossy compression when trying to squeeze a few extra bytes out of an image. The same method of removing parts of a digital image to decrease the size, while not compromising the integrity of the image, can also be applied to audio.

In the example of MP3, a compression algorithm is run through the digital audio and removes parts of the track that normally the average human ear is not able to pick up. A lower bitrate for the MP3 file indicates that more data have been removed from the recording.

While some individuals claim to hear a tinny sound from MP3s due to the missing audio information, most people cannot seem to tell the difference when compared to a lossless digital copy. This makes MP3 a fantastic audio codec to use for your HTML5 audio as you can get incredibly small files that download and stream quickly to your user's browser. This being said, you should be careful to use a decent bitrate for an MP3 file—say 128 kbps. Anything lower may have a tinny sound on quality audio devices (for example, the HTC Rezound). Moving up to 192, 256, or 320 kbps may be useful if it doesn't make the file too big; however, you may find it unnecessary given the relatively small benefits. Over 320 kbps is probably a waste unless your app is built for audiophiles!

For the most part, MP3 is the de facto audio format of the Internet, which is why almost every major browser supports MP3 audio with HTML5 out of the box with no additional plug-ins.

AAC

Advanced Audio Coding, also known as AAC, is another audio format out there on the horizon. If you have ever purchased music off of Apple iTunes, then you have most likely purchased music in this audio format. AAC was developed by several companies— including Sony, Nokia, Dolby, and AT&T. This format, which does achieve better audio quality than its MP3 predecessor, was declared an International audio standard in the spring of 1997.

One of the reasons this audio format is popular with developers, besides the obvious fact of having better sounding audio compared to its competitors, is that no licenses or patent payments are needed to distribute or stream AAC encoded content. Note that this licensing only applies to the actual encoding—you can't take copyrighted material that doesn't belong to you, encode it in AAC, and laugh at the lawyers after you distribute it to the world. Well, I guess you can laugh, but that's not going to help your case!

Ogg

Another up and comer in our quest to conquer HTML5 audio on Android devices is one of my personal favorite codecs: Ogg. The creators of Ogg have stated in the past that they created Ogg to be a format that was not bogged down by restrictions and software patents. This has promoted Ogg's adoption as a default HTML5 audio codec in a majority of browsers out there. There is a good chance that if you encode your audio in the Ogg format that it will not only work on Android devices but it will also work on a slew of other devices and browsers out there on the market today.

While Ogg is a lossy compression format like MP3 and AAC, the framework behind Ogg can be found in several lossless audio formats out on the market, like OggPCM and FLAC. With Ogg, you can have it your way: tiny files or huge lossless files. The sky's the limit.

Using the Audacity Audio Editor

One of my favorite pieces of open source audio software is Audacity (http://audacity.sourceforge.net/). This free cross platform application lets you easily import a wide variety of audio from many different formats. Using Audacity, you can easy splice audio together, cut audio files, record live audio, change pitch and speed of audio files, add noise to audio tracks, reduce the levels of audio tracks that are too high, and a lot of other really cool and useful features (see Figure 11–2).

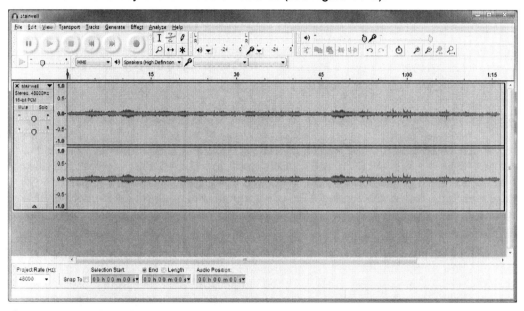

Figure 11–2. *Audacity 1.3 Beta editing a creative commons audio file*

Whenever I am working with audio from a client and I am presented with a large 512MB–1024MB WAV audio file, Audacity is always my first choice for trimming out sections of that audio file that I do not need or converting that audio file to a much smaller and more manageable format.

Since this book is only intended to cover the beginner's aspects of designing for Android mobile devices, I will not go into too much depth about all the features that you can tap into with Audacity. Instead, I'll cover some of the basics such as exporting one audio format to another.

If you are going to want to convert your files to the MP3 format, then you are going to need to download the LAME MP3 Library. You can do this fairly painlessly by going to the preferences in Audacity.

1. Go to the Edit menu and choose Properties.

2. Choose the Libraries option in the left hand section of the Properties window as shown in Figure 11–3.

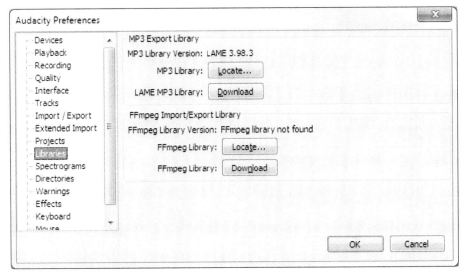

Figure 11–3. *Viewing the Audacity 1.3 Beta Preferences dialog box.*

3. Once there, you can choose to point Audacity to your LAME library if you already have it installed on your computer. If you do not already have the LAME library installed, continue to step 4.

4. Click the Download button, which will take you a site where can download the latest and greatest copy of the LAME MP3 Library, as shown in Figure 11–4.

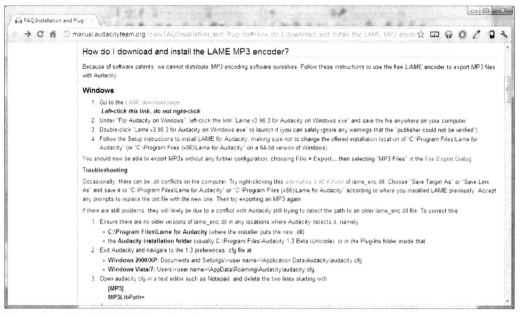

Figure 11–4. *The LAME MP3 Library download page.*

5. Once you download the library and unzip it to your hard drive, you will be all set to record and export audio to the MP3 format.

If you take a look at Figure 11–2 from earlier in this section, you will see that we are already working with a creative commons audio file called stairwell.ogg. What we are going to do is take this Ogg file and convert it to a MP3 file in no time at all. To do this:

1. Click File in the menu bar, and then select the Export item as seen in Figure 11–5.

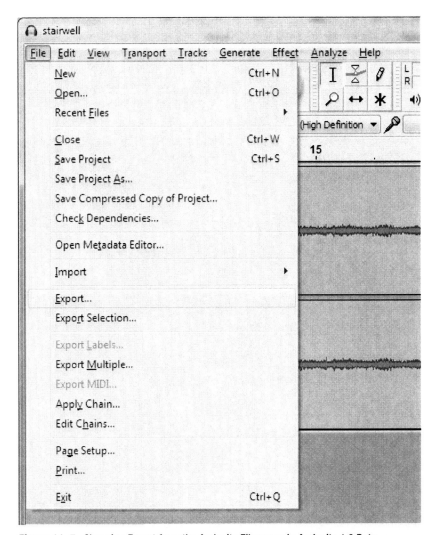

Figure 11–5. *Choosing Export from the Audacity File menu in Audacity 1.3 Beta.*

2. In the drop down box, make sure to change the file format to MP3 instead of the current format of the audio file.

3. Choose where you want to save the file, click the Save button, and you are all done!

See, did I not promise you that would be painless or what? Now that you know how to quickly convert your audio from one format to another, it's time to move on to the fun part of manipulating that audio through the very handy HTML5 Audio Data API.

Audio Data API

Using the Audio Data API, a developer can interact with their audio data in ways that were not possible just a few years ago. Using JavaScript and some HTML, you could easily create your own controls to interact with your audio data, as we can see in Listing 11–3.

Taking a look at the following example, you can see that we are expanding on Listing 11–1 and adding in some new custom built controls to play and stop the audio.

Listing 11–3. *A more advanced look at the HTML5 Audio Data API*

```
<audio id="audioDemo">
    <source src="audio/stairwell.ogg" type="audio/ogg" />
    <source src="audio/stairwell.mp3" type="audio/mpeg" />
    "Sorry, your browser does not support the audio element."
</audio>

<button id="play">Play</button>
<button id="pause">Pause</button>

<script type="text/javascript">
    var audio = document.getElementById('audioDemo');
    var playButton = document.getElementById('play');
    var pauseButton = document.getElementById('pause');

    playButton.addEventListener('click', function() {
        audio.play();
    }, false);

    stopButton.addEventListener('click', function() {
        audio.pause();
    }, false);
</script>
```

When you run this code in your browser, the first thing you would probably notice is the lack of any audio controls on the page at all, except the two buttons we added to the page with the IDs of play and pause. These buttons, while not as pretty as those seen in Figure 11–6, will be our only means of manipulating the audio on the page.

Figure 11–6. *Loading our demo HTML5 audio document on an Android 2.3.4 Gingerbread device*

Now, if you look at the bottom of the Listing 11–3, in the JavaScript, we can examine where the real magic is happening. Here, we declare the variables for audio, playButton, and pauseButton. Next, we add an event listener to each of those buttons so that when the user clicks those buttons, we fire off some code to either play or stop the audio stream. If we'd like, we could include additional buttons for volume, which would take a similar form to the code above, but call audio.volume=X where X would be a number between 0 and 1, indicating volume level percentage (so if you would like to increase the volume by 10%, your code would read audio.volume = audio.volume + .1).

You are not just limited to pausing your audio files at will, either. Using the HTML5 Audio Data API, you can easily control many aspects of playing or enjoying audio in a page, such as manipulating the volume of the audio file, analyzing how many beats per minute are in a track, creating your own audible tones combining the awesome powers of canvas with the Audio Data API, and a lot more.

Adding Video to Mobile Applications

Now that we've covered the wonderful world of audio, it's time to take a walk on the visually appealing side of Internet multimedia with HTML5 video. The video tag is another one of those new HTML5 elements to emerge over the next few years. It was created to make the job of a developer easier and to move us away from our dependency on Adobe Flash. Unfortunately for us, no one can really agree on a video standard and with so many obstacles, codecs, licensing agreements, and patents standing in our way, we are not likely to get any closer to coming up with a universal video format for browser-based consumption anytime soon.

The good news is that since we are only focusing our efforts on Android based devices we do not have to deal with a lot of the frustrations that come with working with HTML5 video in the desktop computing world. Here, it is very simple. A few video codecs out there will work with Android browsers, and as long as you stick with one, or all, of them, you will be able to present your mobile users with a richer multimedia experience.

Using the HTML5 video Tag

Invoking the HTML5 video tag is just as easy as calling the audio tag we discussed earlier in the chapter. Take a look at Listing 11–3 to see how we can use a few lines of code to easily display video to our users.

Listing 11–3. *Basic use of the HTML5 video element*

```
<video width="320" height="240" controls="controls" poster="video/big_buck_bunny.jpg">
    <source src="video/big_buck_bunny.mov" type="video/mp4" />
    <source src="video/big_buck_bunny.ogg" type="video/ogg" />
    <source src="video/big_buck_bunny.webm" type="video/webm" />
    Sorry! Unfortunately your browser does not support the video tag
</video>
```

In this example, we are just calling a video file and setting the width of the video container to 320 pixels and the height to 240 pixels. We are also telling the video to display its controls so the user can play, pause, stop, and manipulate the volume of the video. You can see what this looks like on a mobile device in Figure 11–7.

Figure 11–7. *Viewing an HTML5 video on an Android 2.3.4 Gingerbread device*

You'll also notice that the `video` tag differs from the `audio` tag by having different attributes. The main one that sticks out is the `poster` attribute, which lets us add a screenshot (or any other image we have) to represent the video that is about to be played. This is great for mobile devices because when you go to play a video on an Android device, instead of playing the video in the browser as one would expect after years of using a desktop computer, the Android device will pass the video stream along to its built-in video player, which will play the video for you.

While this feature is fun and handy, it completely takes away a lot of the reasons someone would use the Video Data API, since it plays the video outside of our page—in a dedicated video application. This breaks the user experience and prevents us from controlling exactly what the user will see when they watch our video.

In a moment, we'll give a video example similar to the one we used with the audio API up above. However, we should note that while there are some cool things you can do with the Video Data API, a lot of them tend to be well beyond what most people need. The following are the basics; however, the full API is available to reference at www.w3.org/2010/05/video/mediaevents.html. Now let's take a look at the most useful attributes you can use when developing your next mobile web application that uses video!

- `height`–controls the height of the video being played
- `width`–controls the width of the video being played
- `preload`–If set, will preload the video when the page loads
- `autoplay`–If set, will automatically play the video when it is ready
- `loop`–If set, will loop the video indefinitely
- `controls`–If set, will display controls to the user to control the video
- `src`–The URL which points to the source of the video file

Codecs

Just like we did with audio, video must be encoded into one of a few formats that the native Android web browser supports (mentioned subsequently). Encoding video can be a bit trickier than audio in that you're encoding two things—namely the audio and the video! We'll walk through the formats you can use, and discuss how to move audio and video between them with ease.

h.264/MPEG-4

Over the years, MPEG-4 has become one of the premiere standards in video encoding on the Internet and in our daily consumer lives, especially when it comes to high definition video. Recently, MPEG-4 has come into the public consciousness through the rise of social video sharing sites like YouTube and Vimeo, which allow users to upload videos in this format. The current version of MPEG-4 is properly known as h.264/MPEG-4 AVC, and is the standard for high quality video compression, such as that found on a Blu-ray disc.

Ogg Theora

Theora is a free and open source lossy video compression format created by the same foundation responsible for maintaining the Ogg audio codec, Xiph. Org Foundation. While Theora itself is based on a proprietary video codec called VP3, it was later released into the public domain, making it free for anyone to use as of March 2002.

Ogg Theora is similar in design to MPEG-4 and has quickly been progressing as a technology over the last several years. While it is still not as comparable in quality to MPEG-4 video, it is so close that a lot of developers who previously preferred the wide acceptance of MPEG-4 now opting to go the HTML5 video route have started jumping onto the Theora bandwagon.

WebM

A new contender in the video world is Google's very own WebM video codec. Announced at the Google I/O conference in 2010, WebM is a royalty free video codec that Google put out there in the wild to try and circumvent a lot of the problems that were popping up in the HTML5 audio and video. While everyone is excited to use these new technologies in their web applications and web sites, it is hard to do so without all of the browser makers agreeing on a standard.

WebM is completely royalty free, which means that anyone can pick up the technology and include it with their web browser without worrying about Google knocking on their door in the future demanding a payout. Recall, though, that this refers to the technology—not the actual content. Distributing copyrighted movies will get others to knock on your door demanding a payout!

Even with this royalty-free safety net, WebM has had a pretty slow adoption rate when compared to other video codecs out there, like Ogg Theora.

Using Handbrake to Transcode Videos

Now that you have a better understanding of some of the video codecs out there, I bet you're asking yourself how you go about creating video content to use in your application with them. One of the easiest and hassle-free means of doing so is a nifty little application called Handbrake (`http://handbrake.fr/`). Handbrake is another one of those fabulous open source applications created to make the everyday lives of video enthusiasts, and your average video transcoding consumers, easier.

Take a look at Figure 11–8. This is the default view we are presented when we open the Handbrake application. As you can see, everything here is incredibly user friendly and easy to use. On the top of the application, if you click the movie clapboard icon, you can set the source of the video you would like to transcode, or convert from one format to another. Below that icon, you have an area where you can set the destination of the newly created video as well as change the container you would like to house your video in. The two containers that Handbrake offers are the MKV and M4V video containers. A container is simply the file format that is used to hold the two separate parts of the video (the pictures and the audio).

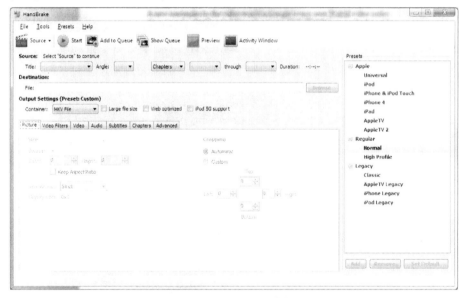

Figure 11–8. *A view of Handbrake after opening it up on a Windows 7 operating system*

The bottom half of the application is a tabbed view that you can use to customize your video even more to your liking. The most important tab here for our purposes is going to be the Video tab. Here, you can set which codec you would like to convert your video to. Handbrake offers you three choices for video conversion depending on which video container you choose—MPEG-4 or Ogg Theora.

The right hand side of the application is where a lot of the magic will be happening for you. Here, you can choose from a variety of preconfigured video settings so all you have to do is input a video source, decide where you want to save your video, choose one of the settings that strike your fancy, and start encoding.

If you take a look at Figure 11–9, you will also notice two little checkboxes next to the video container options. These checkboxes, `Web Optimized` and `iPod 5G Support,` are two options you may want to experiment with when encoding your videos. In some cases, I have found that these settings have helped me create better quality video files for use in the browser. At other times, however, they caused me nothing but heartache. It all comes down to the video file you are using as your source material. Video can be tricky, especially when transcoding it from one format to another. In the end, one must generally "play" a bit with settings to get the best possible result. If your video file is large (therefore needing more time to transcode), you might consider splitting off a small section of it to experiment with. Once you've found the right combination of settings and options, you can then convert the long version of the video, saving yourself some time.

Figure 11–9. *Setting the video source, destination and video container settings within Handbrake for Windows 7*

Figure 11–10. *Selecting the iPhone & iPod Touch preset configuration settings for our video*

Finally, the number of options that you have access to in Handbrake may be a bit overwhelming. If you're looking for something easier, you might want to check out more consumer-friendly (i.e., made for non-developers or power users) solutions such as DoubleTwist (www.doubletwist.com) and Videora (www.videora.com). Both can convert videos to a format that is viewable on a mobile device with very little effort or need to customize.

Now that we've got some basic information covered on creating, displaying, and working with your own audio and video, we'll introduce some areas you might extend your applications by interfacing with different APIs available to programmers.

Exploring on Your Own: Music Service APIs

Many web services offer access to programmers to their platform via an API (application programming interface). In this section, we're going to talk about two popular applications, and the APIs they offer. You might find that by tying your application into one of these services, you not only will have access to some cool tools—you'll also add appeal to your application for users of that service.

"Scrobbling" Tracks to Last.fm

Last.fm is a service that is designed not only to stream music to your computer or phone, but also to learn about your preferences intelligently. One way it does this is by allowing multiple devices (i.e., iOS devices and android phones where the Last.fm client is installed) to send listened track information to Last.fm, a process Last.fm refers to as 'scrobbling'. For instance, I use Google Music to listen to my music collection through my browser. By using an extension for Chrome that scrobbles my tracks to Last.fm, I can view my listening behavior later, and Last.fm knows what sorts of music I like to listen to (Figure 11–11).

jonwestfall

Jon Westfall, 29, Male, United States   Edit ▾

3709 plays since 25 Jun 2009

63 Loved Tracks | 0 Posts | 0 Playlists | 1 shout

Recently Listened Tracks   ⚙ Settings | 🔲

	Third World – Freedom Must Be Now (feat. Mykal Rose)	Yesterday 9:27am
	The Allman Brothers Band – Midnight Rider (Album Version)	Yesterday 9:24am
	Jimmy Buffett – Flesh and Bone	Yesterday 7:53am
▶	Simon & Garfunkel – I Am A Rock	Yesterday 7:50am
▶	Céline Dion – It's All Coming Back to Me Now ＊	29 Feb 9:48pm
	The Wreckers – My, Oh My	29 Feb 9:45pm
▶	Jimmy Buffett – Last Mango In Paris	29 Feb 9:39pm
▶	Lady Gaga – You And I	29 Feb 9:33pm
▶	Tommy Roe – Dizzy	29 Feb 2:53pm
▶	Southern Culture On The Skids – King of the Mountain	29 Feb 2:48pm

Figure 11–11. *My Last.fm recently listened to tracks*

Once a track is recorded, it informs Last.fm about my listening habits. This is useful in telling Last.fm what to recommend to me, and it allows me to find new music I might like.

Imagine that we'd like to present snippets of music to a user in our new app, MusicDiscovery. MusicDiscovery, hypothetically, takes 45-second song clips and plays them for the user. Users rate how much they like the song, and if they rate it high enough, we scrobble it to Last.fm so that it can record their preferences. How would we go about doing this?

First, we need to learn about the Last.fm API. Most web services that offer API access will clearly show how to use it in a section of their website labeled "for developers" or "API access." Last.fm includes an "API" link on the bottom of their home page, which takes one to the API homepage (Figure 11–12).

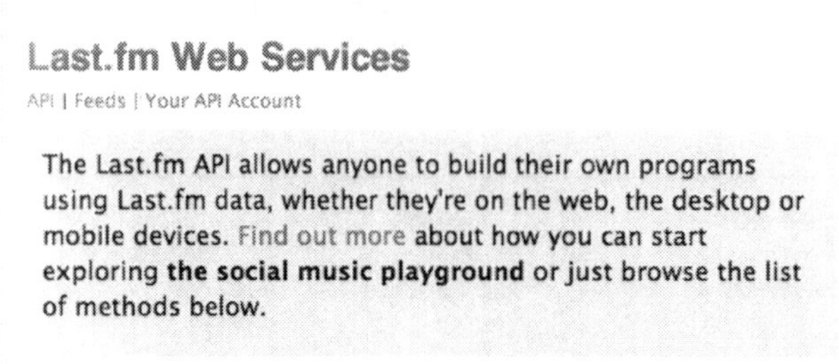

Last.fm Web Services

API | Feeds | Your API Account

The Last.fm API allows anyone to build their own programs using Last.fm data, whether they're on the web, the desktop or mobile devices. Find out more about how you can start exploring **the social music playground** or just browse the list of methods below.

Figure 11–12. *The Last.fm Web Services page*

Looking over the Last.fm API information, it seems to be a two-step process. First, one must apply to be a developer (which involves telling Last.fm what you plan to use their data for, i.e., commercial or non-commercial use), and filling out a bit of basic information about your app. Once that's taken care of, you can explore the use of their API.

The API Intro page lists some essential information, including the API root URL. This is the web address that we'll be sending information to. Most of these requests will make use of AJAX, a technology that we'll discuss in detail in the next chapter. Browsing the documentation, we find examples of how to send data to Last.fm.

As we can see in Figure 11–13, our requests to the Last.fm API take the form of specially formed URLs or HTTP POST requests. The Last.fm API then returns responses using XML.

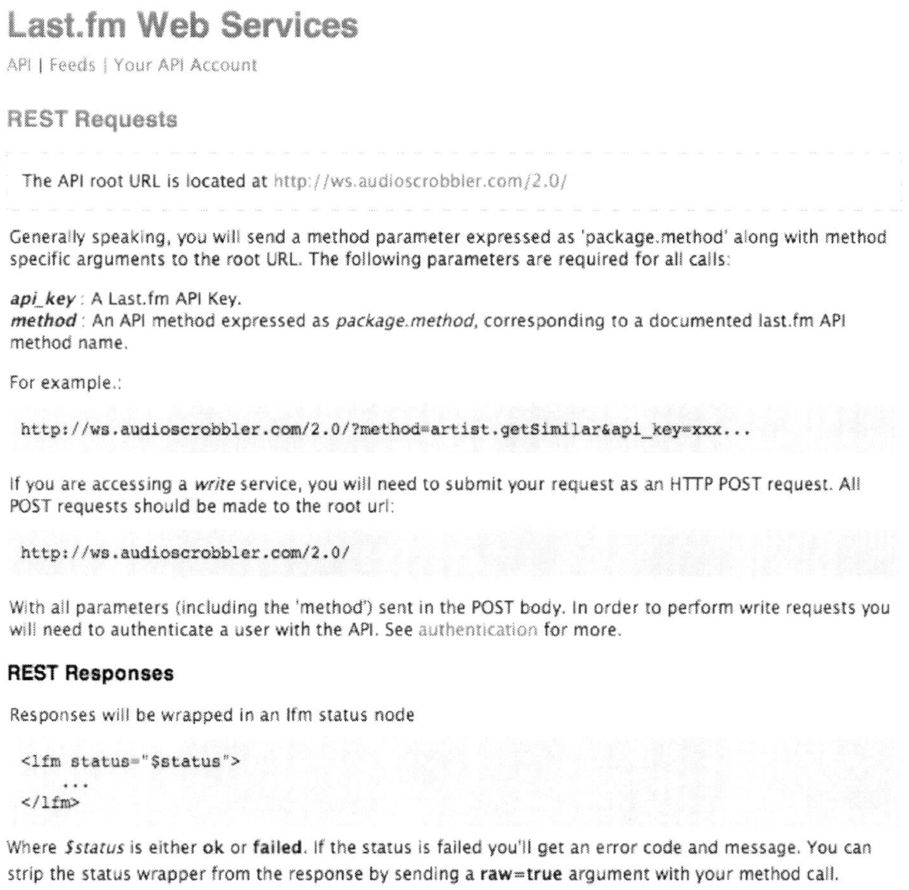

Last.fm Web Services

API | Feeds | Your API Account

REST Requests

The API root URL is located at http://ws.audioscrobbler.com/2.0/

Generally speaking, you will send a method parameter expressed as 'package.method' along with method specific arguments to the root URL. The following parameters are required for all calls:

api_key : A Last.fm API Key.
method : An API method expressed as *package.method*, corresponding to a documented last.fm API method name.

For example.:

```
http://ws.audioscrobbler.com/2.0/?method=artist.getSimilar&api_key=xxx...
```

If you are accessing a *write* service, you will need to submit your request as an HTTP POST request. All POST requests should be made to the root url:

```
http://ws.audioscrobbler.com/2.0/
```

With all parameters (including the 'method') sent in the POST body. In order to perform write requests you will need to authenticate a user with the API. See authentication for more.

REST Responses

Responses will be wrapped in an lfm status node

```
<lfm status="$status">
   ...
</lfm>
```

Where *$status* is either **ok** or **failed**. If the status is failed you'll get an error code and message. You can strip the status wrapper from the response by sending a **raw=true** argument with your method call.

Figure 11–13. *The Last.fm API request documentation*

Now that we know roughly how information will be passed back and forth between our application and Last.fm, we can begin exploring the scrobbling feature. Last.fm's scrobbling documentation (www.last.fm/api/scrobbling, Figure 11–14) lays out the entire process in detail, including which API calls (or functions) to use, and what criteria to use when sending a scrobble request.

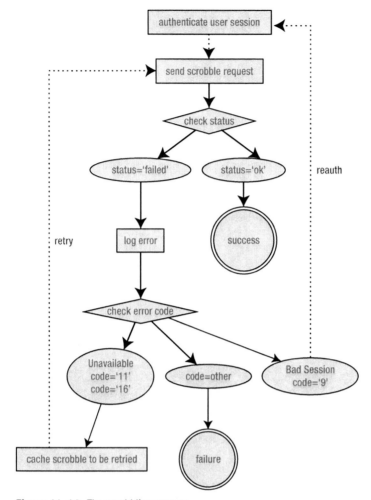

Figure 11–14. *The scrobbling process*

Now that we've got all the pieces, all we'd need to do is write the appropriate JavaScript code to take the current piece of music the user has rated, look it up in Last.fm's catalog, and send the scrobble request. Here's where you can flex your programming muscle and work it out. Along the way, be sure to check out the rest of Last.fm's extensive lookup and recording features. Not only can you enhance your user experience for Last.fm users, you can also use Last.fm data to enhance the experience for your own users who don't use Last.fm!

Tapping into the Power of Amazon's Product Advertising API

Amazon.com started off around 15 years ago as a bookstore. Now they have evolved into a massive retail giant that offers everything from books to cloud computing servers and more. Recently, they've expanded their music offerings quite a bit, and developers who feature music or videos in their apps may want to provide links to purchase these resources through Amazon.

The Amazon Product Advertising API (https://affiliate-program.amazon.com/gp/advertising/api/detail/main.html, Figure 11–15) is a massive web site so we can only highlight its main features here. You could literally spend days exploring everything you can do with Amazon's data, all with the goal of driving revenue through offering Amazon products for sale through your app.

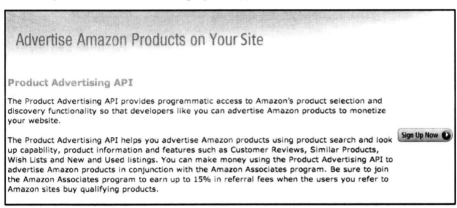

Figure 11–15. *The Amazon Product Advertising API*

Amazon offers not only documentation on their API, but also developer forums where you can ask other developers for help and even code samples, which can get you up and running quickly.

A few quick searches of the code database uncovers a very interesting piece of code for anyone looking to build an application that showcases a particular artist. Say you're in a band and want to build an app for your band. You've decided to build a web app, since that will easily run on everyone's smartphone, and you're storing your concert recordings, demos, and albums in Amazon's S3 cloud storage. How might we go about selling those to fans? There's a demo for it, known as iObjects (http://j.mp/iobjects, Figure 11–16).

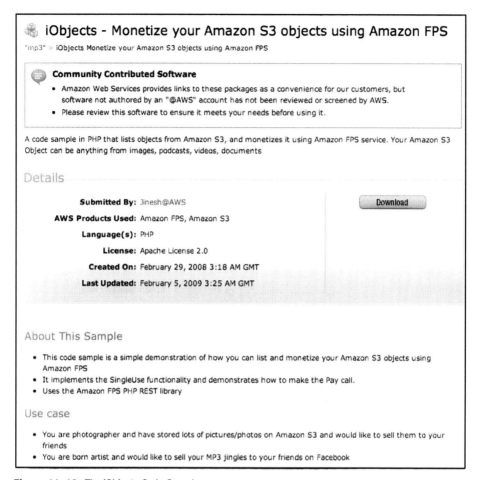

Figure 11–16. *The iObjects Code Sample*

While this is quite a bit more complicated than the Last.fm API we discussed in the previous section, it can really showcase the power of using an API in your application. Now you don't need to worry about payments for your material (since Amazon Flexible Payment System (FPS) can take care of that), and you can easily offer products through your app, through Amazon, which—chances are—your fans are familiar with and use regularly!

As we have seen, using APIs from services such as Amazon or Last.fm can add not only interactivity to your application, but also new revenue streams and ways to innovate. Your band (or your client's band) will certainly distinguish themselves when their users can download the song while still at the concert, and you'll be the developer hero that made it all happen!

Summary

Audio and video can be pretty painless to work with on the mobile HTML5 front because of the limited number of handsets and operating systems that you have to support. However, as mentioned at the beginning of the chapter, they are both technologies that can be easily abused, or quickly turn against you, if not used properly. In this chapter, I hope I have presented you with the tools needed to use these technologies to your benefit.

When it comes to audio and video conversion and manipulation, we have not even begun to scratch the surface in regards to what tools are available for you to use to get the job done. There are just way too many quality audio and video tools out there—we could probably fill an entire book talking just about them. You do not have to use the tools I've suggested in this chapter and I encourage you to do some research and find the best solution that works for you.

Chapter 12

Supercharging the User Experience with AJAX

We're most of the way through the book, and we haven't yet hit explicitly on one chronic annoyance to web users in general, and mobile users especially: the dreaded refresh!

Why dreaded? Well, in the mobile world, as we've learned, speed is everything. The last thing a mobile user wants to do is reload an entire webpage. Even if the "heavier" aspects of the page are cached on the user's phone (such as graphics, fonts, etc.) the phone's browser must still reload them into the browser. This takes an amount of time, processing power, battery power, and the user's patience. Thankfully a series of technologies exist that can help us, known as AJAX.

What Is AJAX?

AJAX stands for Asynchronous JavaScript And XML. Let's break down that name. The first word, Asynchronous, may sound a bit daunting at first, but it's the whole key to what makes AJAX special.

Asynchronous?

Most web pages are programmed to require communication in a send/receive/display series. The user presses a button on a web app, the page sends the required information to the server, the server sends back some response, and the app displays a new page with that response on it. Back and forth it goes, until the user is finished with the app. Each time the user interacts with the app, the page is refreshed completely. This is, for some, the very definition of annoying.

Asynchronous transfer refers to the idea that we can break this chain down into simply send/receive/display/send/receive/send/receive, and so on, instead of including the display portion in each successive round. In other words, we can send and receive data without ever loading a new page. An asynchronous call is simply a request that we make to the web server through this alternate method. For an example of this, we only need to visit Google's search engine on our phone. We start with a blank search page, as in Figure 12–1.

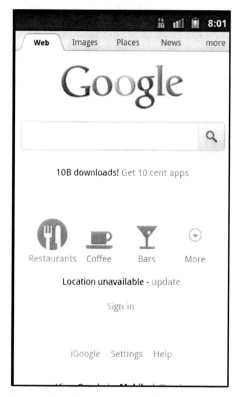

Figure 12–1. *The Google search home page*

Now say it's early in the morning and I want to start my day listening to a great song set to a bunch of pictures of the events the song is discussing. I might begin to type in the name of the song, as in Figure 12–2, and while I do that, Google is using asynchronous calls to try to figure out what I'm looking for. As I type, it's checking each letter against a central database, without requiring me to refresh the page. It's then showing these suggestions below the search bar.

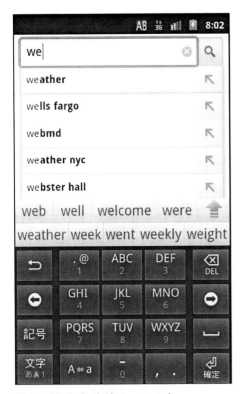

Figure 12–2. *Beginning my search*

At some point, around Figure 12–3, the suggestion matches the whole phrase I'm looking for, and I can simply click on it.

Figure 12–3. *As I type more, the web page tries to fill in likely queries. Interestingly, the Android operating system is also trying to figure out what I'm writing—it's like they're both trying to read my mind!*

Basically, Google has been able to predict what I'm looking for and is giving me a shortcut to access those search listings directly. When I tap on the suggestion that fits what I want, it brings me to the search results I see in Figure 12–4.

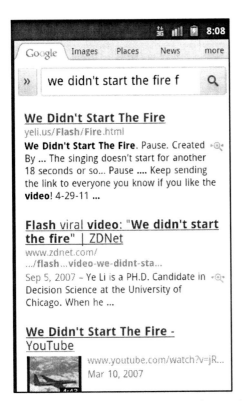

Figure 12–4. *Ah, my results—now I can listen to the flash video I've been searching for*

Prior to Google rolling out these asynchronous calls on the search page, one entered an entire query into the search box, pressed "Search," and waited for the screen to reload. If there was an error in the query, the user didn't know until the new page loaded and Google pointed it out. This took up the user's time (by loading pages needlessly) and Google's bandwidth. Recently, Google has taken this "helping hand" a step further by running the entire search asynchronously—you can type your query and, letter by letter, the search results update within the same browser window.

So What About the JavaScript and XML?

AJAX, technically, can work with any client–side programming language (client–side languages, like JavaScript, process within the user's browser. Server–side languages, like PHP, process on the web server). However, JavaScript is predominantly used as it's become the lingua franca of client–side languages. XML gets in on the game because it's become a simple and easy–to–understand way to move data around. While you could mix other technologies into the AJAX banquet, we'll stick with JavaScript and XML in our examples here.

Now that we've established what AJAX is, let's talk about some neat ways we can incorporate it into some very simple applications. We'll start with a word–of–the–day example, and then move into something a bit more complex, referencing both a web service and our own local database.

AJAX–of–the–Day

It was recently reported that the "word of the year" for 2011 was "pragmatic." This was because one dictionary–serving website found it to be the most looked up word in that year, and thus crowned it the winner. Perhaps you're looking at this going, "I've always wondered what 'pragmatic' means" (or maybe, "What kinda moron doesn't know what 'pragmatic' means?!?"), and wondering why we don't have more web applications bringing us content like this. Well, today is your lucky day, because you're about to write one.

For the word–of–the–day application, we're going to create a rather bare–bones mechanism to provide said word. Later in this chapter we'll discuss how to use AJAX to pull in information from a database or web service, but for now we're going to use a good, old–fashionedflat text file. Named, aptly, `word.txt`:

Listing 12–1. *word.txt*

```
<em>Pragmatic</em>: relating to matters of fact or practical affairs. <i>-<A
HREF=http://www.merriam-webster.com/dictionary/pragmatic>Merriam-Webster.com</A></i>
```

The file `word.txt` has some bits of HTML in it (in this case, we're using simple style tags, however we could use CSS–themed div statements), and if we load it up in our web browser (Figure 12–5), we'll see it displayed as simple text:

Figure 12–5. *The word–of–the–day word.txt file*

Next up, I'm going to build an HTML page that will load up the word–of–the–day when the user presses a button. It's going to look something like Listing 12–2, in code terms. We'll walk through this stepbystep.

Listing 12–2. *word.html, Part 1: The Initial JavaScript Function to Load the Word*

```
<html>
<head>
<meta content="text/html; charset=ISO-8859-1"
http-equiv="content-type">
<title>Word of the Day</title>
<script type="text/javascript">
```

```
function loadword(){
if (window.XMLHttpRequest){
// Modern browsers use this type of request
        request =new XMLHttpRequest();
}else{
// Old Microsoft browsers use this type!
        request =new ActiveXObject("Microsoft.XMLHTTP");
}
```

OK, we're up and running. The first thing we did was create the top of a standard HTML page, and then started a new JavaScript function named loadword, which will do most of the heavy lifting of the page. Inside this function, we first need to figure out if we're using a modern browser (i.e., something released in the last five years, like Firefox, Safari, Opera, Chrome, or newer versions of Internet Explorer) or an older Microsoft browser (Internet Explorer 5 or 6). The reason for this is simple: Older Microsoft browsers don't know what an XMLHttpRequest() object is! For them, we'll ask that an ActiveX object be created, which will give us the same functionality. It's just a funny compromise to the way Microsoft used to code browsers. Let's continue working with the JavaScript for this page in Listing 12-3.

Listing 12–3. *word.html, Part 2: The JavaScript onreadystatechange Function, and the End of the JavaScript Block*

```
    request.onreadystatechange=function() {
if ( request.readyState == 4 &&request.status == 200){
document.getElementById("theword").innerHTML = request.responseText;
}
}

        request.open("GET","word.txt",true);
        request.send();
}
</script>
```

Now that we have our request object, named aptly "request," we can ask it to do some things. This next part of the code is written slightly "backward," in that the code written at the top will be executed after the code written at the bottom. This is because the XMLHttpRequest object, the heart of AJAX, has a special function named onreadystatechange. Anytime the request we're making, processing in the background, does something either expected or unexpected, it fires this function. In essence, this function is where we put the "what do I do with what I get back" code. You can think of the code here as the programming equivalent of "substitute teacher's instructions." You may remember, as an astute student, that when your teacher was absent, he or she would leave instructions for the replacement, perhaps in a special folder. Your onreadystatechange function acts as those instructions, telling the computer (in this case, the JavaScript engine) what to do when you're not around but something happens. Most of the time, these instructions are similar to what we have preceding (in this case, "if the request is processed correctly, display it on the screen"). We can also include instructions for "worst case scenarios," such as when the request cannot be fulfilled, or it throws an error.

In this function, we first test to see what the readyState and status are of our request. The former can return five different numbers, which correspond to where the request is in terms of processing. Returning a code of

- 0 means that the request hasn't been started yet. This is the state in which a new request would be before being sent.

- 1 means that the connection to the server has been initialized. In essence, the pipe is open, and data is moving.

- 2 or 3 means that the request has been sent and is processing, respectively. At this point, all your code can do is sit and wait (or show a "loading" graphic, if you so choose).

- 4 means that the request is complete and ready for the code. You can now do whatever you want to do with the information.We only want to change the text on the page once we reach a readyState of 4.

We also care about the status, which can report 200 (for "OK") or 404 (for "not found"). So the second line of Listing 12–3 translates to: "Only do this if the request is ready and it was done successfully!" From there, it's simply one line that changes the ellipsis, or text placeholder (see Listing 12–4), to the text that was returned by the request.

Finishing up Listing 12–3, we're creating and sending our request. The line starting request.open calls the function that specifies what we're trying to retrieve and how we want to do it. In this case, it's a really simple request—we're just getting data, not sending any data we want the server to parse. We'll use the "GET" method instead of "POST" because it's faster, we'll ask for "word.txt," and we'll set asynchronous to "true," since we want the response in the background, allowing the script to continue running. For a discussion of why we might set this to false, as well as more detail on GET versus POST methods, see the end of this chapter in the "AJAX Considerations" section.

Finally, we simply call request.send(), which fires off our request. Once we get the request back, the XMLHttpRequest object will fire our onreadystatechange and change the line in the webpage.

Finally we finish the page off in Listing 12–4 by creating the basic HTML structure. We've got a special div id called "theword" which holds an ellipsis (...) to begin with. This is what will be replaced by the JavaScript code we wrote at the top. We have a button as well, which fires off our function, loadword().

Listing 12–4. *word.html, Part 3: The Rest of the Page, Consisting of a Simple Body Portion and Text, Along with 'theword' div*

```
</head>
<body>
<span style="font-family: Helvetica,Arial,sans-serif;">Get Today's Word
Of The Day<br>
<div id="theword">
<h2>...</h2>
</div>
<button type="button" onclick="loadword()">Get The Word!</button>
```

```
    </span>
  </body>
</html>
```

When viewed on the Android web browser, the page loads and shows the default state (see Figure 12–6).

Figure 12–6. *The initial page of the Word–of–the–Day example*

Now when the user clicks the "Get the Word!" button, the ellipsis is replaced with the actual word of the day, drawn from `word.txt` (see Figure 12–7). You'll also notice that the text seems to shrink up a bit—this is because the AJAX request is taking up the entirety of the 'theword' `<div>` section, including the `<h2>` tag which normally would provide more spacing. I've done this intentionally to point out that the nesting of tags is important when considering AJAX requests. Placing the `<h2>` outside the `<div>` would preserve the space.

Figure 12–7. *The word is now put into the page, without the page reloading!*

Success! We've changed the content of the page, by making a call to the server, without actually reloading the page. Better yet, if the user hits "reload" on the browser, we'll avoid an ugly error similar to that in Figure 12–8, since we didn't actually send any "POST" data to the server (in the traditional sense).See the "AJAX Considerations" section at the end of this chapter for more information on POST data.

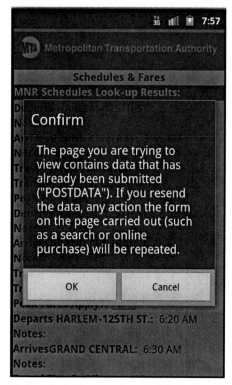

Figure 12–8. *The Android Confirm Reload dialog*

Now that the basics of word–of–the–day are done, we could continue by making it a bit prettier (i.e., using a nice CSS scheme as mentioned previously).For our purposes, though, you should now have a good idea of how flat text files can not only be included through PHP (as shown in previous chapters), but also now through AJAX.Our next stop? The wonderful world of web services, XML, and JSON.

My News!

Our next example calls a few web services to bring us content which won't be stored on our own device. We'll also have to take a slightly ego–centric view of the world, but hey, that comes with the territory of being a programmer!

Let's imagine that we have a number of websites we like to visit, and we want our application to display the most recent news from them. To do this, we need to bring the RSS feeds of these websites together, merge them, and then display them. We'd like the list to update in real time, on our page, without user intervention. Sound complicated? Not really—if you know some tricks!

First: Create a Pipe

Yahoo! Pipes is one of my favorite web services (Figure 12–9, http://pipes.yahoo.com) and it doesn't get too much coverage by most blogs or websites. But the service it provides is pretty awesome—it can stitch together RSS feeds and other data, and provide them in an easy–to–use format of your choosing.

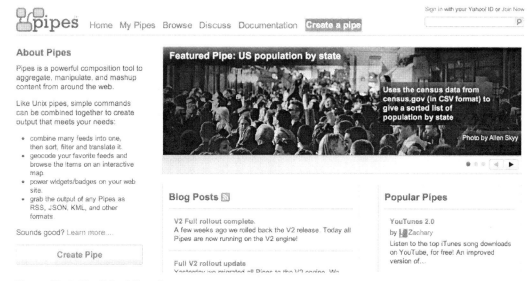

Figure 12–9. *The Yahoo! Pipes homepage*

While other sites allow you to connect things together (Dapper, another Yahoo! property at http://open.dapper.net/, and ifttt (If This Then That) at http://ifttt.com come to mind), Pipes provides the more customizable "output," so we will use it for this example. To get started, click on "Create a pipe" to load the Pipes editor, shown in Figure 12–10. The Pipes editor allows you to organize a series of modules (on the left side) into a logical structure of rules. Each pipe starts with one or more inputs, then uses modules to operate on them (i.e., to change data, or consolidate it), and then outputs the results in a variety of forms.

Figure 12–10. *The Yahoo! Pipes editor*

On the left side you'll find the series of modules that you can drag into the Pipes UI. These modules can be connected to perform the operations you want. I'm going to use three modules—Fetch Site Feed, Union, and Truncate—to bring together the feeds of three websites, merge them together, and then cut off the output after five items (Figure 12–11).

1. Fetch Site Feed takes the URL of the RSS feed for a web site. In this example, I'm going to take three RSS feeds, for three different websites, and link them together. You'll notice in Figure 12–11, I have three "Fetch Site Feed" modules.

2. Union simply combines up to five inputs into one feed. Here the union is combining the three feeds that I've entered. If desired, I could have multiple unions and feed more than five pipes by "union–ing" to a union, and so forth.

3. Truncate tells Pipes that I only want five items output. This is useful to speed up response time, as Pipes only needs to export a few items, and not the tens or hundreds that multiple feeds may provide. Here it's the last thing I've connected up before the Pipe's output module.

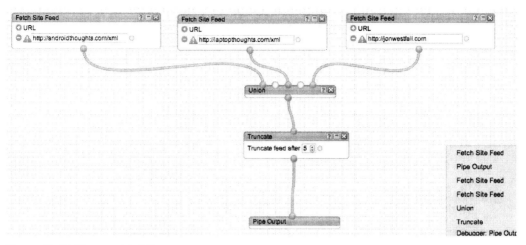

Figure 12–11. *The completed Pipe*

In the debugger window (Figure 12–12), I can see what the output will look like for either the whole Pipe or individual parts along the way. The following output (in Figure 12–12) is shown when I click on "Pipe Output." If I had clicked on the Union instead, I would see all of the feed items, not just the five shown after the Truncate command. This intermediate level of debugging is useful when debugging pipes to see which component may be causing a problem.

Time taken: **1.092s** Refresh
  ▷ **Thanksgiving Thank-Yous 2011**
  ▷ **All-in-One Blog Backup Script**
  ▷ **Keep your Android Tablet Up To Date Daily With Increased Battery Life!**
  ▷ **A Subtle Endorsement of Dancing!**
  ▷ **Graduate School Superstars**

Figure 12–12. *The entire output of my pipe, given that we've truncated after five items*

Once you're done, click "Save" and give your Pipe a name. Then click on "Run Pipe" to see the output (Figure 12–13).

Book Pipe

Click to add description

Pipe Web Address: http://pipes.yahoo.com/pipes/pipe.info?_id=0a1f972788e5ee484b335cb892fc85be (edit)

Figure 12–13. *The book Pipe I created*

You'll notice that Yahoo! Pipes gives me options for how I want to access my Pipe. I can access it as an RSS feed itself, or I can get it as a JSON result output. Under "More Options" I can also configure to get my results by e-mail or through PHP. For this example, I'm going to want to get my results as JSON. You'll recall that we've used JSON earlier in the book, in our apps in Chapters 2 and 3. Here, we're using it again to get the output of our Pipe. Clicking on the JSON button gives me a fairly ugly screen full of content, but it's really the URL that I want to remember. It looks something like `http://pipes.yahoo.com/pipes/pipe.run?_id=0a1f972788e5ee484b335cb892fc85be&_ren der=json` and it can be called through my AJAX web page.

Second: Get the Output and Display It!

We're going to modify our word–of–the–day example to pull the JSON output and display it. While there are easier ways to do this (most notably using JSON's getJSON function, and looping the list items), the code in Listing 12–5 is a bit more drawn out, which makes iteasier to see exactly what we're doing to parse each item. Later, as a flex of your JavaScript skills, you can rewrite this code using getJSON if you'd like.

Listing 12–5. *mynews.html*

```html
<html>
<head>
<meta content="text/html; charset=ISO-8859-1"
http-equiv="content-type">
<title>My News</title>
<script type="text/javascript" src="jquery-1.7.1.min.js"></script>
<script type="text/javascript">
```

```
function loadnews() {
    if (window.XMLHttpRequest) {
        // Modern browsers use this type of request
        request = new XMLHttpRequest();
    } else {
        // Old Microsoft Browsers use this type!
        request = new ActiveXObject("Microsoft.XMLHTTP");
    }

  request.onreadystatechange=function() {
        if ( request.readyState == 4 && request.status == 200) {
var resp = jQuery.parseJSON(request.responseText);
var lister = "<ul>";
            lister += "<li><A HREF=" + resp.value.items[0].href + ">" +
resp.value.items[0].title + "</li>";
lister += "<li><A HREF=" + resp.value.items[1].href + ">" + resp.value.items[1].title +
"</li>";
            lister += "<li><A HREF=" + resp.value.items[2].href + ">" +
resp.value.items[2].title + "</li>";
            lister += "<li><A HREF=" + resp.value.items[3].href + ">" +
resp.value.items[3].title + "</li>";
            lister += "<li><A HREF=" + resp.value.items[4].href + ">" +
resp.value.items[4].title + "</li>";
            lister += "</ul>";
            document.getElementById("thenews").innerHTML = lister;
        }
    }

request.open("GET","http://pipes.yahoo.com/pipes/pipe.run?_id=4659b1f4f4bfdb96c3775b61be
8ca3b8&_render=json",true);
        request.send();
 }
</script>
</head>
<body>
<span style="font-family: Helvetica,Arial,sans-serif;">Get the News!<br>
<div id="thenews">
<h2>...</h2>
</div>
<button type="button" onclick="loadnews()">Get The News!</button>
</span>
</body>
</html>
```

You'll notice that much of this code is the same as the code we used in word-of-the-day. Notably, we've changed a few things, which are bold in our code.

- We've changed the request from word.txt to the URL of the Yahoo! Pipes JSON output.

- We're now using jQuery, a library we've used before which contains some helpful functions to read and decode JSON output. Using jQuery means we have to add in the reference to the jquery-1.7.1.min.js file at the top.

- We're now using jQuery.parseJSON to parse the text we get back from our XMLHttpRequest.

- And we've got an HTML formatted list that will be displayed once we've retrieved the JSON.

The finished product looks like this in our browser (Figure 12–14):

Figure 12–14. *The My News application*

And when we click on "Get the news!" the following is displayed (Figure 12–15):

Figure 12–15. *The news is now loaded!*

Now that we've loaded data from our server, and loaded data from a web service, we can turn to the final installment: a back–and–forth interaction between a web page and a database.

Username Availability

One of the nicer things that websites have done in the last few years is the "instant username availability" field. This is done using AJAX, by checking what the user is entering into the "username" field and simultaneously checking on its availability in the database. We'll create this experience using AJAX, communicating with a MySQL database using PHP on the back–end. This is similar to what Google does with its instant search results, the feature we discussed earlier. We'll start by creating the database, using the schema in Listing 12–6. This listing begins by creating a table, and then populating it with several test usernames ("hardcore,""dinosaur," etc.).

Listing 12–6. *the SQL Schema for the Users Table*

```
CREATE TABLE IF NOT EXISTS `users` (
  `name` varchar(25) NOT NULL
) ENGINE=MyISAM DEFAULT CHARSET=latin1;


--
-- Dumping data for table `users`
--

INSERT INTO `users` (`name`) VALUES
('hardcore'),
('dinosaur'),
('yelius'),
('tep');
```

Use the preceding schema to create the users table in your MySQL database. (MySQL is available at `http://www.mysql.com/products/community/`.) Note that you can name the database whatever you wish, but in this example it's called "datab." Now we need a simple PHP script which takes a value and checks it in the database. Listing 12–7 shall do nicely.

Listing 12–7. *The check_name.php Script*

```
<?php
$name = $_GET['u'];
$user = "root";
$pass = "";
$server = "localhost";
$db = "datab";
mysql_connect($server,$user,$pass) or die("Can not connect");
mysql_select_db($db) or die("No such database");
$query = "SELECT * FROM `users` where `name` = '$name'";
$result = mysql_query($query);
if (mysql_num_rows($result) == 0)
{ echo "<font color=green>Available!</font>"; } else { echo "<font color=red>Not
Available :( </font>"; }
?>
```

The preceding script is fairly simple. It connects to the database and does a simple query to see in how many rows the name is entered. If the name is not found on any rows, then it's available; the script sends back "Available" (and there is presumably much rejoicing). However, if it's not available, because the database already has a row with the name in it, the script returns the considerably sadder "Not Available." You can test this by visiting the `check_name.php` script in your web browser, including `&u=test` with some sort of test username. For example, in my testing environment, `http://localhost/~jon/uname/check_name.php?u=dino` returns "Available," while `http://localhost/~jon/uname/check_name.php?u=dinosaur` returns "Not Available." If this is working for you, then you're ready to proceed.

With the back–end complete, we'll now build a very simple form that will check the username as the person types, and tell him or her if the desired name is available.

We'll accomplish this with the code in Listing 12–8.

Listing 12–8. *The checkname.html Page*

```
<html>
<head>
<title>Registration Page</title>
<script type="text/javascript">

function checkusername($name) {
    if (window.XMLHttpRequest) {
        // Modern browsers use this type of request
        request = new XMLHttpRequest();
        } else {
        // Old Microsoft Browsers use this type!
        request = new ActiveXObject("Microsoft.XMLHTTP");
        }

request.onreadystatechange=function() {
        if ( request.readyState == 4 && request.status == 200) {
            document.getElementById("theres").innerHTML = request.response;
            }
        }

        request.open("GET","check_name.php?u=" + $name,true);
        request.send();
    }
</script>
</head>
<body>
<form name="theform">
<span style="font-family: Helvetica,Arial,sans-serif;">Register!<br>
<div id="theres">
<h2>...</h2>
</div>
<input type="text" name="un" onkeyup="checkusername(this.form.un.value)">
</span></form>
</body>
</html>
```

You'll notice that, like last time, we're building off of the same format we used with word–of–the–day. This time we've changed the function to accept an argument (the name we need to check), and we've changed the button to a text field. This text field checks the name every time a key is released (the onkeyup event), and the result updates. When loaded, the page looks similar to Figure 12–16.

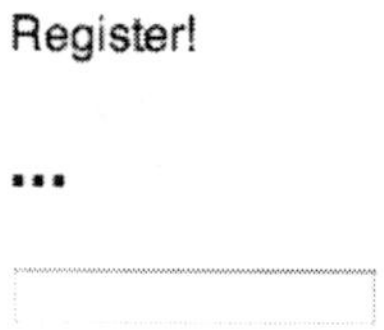

Register!

...

Figure 12–16. *The check username page*

If you enter a name that's open, like "skip," you'll see a message of success, as shown in Figure 12–17.

Register!
Available!

Figure 12–17. *Sweet victory*

If, however, the username you want has already been taken by some awesome person, then you'll see a sad message such as the one in Figure 12–18.

Register!
Not Available :(

dinosaur

Figure 12–18. *The "not available" screen*

Incorporating this technique across an entire web form will allow you to not only check usernames on the fly, but also validate information so that the user never has to hit a "submit" button only to find that he or she has put in an invalid number, e-mail address, or username.

Before we finish, there are two quick tips regarding forms that you might find helpful. The first is to consider to what event you would like to bind the AJAX checking code. In this example, we've bound to the onkeyup event on the form field that we're checking (the username). However, this causes a lookup action on each keypress, something that might bog down your script. An alternative would be to place the function code in the next element (e.g., perhaps a password field) in the onfocus event instead of onkeyup. This will cause the AJAX request to fire after the user has moved to the next field on the form, reducing load. A second consideration involves validation and auto–submission of forms. It can be tempting to make a form auto–submit once the last field is completed. After all, you might be validating information as users enter it, so why make them wait after they finish the last field. This could be a problem though, as some people may wish to check their answers before they continue. It might be best to keep a "submit" button on the page, and let users continue when they are ready.

AJAX Considerations

The examples we've used in this relatively short chapter span the three major types of data with which you'd be interacting while using AJAX. We've taken data from our server and put it into a page without refreshing, we've queried a web service to get RSS headlines, and we've checked usernames to make sure they're available. At this point, you've got the basic tools that you need in order to write applications that leverage the power of AJAX. There are a few things one should consider when building out from here, which we'll highlight next.

POST vs. GET

You'll notice that in our examples, we're consistently using the GET method versus the POST method, as first seen in Listings 12–3 and 12–4. The reason for this, primarily, is speed. GET is much faster than POST because of the simpler format it uses. If you're wondering why, it's most likely due to the original intent of GET—it was designed to be for "idempotent" data only. This simply means that the information isn'tmeant for lasting use (i.e., itshould simply be a lookup value, not data to be entered into a database or processed in any way).

However, there are times when POST will be appropriate. First, POST doesn't have the size limitations that GET does, so if you're passing a lot of information to the server, you'll need to use POST. Second, POST should be used whenever you're changing something on the server (such as a database update), versus referencing static or cached content. Simply put, use GET if you're passing data that won't be needed again. Use POST if you're passing data that should be processed or entered into a database, e-mail, or file.

Using POST is slightly more complex than GET. You'll need to set a request header, and send information through the send function. This is because POST data are encoded in a message body, whereas GET data are simply tacked onto the URL. This is why the Android browser in Figure 12–8 mentions resending POSTDATA—it's referring to this specially encoded message. If we wanted to changeour username example to use POST, we could change the following lines:

```
request.open("GET","check_name.php?u=" + $name,true);
request.send();
```

The change would result in the lines shown in Listing 12–9.

Listing 12–9. *Using POST in the Username Availability Example*

```
request.open("POST","check_name.php",true);
request.setRequestHeader("Content-type","application/x-www-form-urlencoded");
request.send("u="+$name);
```

We would also have to alter the PHP script (see Listing 12–7), changing the first line from `$name = $_GET['u'];` to `$name = $_POST['u'];`.

Setting Asynchronous to False?

As you've seen from the preceding examples, the third argument of the open function for our XMLHttpRequest is normally set to "true." It makes sense this way—after all, why would we want to set it to false anyway? Well, the answer is that there are very few times we would! Still, in some circumstances you might. For example, if you're writing a script and you absolutely do not want something to happen until the request is returned and ready for processing, it would be permissible to set this to false. An example that comes to mind involves a username check form, similar to the one in Figure 12–16, that should only allow the user to continue with the form if the username is available (perhaps so that other options can be customized based on it). In this case one might disable or hide all subsequent form fields, then wait until the request is returned; if it is successful, the fields could then be re-enable or shown. But be mindful that your entire script will be held up, so doing this with larger amounts of data will not be a good idea. One could imagine the entire browser "stuck," something frustrating on any platform, but especially vexing on a mobile device where the demand for speed is already greater than its availability.

Also be aware that if you decide to set asynchronous to false, you don't need (and shouldn't use) the onreadystatechange function. This is because there is no ready state to look for—the code will continue processing after the request is ready. Simply put the rest of your JavaScript code after the send function, and it will process sequentially.

Finally, before setting asynchronous to false, you may wish to ask yourself if AJAX is really the best solution for what you're trying to accomplish. Sure, it will probably look cool, but if you need to force the user to wait for something, perhaps it would be easier to implement your code in a different way. For example:

- If there is the possibility that your users may disable JavaScript, requiring JavaScript to complete a form will render the page useless for them. Using AJAX with asynchronous set to true will generally avoid this problem.

- A long form that requires complex validation (e.g., database lookups) after several options might work better as a multi-page form, allowing users to create an account on page one, and then return to subsequent pages at their leisure. Each page could save the progress of the form, allowing users to jump back in where needed, while also providing adequate validation.

Given these thoughts and your own experience in testing, you'll be able to get an idea about not only the best form submission method, GET or POST, but also about whether using the uncommon method of setting asynchronous to false is a good idea for your script.

Summary

In this chapter we've taken a big step forward in making our users' lives easier. We've started doing some of the processing on our forms or our pages in the background, so that users do not need to refresh pages, submit forms, or reload content needlessly. By implementing the ideas and concepts outlined here across your projects and even in our previous examples, you'll be able to create awesome "supercharged" designs in no time!

Chapter 13

PackagingYour Applications

So it has at last come to this: the final chapter. Throughout this book we have reminisced about the days of old (also known as the 1990s), and we have learned about the magical wonders of CSS3, HTML5, and JavaScript. We have played around with audio and video. We have learned the joys of using JavaScript frameworks to increase our productivity and provide our users with stunninglyeasy–to–create page layouts. We have even created a slew of beginner applications, one of which ended up turning you into an International Man of Mystery, to get you started on your future path of stardom. Hopefully, after going through this book, we have even managed to hammer home the importance of optimizing your code and approaching development mindful of the limited bandwidth a lot of mobile users are stuck with.

Like all good things, however, our time is quickly coming to an end. Before we call it quits, though, there is still a bit more information that I will present to you. While we have gone through and built an arsenal of fun applications, we have still not covered what to do with those applications when they are built! For the rest of this chapter we will cover everything from packing and compressing your applications to get them ready for the Internet; to picking a proper hosting service to store your applications; to transferring your files to whichever hosting service you use; and even to skipping the whole hosting service solution altogether in lieu of wrapping your trusty HTML5 code in a framework like PhoneGap or Appcelerator's Titanium Mobile, so that your code will work just like a native application your users can install on their devices from the Android Market!

Compressing Your Application

Now that you have finished writing your code and testing it in a local development environment, you are probably excited to upload your application to the Internet and start telling every person you know to go check it out. Getting to this stage in any project is an accomplishment, but just because you are code complete does not mean you don't have any work left to do. Throughout this book I have tried to hammer home the importance of coding smarter; and doing things such as using CSS3 to create fabulous gradient effects, and custom web fonts (courtesy of Google's amazing web font directory) instead of images or other "heavy" resources such as Flash movies. These things end up helping your code load fast on a user's device.

Sure, we are on the cusp of having nationwide fourth generation mobile Internet available to anyone who wants it, but in reality it does not matter how fast your carrier's broadband service is since mobile networks suffer greatly from poor latency (the amount of time it takes for your phone to communicate with the site or service you are trying to load before data are transferred.) To help our code get to our user faster, and in turn help relieve stress on our poor web servers, we will do something often referred to as minifying our code. Minifying, or compressing, our code consists of running our CSS and JavaScript files through an application or service that will take that code and remove all of the line breaks and unneeded white spaces to make the end product a fair bit smaller than it was before.

What Is Compression?

Let us once again take a look at the ever–popular jQuery framework that many web developers use. As you can see in the Figure 13–1 following, we have two versions of the main jQuery library. One version of the script is uncompressed and comes in weighing a massive 231KB, and another version has been compressed and went through a round of obscurification, bringing the total weight down to a still high, but more manageable 90KB. Opening up our JavaScript documents in a code editor we can see the difference between the two files immediately. The development version of jQuery, as seen in Figure 13–2, is formatted really nicely and has a bunch of really helpful comments sprinkled throughout, while the smaller production–ready version of jQuery almost looks like a weird alien language and is nearly impossible to understand. Take a look at Figure 13–3 to get a better idea of to what I am referring. This is what obscurifying code does. Not only are we taking away all of the line breaks and pretty formatting, but here the code itself was shrunken and manipulated to obscure the code and make it harder to understand.

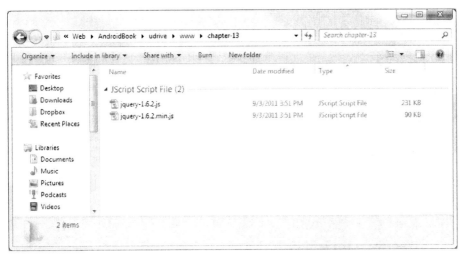

Figure 13–1. *Here we are examining the file sizes of two different versions of jQuery 1.6.2*

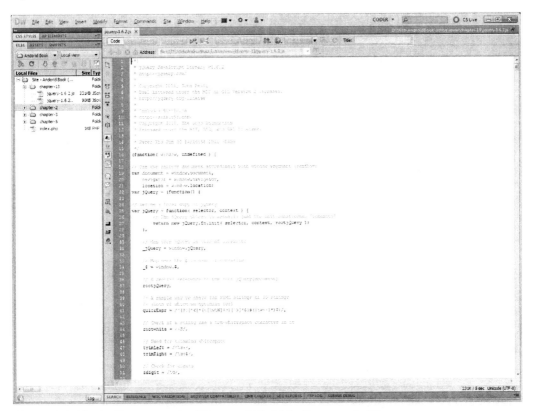

Figure 13–2. *Viewing the uncompressed jQuery script in Adobe Dreamweaver 5.5*

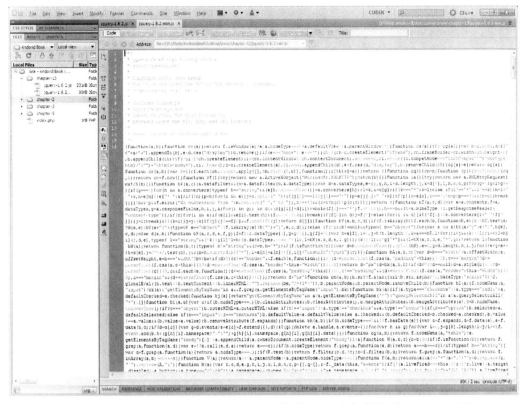

Figure 13–3. *Viewing the compressed, obscured, and alien–like jQuery code in Adobe Dreamweaver 5.5*

One might ask why we want to obscure code—after all, don't we want others to see our neat tricks? Well, in a book like this we sure do, but in real life it can become very important to keep a few things "close to the vest." While obscuring code isn't going to stop intrepid code–readers from figuring out all of your secrets (hence, don't ever rely on obscured code to guard things like passwords, credit card numbers, nuclear launch codes, etc.), it will stop those with a small amount of knowledge from stealing code you've worked long and hard on just to re-use your neat transition or cool layout.

Compression Tools and Utilities

There are plenty of programs out there and available on the trusty ol' Internet to help you make your production–ready code smaller and less hefty on your servers' and users' resources. One of the most popular is Yahoo!'s YUI Compressor (Figure 13–4). Unlike some other compression solutions, YUI Compressor is an application written in Java that will have to be run on your development workstation. After running the application and giving it the options you desire from your command line, the application will take your code, compress it as we have discussed, and even combine your many different JavaScript or CSS files into one super–compressed document, ready to be uploaded to your server. You can find the YUI Compressor at http://developer.yahoo.com/yui/compressor/.

```
$ java -jar yuicompressor-x.y.z.jar
Usage: java -jar yuicompressor-x.y.z.jar [options] [input file]

  Global Options
    -h, --help                  Displays this information
    --type <js|css>             Specifies the type of the input file
    --charset <charset>         Read the input file using <charset>
    --line-break <column>       Insert a line break after the specified column number
    -v, --verbose               Display informational messages and warnings
    -o <file>                   Place the output into  or a file pattern.
                                Defaults to stdout.

  JavaScript Options
    --nomunge                   Minify only, do not obfuscate
    --preserve-semi             Preserve all semicolons
    --disable-optimizations     Disable all micro optimizations

GLOBAL OPTIONS

  -h, --help
      Prints help on how to use the YUI Compressor

  --line-break
      Some source control tools don't like files containing lines longer than,
      say 8000 characters. The linebreak option is used in that case to split
      long lines after a specific column. It can also be used to make the code
      more readable, easier to debug (especially with the MS Script Debugger)
      Specify 0 to get a line break after each semi-colon in JavaScript, and
      after each rule in CSS.

  --type js|css
      The type of compressor (JavaScript or CSS) is chosen based on the
      extension of the input file name (.js or .css) This option is required
      if no input file has been specified. Otherwise, this option is only
      required if the input file extension is neither 'js' nor 'css'.

  --charset character-set
      If a supported character set is specified, the YUI Compressor will use it
      to read the input file. Otherwise, it will assume that the platform's
      default character set is being used. The output file is encoded using
      the same character set.

  -o outfile

      Place output in file outfile. If not specified, the YUI Compressor will
      default to the standard output, which you can redirect to a file.
      Supports a filter syntax for expressing the output pattern when there are
      multiple input files.  ex:
          java -jar yuicompressor.jar -o '.css$:-min.css' *.css
      ... will minify all .css files and save them as -min.css

  -v, --verbose
      Display informational messages and warnings.

JAVASCRIPT ONLY OPTIONS

  --nomunge
      Minify only. Do not obfuscate local symbols.

  --preserve-semi
```

Figure 13–4. *A quick look at the YUI Compressor help screen as would be seen in a command line interface*

Using YUI Compressor can seem intimidating (when looking at all the options, as seen in Figure 13–4),but it's fairly straightforward. For example, assume I'd like to compress the main.js file from our "Who's That Tweet?" app from Chapter 2. First I'd download the YUI Compressor from its website. Then I'd extract the files, open a command line window, and change to the directory containing the Java JAR file (yuicompressor-2.4.7.jar in this case; this name will change depending on version). Next I'd copy over the files that I'd like to compress (into my current directory) and run the compression command. The command I'd use to do this is:

```
java -jar yuicompressor-2.4.7.jar main.js -o main.small.js
```

This tells YUI Compressor to compress main.js into a smaller file named main.small.js. In this case, the compressor cut the file size from 3,763 bytes to 1,946— a little more than half!

There are a few other compressing applications out there that are definitely worth mentioning. The first one I would like to take a look at is a handy little application created by Dean Edwards called Packer (http://dean.edwards.name/packer/) shown in Figure 13–5. This web service will allow you to copy your development JavaScript into a textarea field on the site and with a quick click of a button spit out shrunken JavaScript code that you can just copy and paste into a blank text file and be on your way. If you believe that YUI might be a bit of overkill for your particular needs, Packer might be a great and extremely simple–to–use alternative.

One should note, however, that while Packer is a great tool for shrinking code, it is also quite easy to unobscurethis code by simply disabling the JavaScript that prevents you from pasting code into the "Copy" box and hitting "decode"! Therefore one should use it as simply a compressor, not a security mechanism.

Figure 13–5. *Using Packer we can painlessly minify our "Who's That Tweet?" JavaScript code from Chapter 2, which is in the top textarea field, into something that is just a tiny fraction of the original document size as seen in the bottom textarea*

The last fantastic piece of software I would like to discuss is a little collection of code and apps called the HTML5 Boilerplate created by Paul Irish and found at `http://html5boilerplate.com/`. Although it is not a compression tool specifically, it is a very useful framework you might consider using for app development and which includes its own compression utility. HTML5 Boilerplate is afairly young project (it was launched on August 10, 2010) and is a great starting point for developers that don't want to be bothered with writing the same old basic code over and over again because it is included in almost every project they create. There are those that like to confuse the HTML5 Boilerplate with a framework, but in reality it is far from that. I like to think of this project as more of an organization structure and toolbox (Figure 13–6); it helps you keep your project files in order, and lets you avoid duplication of effort by providing an easy way to implement a lot of things developers have to do repeatedly (such as specifying certain files, JavaScript libraries, etc.).

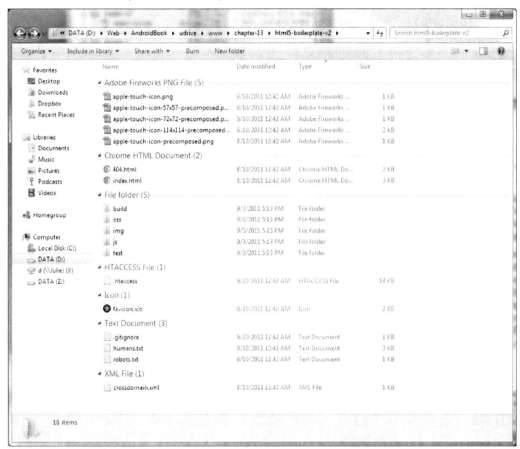

Figure 13–6. *A look inside the HTML5 Boilerplate folder structure. All of the magical compression goodness takes place inside the "build" folder.*

Inside the Boilerplate package, which is currently version 2.0 as of this writing, one can find a ton of useful items and features, such as an already coded barebones skeleton layout of your `index.html` and `404.html` files; the latest copy of jQuery; some predefined CSS styles used to reset styles across the vast array of web browsers out there in the mighty Sea of the Internet; special optimizations to be used in an mobile environment; and even a nifty little code compressor which will compress your HTML, CSS, and JavaScript files for you when you are ready to launch a production version of your application.

To compress your files with the built–in tools, which includes such compressors that we discussed earlier like YUI Compressor, all one has to do is edit the `build.xml` file located within the build directory (see Figure 13–7). Here you will find an agglomeration of options that you can specify to compress your web application to your heart's content. It might take you a little while to get comfortable with messing with this file, but once you have everything set up the way you want it, all you have to do is run the `runbuildscript.bat` file and your code will swiftly be compressed and optimized.

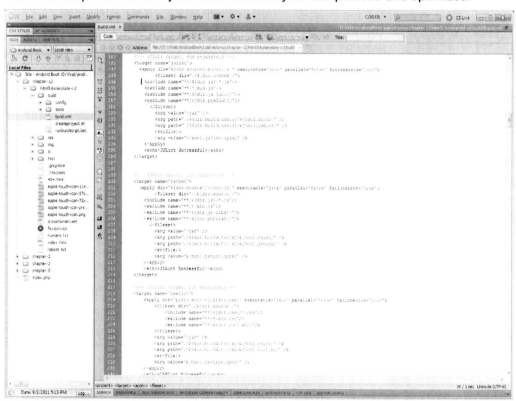

Figure 13–7. *Configuring the HTML5 Boilerplate build settings in Adobe Dreamweaver 5.5*

Finding a Hosting Solution

Now that we have managed to squeeze every last bit of unneeded bytes from our code, making it as small as possible, it is time to upload that thing of beauty to the Internet for the whole entire world to see. Finding a hosting solution that works for you and your project can at times be a frustrating thing, especially if you are not sure what it is you are looking for exactly. Here we'll talk about three of the largest hosting companies out there and our impressions of them as well as the features they offer. First though, let'sconsider the process of choosing a host.

Evaluating Hosting Providers

Not every provider is the same, and a service that works well for one developer may not serve the needs of another. You need to know about the provider and be clear about your own needs and goals. The following questions are a good starting point when evaluating any host:

1. **How many domain names or sub-domains do I get?** Back when many web developers got started, the biggest question was, "How much space do I have?" or "How much transfer (the amount of data you can send each month without getting an overage charge—basically how many visitors you can have)?". However, most web hosts now provide ample space and transfer for beginning programmers and even some advanced ones. The bigger question might be, how many domain names (whatever.com) or sub-domains (something.whatever.com) are offered? The reason is simple: developers rarely have just one client at a time. You'll probably be setting up multiple projects, multiple clients, and even running multiple public sites for apps or other products you build. You'll want to brand each one differently, so getting newname.com is much nicer than yourname.com/newname— and easier to remember.

2. **How responsive is their tech support? Are FAQs or Knowledge Bases available?** In the six years I've used my current web host, and the ten years I used the previous one, I've had to e-mail tech support perhaps five to ten times for various issues ranging from the minor ("does the server support...?") to the major ("all of my sites are down."). Each time I've wanted an answer immediately, especially in the case of the latter, as any time spent waiting is too long. Better yet though, my current web host offers a very good FAQ and Knowledge Base that covers far more than just how to reset a password or create a new e-mail account. It discusses things like PHP versions, server software, shell access, and more. Point being: You want to make sure information is either already available to help you when you run into trouble, or that help is a quick e-mail response away.

3. **What management tools are available?** You'll want to choose a web host that has sufficient manageability in terms of what you can do with the account. Some hosts might prefer that you contact them each time you need to set up a new domain, database, or anything else for that matter. Others might fully automate the process through a control panel. I tend to prefer the latter, since the former is usually always available. My current host even allows me to cancel domains or my entire account online, saving me an awkward phone call if I should ever decide to leave.

4. **What happens if I outgrow my plan?** It's possible that after a few years you'll need access to greater features or more resources. Following, in our discussion of Dreamhost, we note that it offers certain features to "scale" or "upgrade" your package. If you're concerned about the future, you might investigate or ask prospective hosts how hard it would be for you to switch plans or upgrade. If they say you'd have to set everything over again, you might want to find a host that would migrate everything for you or simply upgrade you without any changes necessary.

5. **Do I have shell and/or CRON access?** This last one is a bit technical, but can be important if you're doing some kinds of development work. Shell access, or a shell account, refers to the ability for you as the client to log into your host's server interactively. Normally through a service called SSH, a shell account lets you run commands directly on the server, like a command prompt or terminal window on your computer allows now. CRON is a special software package on the server that lets you schedule commands to be run later or periodically. This might be really useful to you if you create an application that needs to periodically check on itself—say an application that sends out e-mails to your users. Every 20 or 30 minutes you might need to run a script automatically to check whether there is any e-mail to send. CRON access lets you do this. However, CRON can also be abused, which is why some web hosts do not allow you to use it, or allow you to log into the server interactively at all.

In addition to the preceding guidelines, one can also consult review websites when deciding what host to choose. Beware though: Some of the reviews on those sites that are overly glowing or overly negative might not be indicative of the actual service.And at the end of the day, we will always trust the recommendations of people we know have truly used a service over that of a sketchy review, which is why we will quickly take a second to go over some of the hosting providers that we have used or worked within the past to give you a good jumping–off point in your quest to find one that is perfect for you.

Please note that the following sections discuss features that many hosts offer, and the specific hosts we mention are simply ones we've used personally. While we're obviously happy with the services, we'd never assume they're right for everyone. Take what you read in the following paragraphs, consider your options and price range, and find the host that is right for you!

Dreamhost

For the past six years, I (Rocco) have personally been a huge fan of the hosting company Dreamhost (http://dreamhost.com/) which is a great little company created by four very ambitious Computer Science undergraduates back in 1997 (see Figure 13–8). Dreamhost has been around for a while, and while they have had some growing pains in the past, the service that they provided for me has been rock solid, with very little hiccups. Their prices are extremely competitive, usually coming in at a base of $9USD a month, and they even offer their customers unlimited bandwidth and unlimited storage.

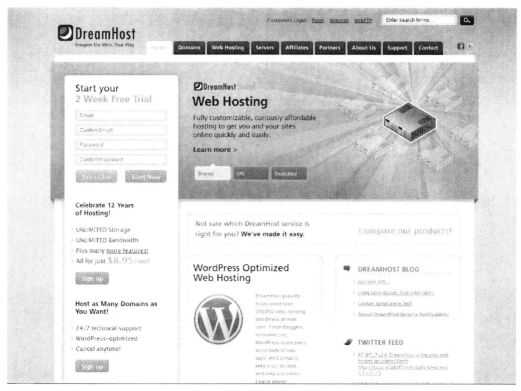

Figure 13–8. *Dreamhost has been hosting millions of sites on the Internet since 1997. Currently they host over 500,000 sites running on the WordPress open source content management solution*

Dreamhost offers a variety of hosting with the basic form of hosting being in a shared environment. While shared hosting is fine for basic projects, there are some major limitations to going that route. For starters, you're sharing an environment with everyone else on that server and if someone uploads a script to the server that somehow manages to hog up a bunch of the server's resources or even crash the server, then everyone on that server suffers. On top of that, there is very little customization you can perform on a shared server. You cannot install custom applications or services to run in the background, and you cannot make any changes to the web server configuration files.

If you're a control freak like me, you would probably want to look at getting yourself a Virtual Private Server or a Dedicated Server. A Virtual Private Server is basically a computer running inside of a computer. Using special virtualization software one can emulate the hardware of a computer within a safe and sandboxed software solution that allows you to install and run an entire operating system inside of another operating system as if it was its own separate computer. When you are renting a Virtual Private Server (VPS) from Dreamhost you are still using it in a shared environment with other people, but you have the *huge* benefit of being sandboxed, or protected, against the harmful actions of anyone else with whomyou are sharing that physical server.

Not only do you not have to worry about having your site go down because of someone else's negligence, but your resources are protected as well. Using a dead simple slider in the Dreamhost administration panel, you can assign as much RAM and CPU processing power to your server as you want, on the fly, in real time (see Figure 13–9). Adding more RAM and CPU power to your service, however, does increase your monthly fee; but if you have an application that you know needs a dedicated 1GB of RAM and CPU power to quickly serve all of your users in a timely manner, it is wonderful to know those resources are automatically safeguarded for you and only you. If you are interested in setting up a VPS on Dreamhost, it offers you the first week free so you can scale your server as high or as low as you want to find the optimal amount of resources your site needs.

Figure 13–9. *A sliding scale is used to determine how much a Virtual Private Server would cost with the selected amount of RAM*

Dreamhost also gives you the option to have your own dedicated environments as well. Usually these machines are relatively beefy servers that have between two and four CPU cores and even up to 12GB of RAM. Chances are you are not going to need that much processing power if you are a new developer, but when you do need it one day, you now know where to look.

On top of having plenty of options at your disposal for hosting your site with Dreamhost, you also get access to a very responsive tech support team. If you have a problem or something is going bonkers on your server in the middle of the night, in most cases you can hop on a text chat with a technician in a matter of minutes and get your problem taken care of swiftly. Out of all the hosting companies I have used in the past,Dreamhost has been one of my favorites when it comes to getting help when you need it.

1and1

Switching authors (Jon here), it's now time to hear about my web host for the past six years, 1and1. 1and1 is actually a fairly large host which has lukewarm reviews by most in the industry. It's not the best (although it is debatable who is), and it's not the worst. Many of the features Dreamhost offers, which Rocco discussed, are also available from 1and1 (and many other hosts, for that matter), so I feel it's probably best to simply outline what I find truly useful about 1and1. That falls into two categories: documentation and reliability. Documentation refers to the 1and1 FAQ section, which surprised me by having in the general questions that detailed information I wrote about earlier. I was having an issue with a script, and was amazed when the 1and1 FAQ site had very specific information about the server setup, PHP version, and available software. I was able to debug my problem without having to write a long, complicated e-mail. The second feature I really have liked about 1and1 is the reliability of my service. While no one can boast 100% uptime (the industry standard term for a server or service being available), from what I've seen 1and1 gets pretty close. As a bottom–of–the–list client (i.e., I pay around $9 a month on a basic shared hosting package), it wouldn't surprise me if I had spotty service here and there. In fact, the opposite has happened— my sites have remained up without much fail the entire time I've been there.

If you're considering another host and want to know how it does in reliability, you might find a friend or person on a forum who uses it and ask what their domain name is. From there, I'd suggest setting up a free account with a service such as Pingdom (`http://www.pingdom.com`), an uptime monitoring service. Pingdom will let you monitor one web site for free, so go ahead and point it at your friend's web site. After a few weeks or months, you'll have reports you can consult to see if the host is reliably up or not.

So there you have it, 1and1 has been reliable and thorough for me. Now back to Rocco to discuss one last host!

Media Temple

Another hosting company that I (Rocco) have used in the past, and the third one I will discuss with you in this chapter, is an industry favorite called Media Temple (`http://mediatemple.net/`). In a lot of ways the services Media Temple offers can be considered better than Dreamhost for a more technical user. Media Temple offers an expanse of solutions, beginning withthe basic Grid Server package (see Figure 13–10), which hosts your site on a cluster with hundreds of other servers powering that cluster. It also offers dedicated virtual servers, as Dreamhost does, and a wide range of very powerful dedicated servers.

My only real problem with Media Temple is that it tends to be a fair bit more expensive than other providers such as Dreamhost, but it does have the option of providing you with much nicer hardware and the same thumbs–up tech support that you would get from a company like Dreamhost; so if power is what you are looking for, make sure to check out what Media Temple has to offer.

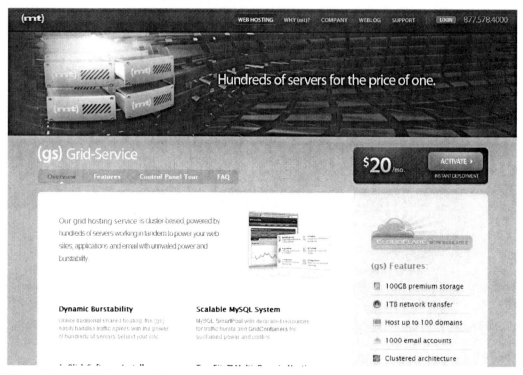

Figure 13–10. *Media Temple's Grid Service landing page*

File Transfer Protocol

Now that we have pointed you in the right direction in finding a hosting provider that meets your needs, we have to get those files that we created on our local development server up onto our shiny new production server. This step is usually completed with a File Transfer Protocol (FTP) application. FTP is a standard protocol in networking that is used to transfer files and documents from one computer to another. On your hosting machine there is an FTP server running that will allow you to connect to that machine using an FTP client on your desktop or workstation. There are tons of free FTP programs out there, but my personal favorite is a free open source piece of software called FileZilla (http://filezilla-project.org/), shown in Figure 13–11.

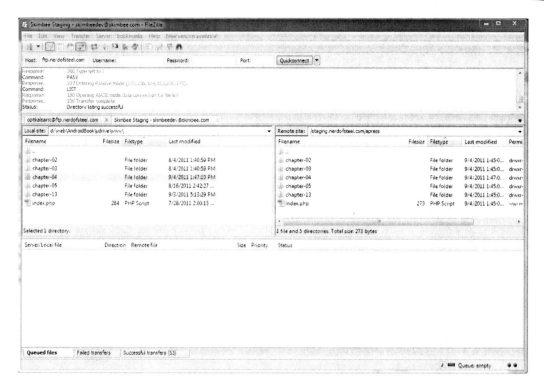

Figure 13–11. *Using FileZilla to transfer code for the book to one of my staging servers for testing*

One of the main reasons I love FileZilla is because the software is constantly being updated and the developers associated with this project work their buns off to make sure that it is one of the fastest and most stable FTP programs in the wild.

Using an FTP client is actually pretty easy and really straightforward. Once you sign up for a hosting solution you will be given credentials to plug into your application, and once connected, if your FTP client supports the feature, you can just drag and drop the files you want into any folder on the server that you have permission to access. Here is an example of what some FTP credentials might look like:

```
url: ftp.myawesomesite.com
user: testuser112
password: psswOrdz
port: 21
path: /var/www/myawesomesite.com/
```

If you've never done this before, it might seem a bit confusing. In the next section, we'll walk through deploying an app from start to finish.

Deploying an Application Using Secure FTP

In this example, we're going to walk you through uploading an entire application to a web hosting service using SFTP. We're going to be using FileZilla on a Windows machine, but if you're using a Mac, you could use a free donation–supported program named Cyberduck. The steps are roughly the same, although the screens will appear different on a Mac.

First, you'll need to gather the following information:

- The connection method your web host requires. Some web hosts no longer support FTP, preferring the encrypted version, SFTP. You'll need to know your FTP address (this is usually ftp.yourdomainname.com, where yourdomainname is your personal domain, like jonwestfall.com), your FTP username, and FTP password.

- You'll need to know if the files for your domain are under any particular directory on your web host. Many web hosts will have your FTP information place you into your root directory by default (i.e., once you log into the server, the files you see under "/" are the same as under your domain name. So /test.txt corresponds to http://jonwestfall.com/test.txt). Other hosts may place your files in a directory named after the domain (i.e., /jonwestfall.com) or a directory named /public_html or /web.

- You'll also need to consider where you want your files to live. In this case, I want "Who's That Tweet?" to live at http://jonwestfall.com/whosthattweet, so I'll need to create that directory and upload my files to it.

Once you have the information you need, download and install FileZilla client (from http://filezilla-project.org/download.php). After it is installed, you should find it under the FileZilla FTP Client group in your Start menu. Open FileZilla, and you should see a screen similar to Figure 13–12.

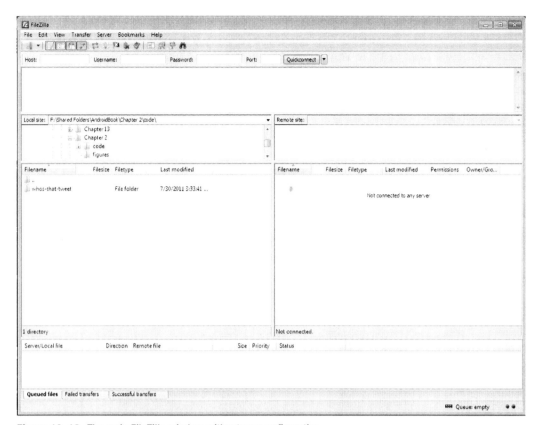

Figure 13–12. *The main FileZilla window without any configuration*

You'll notice it's pretty empty and separated into six panes. The top pane shows the FTP commands that FileZilla is sending to the server. The left–hand panes show files on your computer (both in tree format and listing the files in the directory you're looking in), and the right–hand panes will show files on your server (in the same arrangement, after we've connected). The bottom shows files that we're currently transferring from one side to the other (either from our computer to the server, or vice versa).

Start by entering your FTP host name in the Host box at the top, your FTP username, and your FTP password. If your host supports SFTP, the more secure way to go, you'll want to enter the port number for SFTP, which is typically "22" inside the Port box. If, however, you can only use regular FTP, you'll use the FTP Port number, typically "21." (Note: If your host changes these values, which is very rare for a host to do, you should be able to find them in its FAQ section or Knowledge Base.) After you have all of your information entered, press "Quickconnect" to connect to the server (Figure 13–13).

Figure 13–13. *FileZilla host connection information for SFTP*

If this is the first time you've connected to this server, and you're using SFTP, you may see the following box (Figure 13–14) asking you to verify the server identity. Typically you won't know what value to verify, but you might want to note it the first time to make sure it's always the same. This is a security feature to ensure that you're always connecting to the right machine.

Figure 13–14. *FileZilla Unknown Host Key prompt*

Once you are logged in, the panes on the right hand side of the screen change to show the files on the server. Click on the folders until you find where you would like to upload your files. In my case, I'm going to go to the /new-jonwestfall.com directory (where the web files for jonwestfall.com live) and create a whosthattweet directory. I can do this by double–clicking on new-jonwestfall.com in the right–hand pane, and right–clicking on the white space next to the files. In the menu that appears (Figure 13–15), I choose "Create Directory," and in the next window (Figure 13–16), I give it a name.

Figure 13–15.*Right–clicking shows the Context Menu, allowing you to create a directory*

Create directory

Please enter the name of the directory which should be created:

/new-jonwestfall.com/whosthattweet/

OK   Cancel

Figure 13–16. *The FileZilla "Create directory" dialog*

Now I make sure that I have the directories properly set up: the files I want to move on the left side, and the targetlocation on the right side,as in Figure 13–17.

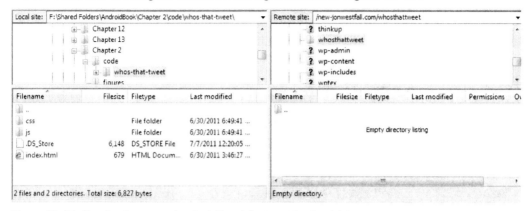

Figure 13–17. *Showing the source (on the left) and the target (on the right)*

Now it's a simple matter of selecting the files on the left, right–clicking on them, and choosing "Upload" (see Figure 13–18).

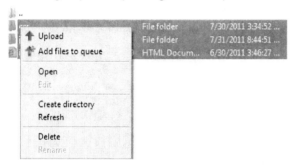

Figure 13–18. *I can now click the "Upload" option to upload the files to the server*

After I do that, I should see the same files in both panes, as in Figure 13–19.

Filename	Filesize	Filetype	Last modified		Filename	Filesize	Filetype	Last modified	Permissions	Owner/Gro...
..					..					
css		File folder	7/30/2011 3:34:52 ...		css		File folder	2/7/2012 11:30:..	drwxr-xr-x	5434456 600
js		File folder	7/31/2011 8:44:51 ...		js		File folder	2/7/2012 11:30:..	drwxr-xr-x	5434456 600
index.html	679	HTML Docum...	6/30/2011 3:46:27 ...		index.html	679	HTML Doc..	2/7/2012 11:30:..	-rw-r--r--	5434456 600

Figure 13–19. *The files from my computer (on the left) are now on the server (on the right)*

Now comes the big test. Now that the files are accessible, I should be able to view them in my mobile browser (or on the desktop) by going to the appropriate address. In this case, the address is http://jonwestfall.com/whosthattweet/index.html. By visiting this in a desktop web browser, I can see that the files are online,as in Figure 13–20. This might look pretty ugly since the files are meant to be viewed on a mobile web browser;

however, we've verified that the files are online and accessible! Congratulations—
you've uploaded your project to the Web!

Figure 13–20. *The game doesn't render properly on the desktop browser, but this test verifies that the files have been properly uploaded*

Versioning Your Software

FTP normally works well for small development projects with one developer, especially when the project is not very complex. However, for instance, let's say you are working on a project with a team of developers and every single one of them has access to the FTP server and uploads and changes things whenever he or she wants. Eventually you will run into a situation where one user ends up making changes to a file and then a minute later someone uploads changes they made to the exact same file, completely overwriting the first person's work that was just uploaded.

This is a very frustrating situation, and in reality stuff like this is actually fairly common and happens all the time when programmers are not organized. One easy way to prevent this is by using some form of software versioning, like Subversion, to essentially back up and version your files for you. This way, let's say Jon makes a few changes to a file that we are sharing and I accidentally check in a new version on that file that does not have the code Jon added. Instead of freaking out and panicking, which would have been our only two options before, we can easily revert the file to an earlier version of itself and save that code we thought we lost. Heck, using versioning you can even merge two previous versions of a file together and make one super–file.

There are tons of versioning solutions out there just waiting to be used, but the two most popular solutions are Apache Subversion (http://subversion.apache.org/) and Git (http://git-scm.com/). Subversion, also known as SVN, has been around for a long time and is a very mature product with a wide range of support in almost every single hosting solution I have used in the past. The best part is there is a really nifty Windows application that adds all of the SVN options into your right–click menu, which would do wonders at helping newer developers that are intimidated by using the command line.

As much as I love SVN, over the past few years I have been moving more toward using Git for all my versioning needs. Git is another free and open source software solution for versioning that is insanely fast when you compare it to SVN, and really easy to use as you can see in Figure 13–21.

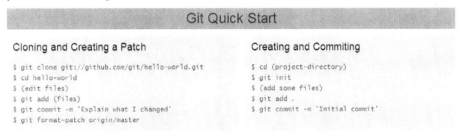

Figure 13–21. *A quick start guide to getting up and running with Git in a few easy keystrokes*

Git also tends to be more user friendly due to the ever popular web siteGitHub (https://github.com/), which markets itself as a social coding hub, playing off of the Web 2.0 modus operandi of having everything be as "social" as possible (see Figure 13–22). With GitHub you are able to store all your projects in the GitHub cloud free of charge; you thenare able to have other developers fork, or copy, your repository so they can make whatever changes they want to it while keeping those changes completely separated from your work. It is a bit gimmicky, but Git itself is such an awesome technology that you learn to ignore the whole social thing if that isn't your cup of tea.

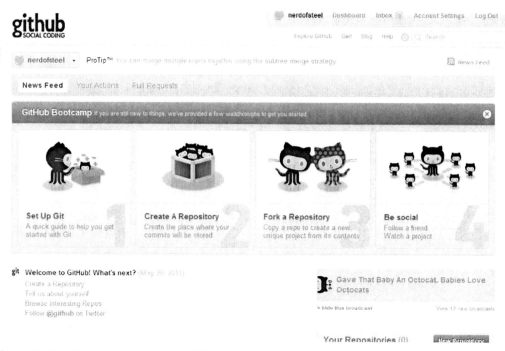

Figure 13–22. *Using the social coding hub, GitHub*

It is best to think of versioning as a way of backing up your code and application. In fact, even if you are the only developer working on your project, it is always best to version your application the moment you create that first folder or file for it. This way if anything happens along the way, like your laptop explodes, or your toddler decides your computer looks thirsty and drowns it in apple juice, you will be able to recover that code and pull it down to a new machine to continue working on it. Even if your computer doesn't explode, once you are ready to deploy your project onto your server, all you have to do is log in and run a simple command in your prompt to copy the contents of your versioned program to your production server (i.e., your webhost) without the need to ever touch an FTP program.

If your computer teachers were like my teachers growing up, they probably hammered home the importance of constantly saving your work. Just like in college when you never want to be caught by the power going out in the middle of writing a giant essay so that you lose everything, make sure to save your work often and then push those new revisions out to your choice in versioning solutions.

Going Native

So now we have built an application, optimized the application's size by compressing the everlasting life out of it, found ourselves an acceptable hosting solution, and learned how to transfer files to that server by using FTP, SVN, or Git—but what if you don't want to package your application up to be used on the Internet from a data connection? What if you are building an application that you know will be used in areas where there is no data coverage whatsoever? What if you know your application is really resource heavy and contains a lot of audio files or images that you do not want to sit around and wait to load onto a device? What if your project is so awesome that you don't want to give it away for free and want to sell it to your users instead? Well, do not fret because we have solutions for you to turn that incredible HTML5 and JavaScript application into a full–fledge native application that can be run on your users' phones without the need to ever open their Internet browsers.

On top of that, going the native route opens up many avenues to you that were not available beforehand by giving you access to many of your handset's features (such as accessing the handset's contacts, or creating a game that makes use of the phone's or tablet's accelerometer, or creating files on the handset's file system). These are features you normally are not allowed to access when going through a standard web browser, and for good reason too! If anyone was able to modify your computer's, tablet's, or phone's file system from the Internet, it would be mass hysteria all around the planet. If you think the computer world has problems with viruses and trojans now, imagine how it would be if you visited Amazon.com and an angry rogue developer decided to use his file system access rights to delete all the files on your computer? Yeah, I told you, mass hysteria. This is why your browser is locked down as we discussed when creating our Twitter applications "Who'sThat Tweet?" and "I Love Ham."

There are times, though, when this access is needed, and that is where frameworks like PhoneGap (http://www.phonegap.com/) and Titanium Mobile (http://www.appcelerator.com/products/titanium-mobile-application-development/) come into play. Both of these application frameworks let developers take their existing HTML5 and JavaScript code and turn it into a full–fledged application that can be uploaded to any mobile application store of your choosing. While both of these products allow you take your application down the native path, they each do it in pretty different ways that I feel are worth mentioning.

PhoneGap

PhoneGap is a free and open source solution, like many popular web development solutions, which has come a long way in a very short timeframe. Created by Nitobi Software during a 48 hour coding spree at iPhone Dev Camp in 2009, PhoneGap came into existence and has been a fan favorite of web developers looking to hop into the mobile development scene without spending a lot of time learning a new programming language.

With the recent release of Adobe Dreamweaver CS5.5, Adobe has integrated the PhoneGap framework into Dreamweaver so a developer can create a native application, and test it in an Android emulator, with just a simple click of the mouse (see Figure 13–23). This partnership with such a massive development powerhouse gives PhoneGap a huge advantage over its competitors in the "write once run anywhere" mobile space.

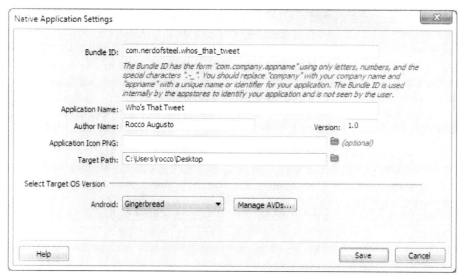

Figure 13–23. *Configuring Adobe Dreamweaver CS5.5 to build out our HTML5 application as a native application with PhoneGap*

Let's take a quick look at some code, in Listing 13–1, from a PhoneGap sample so you can get a feel for how to structure your HTML5 PhoneGap application.

Listing 13–1. *PhoneGapExample*

```
<!DOCTYPE HTML>
<html>
<head>
<meta name="viewport" content="initial-scale=1.0, user-scalable=no, width=device-width"
/>
<title>Training App</title>
<linkrel="stylesheet" href="assets/css/master.css" type="text/css" media="screen" />
<scriptsrc="phonegap.js" type="text/JavaScript" charset="utf-8"></script>
<scriptsrc="assets/js/xui.js" type="text/JavaScript" charset="utf-8"></script>
<scriptsrc="assets/js/lawnchair/adaptors/LawnchairAdaptorHelpers.js"
type="text/JavaScript" charset="utf-8"></script>
<scriptsrc="assets/js/lawnchair/adaptors/DOMStorageAdaptor.js" type="text/JavaScript"
charset="utf-8"></script>
<scriptsrc="assets/js/lawnchair/adaptors/WebkitSQLiteAdaptor.js" type="text/JavaScript"
charset="utf-8"></script>
<scriptsrc="assets/js/lawnchair/Lawnchair.js" type="text/JavaScript" charset="utf-
8"></script>
<scriptsrc="assets/js/dsl.js" type="text/JavaScript" charset="utf-8"></script>
<scriptsrc="assets/js/app.js" type="text/JavaScript" charset="utf-8"></script>
</head>
<body>
<div id="title_bar">Phone<strong>Gap</strong> Training App</div>
<div id="welcome" class="view">
<div class="app_button" id="map_button">Show My Location</div>
<div class="app_button" id="settings_button">Settings</div>
</div>
<div id="map" class="view">
<div class="map_image"><img id="static_map" src="assets/img/staticmap.png"></div>
```

```
<p>This is where you are</p>
<div class="app_button" id="welcome_button">Go Back</div>
</div>
<div id="settings" class="view">
<form id="settings_form">
<fieldset>
<legend>Map Type</legend>
<input type="radio" name="map" value="roadmap" checked>
     Road Map<br/>
<input type="radio" name="map" value="satellite">
     Satellite<br/>
<input type="radio" name="map" value="terrain">
     Terrain<br/>
<input type="radio" name="map" value="hybrid">
     Hybrid<br/>
</fieldset>
<fieldset>
<legend>Zoom Level</legend>
<input type="radio" name="zoom" value="10">
     Super Far<br/>
<input type="radio" name="zoom" value="12">
     Far<br/>
<input type="radio" name="zoom" value="15" checked>
     Normal<br/>
<input type="radio" name="zoom" value="18">
     Close<br/>
<input type="radio" name="zoom" value="20">
     Super Close<br/>
</fieldset>
<button id="save_button">Save</button>
</form>
</div>
</body>
</html>
```

As you can see from the preceding kitchen sink example, there is not a whole lot going on here that is different from how you would normally structure a page. For all intents and purposes this is an HTML document, and this is where PhoneGap starts to fall short when compared to its competitors. See, when using a PhoneGap application on your handset, even though the application is now native and can hook into the operating system with permissions to which a normal Internet–hosted web application will never have access, you are still just loading a web page on the device. This is fine in most cases, but on Android devices we do have to acknowledge that the browser is not hardware accelerated like the iPhone browser; so, if you have a lot of fancy effects and animations in your app, it will still be as slow and sluggish as it is when viewing it in a web browser. Just because you are wrapping your application in such a way that we can call it "native," it really isn't native in the true sense of the word. This is where my favorite mobile platform comes into play: Titanium Mobile!

Titanium Mobile

For years I have been a huge supporter of the work that Appcelerator is doing with Titanium Mobile. They started off taking the same approach as PhoneGap, allowing users to create content in pure HTML and JavaScript, but quickly realized that sometimes it is best to go fully native for increased performance and speed. Somewhere around the time the Titanium Mobile software matured into the production–ready 1.0 release, Appcelerator released a new set of APIs that would still allow developers to use HTML5 to create applications in a web view, but with the addition that now they could skip HTML5 altogether and create their applications in pure JavaScript.

Doing this they are able to take those JavaScript files at build time and completely transform them into a *real* native application using the operating system's own code to generate layouts of the pages. That means that instead of creating your own set of buttons or styles to use in your app, you can make your application look more like a real native app by using native user interface elements for whatever platform you are using.

Not to be outdone by PhoneGapwith its integration into Adobe Dreamweaver, the good folks over at Appcelerator purchased the integrated development environment (IDE) company Aptana and created their own full–fledged IDE for use with their framework. Since Titanium Studio was released early in 2011, working with the Titanium Mobile environment has been a breeze.

While Titanium Mobile is an open source project and free to use, there are special modules that that are only offered to paying customers. Being a paying customer of Titanium Mobile has its perks, like getting early access to the newer versions of Titanium Mobile and using modules that would give you access to APIs from companies like AdMob for in-app advertisements and Paypal for in-app purchasing. Becoming a subscription member to Titanium Mobile is pretty easy on the pocket book as well, with free basic membership and paid memberships starting at $49.99/month.

If you can afford it and want access to certain modules like the GameKit and OpenGL gaming modules, then hopping on the basic indie plan is a no brainer. If you want to just fiddle around with the software and create applications without fancy modules, then you can do that as well, free of charge! With Titanium Mobile you will be able to use either pure JavaScript or a combination of HTML5 and JavaScript to create truly incredible mobile applications in no time at all.

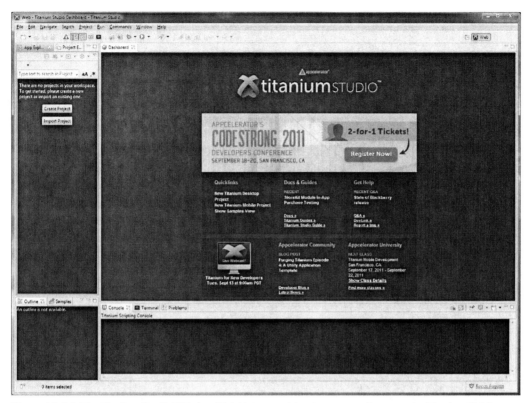

Figure 13–24. *The Titanium Studio IDE, the official integrated development environment for Titanium Mobile*

Closing Time

Now that we have gone through the entire gauntlet of everything one would need to know to get up and running in the mobile development world, it is time to say goodbye, turn off the lights, and slowly walk away while the theme song to the late 1970's TV show *The Incredible Hulk* is played on a piano somewhere in the distance. We have really enjoyed sharing all of this knowledge and information with you and hope that you can use it in the near future to turn yourself into a Level 10 Web Shaman and defeat any tricky development situation that crosses your path. We are sure you are currently grinning from ear to ear, ready to go hop on your computer and start coding out your next project, and we're grinning from ear to ear because we're excited for you; but before leaving you today weare going to once again remind you of a little bit of friendly advice that was given to Rocco almost two decades ago—keep it simple, stupid!

Thanks for taking the time to read this book, and if you happen to know of any budding developers out there that can benefit from the contents of this tome about mobile web development, then feel free to lend them your copy and pass this knowledge and information on to someone else. Take care, and happy coding!

— Jon, Rocco, and Grant

Index

CPSIA information can be obtained at www.ICGtesting.com
Printed in the USA
LVOW062338200213

321054LV00003B/88/P